IMAGES
of America

AROUND MULBERRY

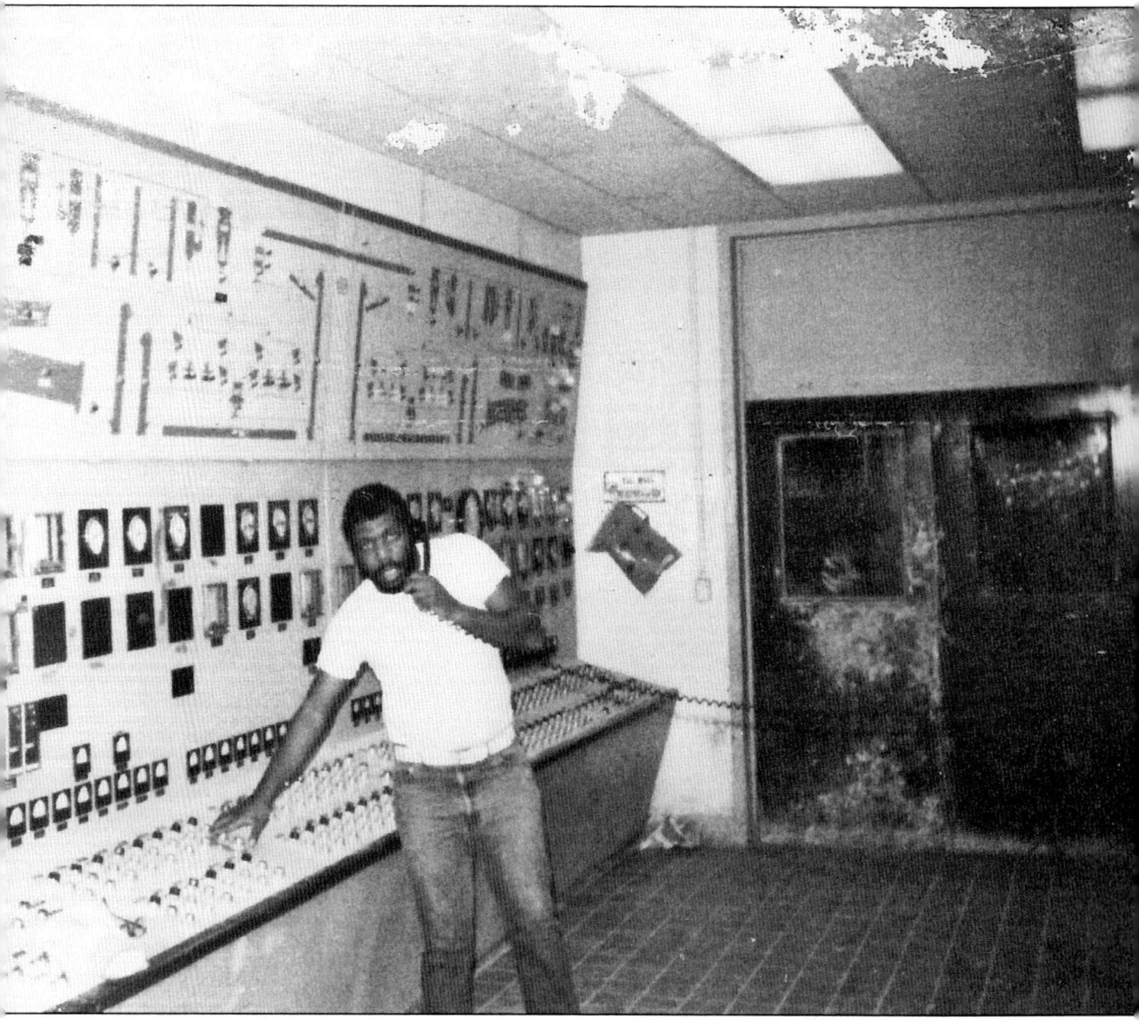

Joseph "Bob" Lee Jones Sr. (1939–2007) worked at the Brewster and Farmland Industries mines as a DAP (dia ammonia phosphate) "dry product" fertilizer operator, monitoring the panel board. He worked in the industry for 33 years and served in the U.S. Army for two years. Together with Nila Helper Jones, he raised six children: Stephanie, Tanya, John, Cedric, Lil Gene, and Christopher. (Nila Helper Jones.)

On the Cover: A crew of six men were required to operate the 95-ton Bucyrus railroad steam shovel pictured. The phosphate industry used this machinery, which typically had a 3.5-cubic-yard dipper, to remove overburden near Mulberry around 1910. (Mulberry Phosphate Museum.)

IMAGES
of America

AROUND MULBERRY

Stephanie L. Dukes, Essie N. Helper Morgan,
and the Mulberry Historical Society
with a foreword by Dr. Frank Satchel Jr.

ARCADIA
PUBLISHING

ISBN 978-0-7385-5370-2

Published by Arcadia Publishing
Charleston, South Carolina

Printed in the United States of America

Library of Congress Catalog Card Number: 2007939938

For all general information contact Arcadia Publishing at:
Telephone 843-853-2070
Fax 843-853-0044
E-mail sales@arcadiapublishing.com
For customer service and orders:
Toll-Free 1-888-313-2665

Visit us on the Internet at www.arcadiapublishing.com

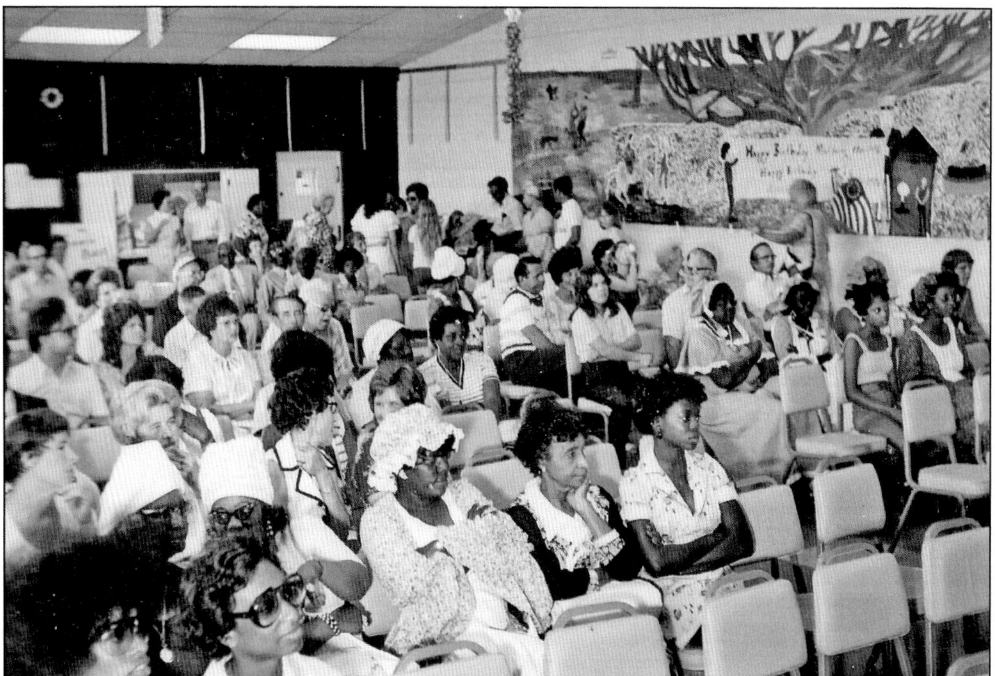

Above are members of the Mulberry community. This book is dedicated to all the families that lived and died, dragged and mined, educated and communicated, saved and served, and to all who preserved that rich heritage—especially historians Raymond L. Driver and Essie N. Helper Morgan. (MBS.)

Contents

ACKNOWLEDGMENTS

I would like to thank all who inspired us to document the history of Mulberry through the use of their pictures and knowledge. The response from the community at large was overwhelming, the selection of images exhausting and extremely difficult.

Special thanks go out to Raymond L. Driver and Essie. N. Helper Morgan, lead historians; Robert Keim, president of the Mulberry Historical Society; and other members of the society: Irene Keim; Ron Thomas; Belle Roberts; Averil Jane Townsley; Alva C. Pipkins; Henri Harned Sparkman; Richard A. Fifer, contributing writer of chapter two; Lewetta "Lou" Haag, director of the Mulberry Phosphate Museum, and assistant curator Elly South; Michael Borders, president of the Kiwanis club; Ruenea Boyd Bigham; Robert Histead of the *Mulberry Press*; Sharron Jones of the Mulberry Chamber of Commerce; Mary Ellin Barrett, director of the Dr. C. C. Pearce Municipal Library; Vanessa Baker, Mulberry's city clerk; Rev. Eugene and Wanda Kendrick; Mosaic; C. F. Industries; Badcocks and More; Clark Environmental, Inc.; Digitech Graphics Group; the Moseley House Museum; Rev. Daniel Lavan Sr.; Vera Mae Hardee; Sandra Brown; John and Ruth Glover; Roosevelt and Lillie Baker; Mike Woodfin; Stephen Jackson; Everee J. Clark of the Pleasant City Family Reunion Committee; the Polk County Historical Society; Wilbert, Rosa, and Harriet Brown; Clarriet Brown-Gray and Charles Gray; Bernard White; the Woodard family; Sharon Helper Mobley; Lauren Helper Scavella; Palmer Francis Jr.; John Fitzgerald Dukes; Cedric Jones; Frederick M. Ross; Dr. Linda Ray; Rev. John W. and Dannie Dukes; Essie N. Helper Morgan; Ermase L. Evans, who turns 105 years old on August 4, 2008; Nila Helper Jones; other brothers and sisters, uncles and aunts, and our nieces and nephews who constantly asked, "Have you finished yet?"

Thank you to Luke Cunningham, our editor, for his patience during the family's mourning of the passing of Joseph L. Jones Sr. Thanks also to publisher Lauren Bobier, production coordinator David Mandel, and to all of the production editors who worked on the book.

PHOTOGRAPH CREDITS

State Library and Archives of Florida: SLAF
Mulberry Phosphate Museum: MPM
Richard A. Fifer: RF
Mulberry Bicentennial Scrapbook: MBS
Mulberry Chamber of Commerce: MCC
Mulberry Press: MP

In Loving Memory of Joseph Lee Jones ("Dad")

FOREWORD

It is with a spirit of humility that this foreword is written about the wonderful city of Mulberry, Florida. Words alone cannot express the true feeling of warmth that permeates our community. Unique is a simple way of summarizing the many great things that have happened, are happening, and will continue to happen in this community. The city of Mulberry is surrounded by several smaller communities, hence the book's title: *Around Mulberry*. These communities include Fuller Heights, Nichols, and the now extinct community of Peddy to the west; Pierce/Rolling Hills, Bradley, and the now extinct community of Brewster to the south. No matter what events or circumstances occur within the community, we all rally to the cause of those in need and desire to be of assistance. This is the community where love abounds.

Strange and phenomenal things happen in and around Mulberry, Florida. This area was part of the territory known as Bone Valley. During the Cenozoic Era, also known as the Age of the Great Mammals, animals such as saber-toothed tigers, four-tusked mastodons, rhinoceros, large mammoths, long-nosed camels, and others animals roamed this area. Evidence of their existence was uncovered in the fossils discovered during the mining of phosphate. Artifacts such as fluted spear points, clay vessels, and other pottery place the earliest humans in this area as being the "St. John men," around 4700 B.C. The described collectibles and others are on display daily for public viewing at the Mulberry Phosphate Museum. The museum also features a fossil pit and invites visitors to participate in finding 10- to 15-million-year-old fossils that they may keep to start their own collections. Different Native American tribes are documented to have occupied this area, from the Glades Indians known as Timucuas, according to Marjorie Stoneman Douglas's book entitled, *Florida: The Long Frontier*; and the Carib tribes which, in 1796, were deported to the St. Vincent and Dominica Islands by the British, according to Raymond L. Driver's book *Bone Valley Comes to Life*.

The resources of our area provided for turpentine, rosin, lumber, cattle rising, and phosphate, which brought settlers to the areas as late as the 1840s. In 1887, companies began to mine for phosphate in the Bone Valley area. They first dug with pickaxes and shovels, but these methods were replaced by mule-drawn scrapers, steam shovels, hydraulics, steam- and diesel-powered draglines, electric draglines, and finally the modern-day draglines. In later years, some pits were filled with water and stocked with fish. Some local churches are known for using these water-filled pits as baptizing pools.

The absence of local law and order in the 1880s and a growing population created an atmosphere similar to living in the Wild West. Most men were known to carry a firearm. The story is told that every Monday morning, a coroner's inquest was held for the outlaw activities that occurred during the weekend. As people migrated to the frontier area, mining companies developed company towns to supply transportation, medical care, shopping, education, and housing. An African American author for the Federal Writers' Project (1935) gave this description of the African American quarters: "Mostly comfortably furnished homes . . . well-equipped schoolrooms . . . and automobiles of the latest makes." Rising company costs for these communities and the development of towns such as Mulberry in close proximity to the mines encouraged companies to offer their employees an opportunity to purchase one of the company-provided houses and to resettle farther away by moving the house to an adjourning town.

A city was created to bring justice and peace to the place where the Alafia River begins to flow toward the Tampa Bay; where the natural resources of lumber, citrus, and phosphate demanded the formation of railroad lines to decrease transportation time of goods and services; and where the mail drop location was the site of the eponymous mulberry tree. From 1901, the official date of incorporation of our city, in the county of Polk, in the state of Florida, our citizens were successful in developing this town into an enthusiast and charming community.

In May 1900, with the closing of Kingsford's post office three years earlier, Mulberry's first post office was established. Public school was established in Mulberry in June 1894, according to school board minutes. The Mulberry School began classes as a high school in 1907 and became the third oldest school in Polk County (Bartow and Lakeland are the others), presenting the three students of its first graduating class in 1911. Mulberry High School was chosen as a model school for implementing the decision of *Brown et. al. v. Board of Education* of Topeka, Shawnee County, Kansas. In 1966, the first integrated class graduated from Mulberry High School.

In 1907, our first bank, the Bank of Mulberry, was founded, and the city experienced its first electricity with the forming of Mulberry Electric Company. Many families could purchase an ice box with the opening of the Mulberry Ice Company in 1907. During this year, communication came to Mulberry in the form of the telephone. Mulberry had 24 subscribers with Peninsular Telephone Company, making the city the third exchange in Polk County.

Mulberry's first paved asphalt roads were constructed in 1918. This improved transportation route extended on the north side to Lakeland, on the south side to Brewster, on the west side to the Hillsborough County line, and on the east side to Bartow. A progressive Mulberry city council passed an ordinance in 1919 to handle the new road system by stating that "anyone under the age of 16 must be accompanied by the car owner, a parent or guardian when driving an automobile." This was a bold step, considering that the State of Florida did not start issuing driver's licenses until 1936.

Mining and the processing of phosphate earned Mulberry the title as the official Phosphate Capital of the World. Mulberry is home of the largest foam cup and container plant, Master Containers, Inc. The headquarters of the Badcock Home Furniture is located here in Mulberry; Badcock is more than 100 years old with more than 356 stores. Keeping up with the times, Mulberry is now the location of a store that has become a worldwide household name: Wal-Mart.

As readers take this pictorial journey through the pages of this book, they will truly enjoy reading, seeing, and hearing about the monumental feats of our citizens. I deem it as a joy and a blessing from above to be able to write this foreword. The accomplishments of community members are the results of the untiring prayers, faith, and the endless love of our forefathers.

My sincere thanks and appreciation to all who have played a role in making Mulberry, Florida, the kind of place we all love to call home.

—Dr. Frank R. Satchel Jr.

One

Prehistoric Times

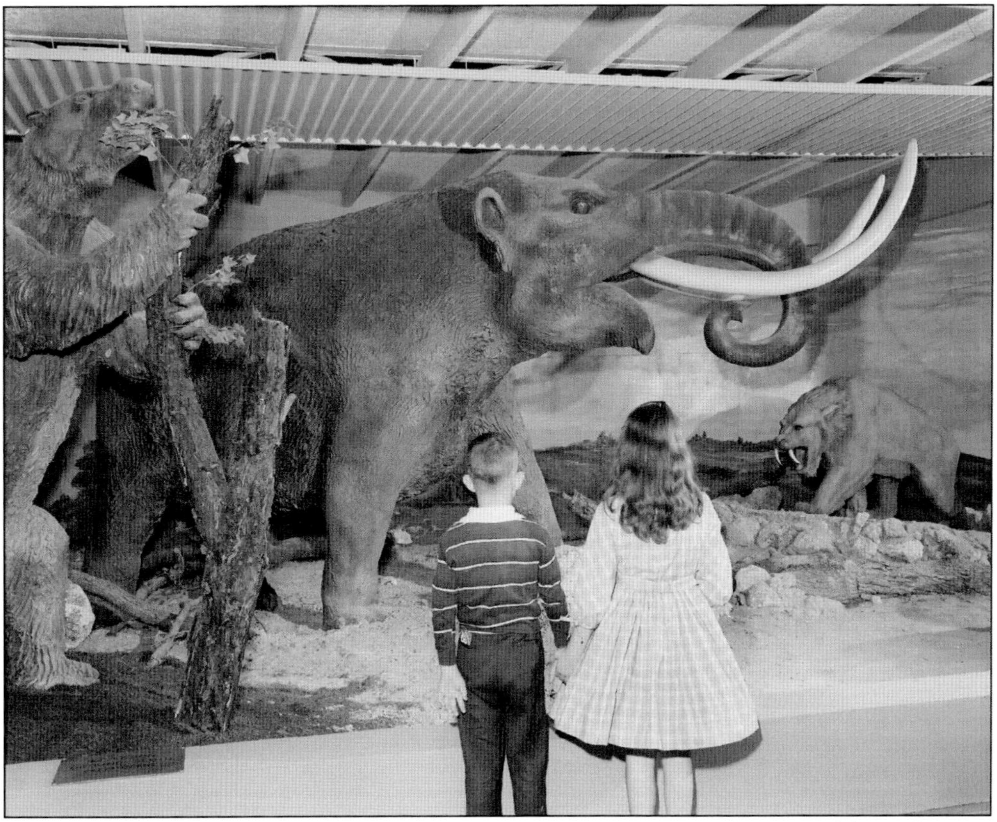

Central Florida's phosphate mining area became known as Bone Valley because of the prehistoric animal bones found in the area. Shown above are life-size replicas. These and other statues, paintings, and dioramas created by Henry de Reus in the 1950s are on display at the Mulberry Phosphate Museum. To preserve this rich history, a phosphate museum was established in Bartow, Florida. After the museum closed, Joe Larned opened a private collection in Bradley, Florida. Upon his retirement, he offered the collection to the City of Mulberry. (SLAF.)

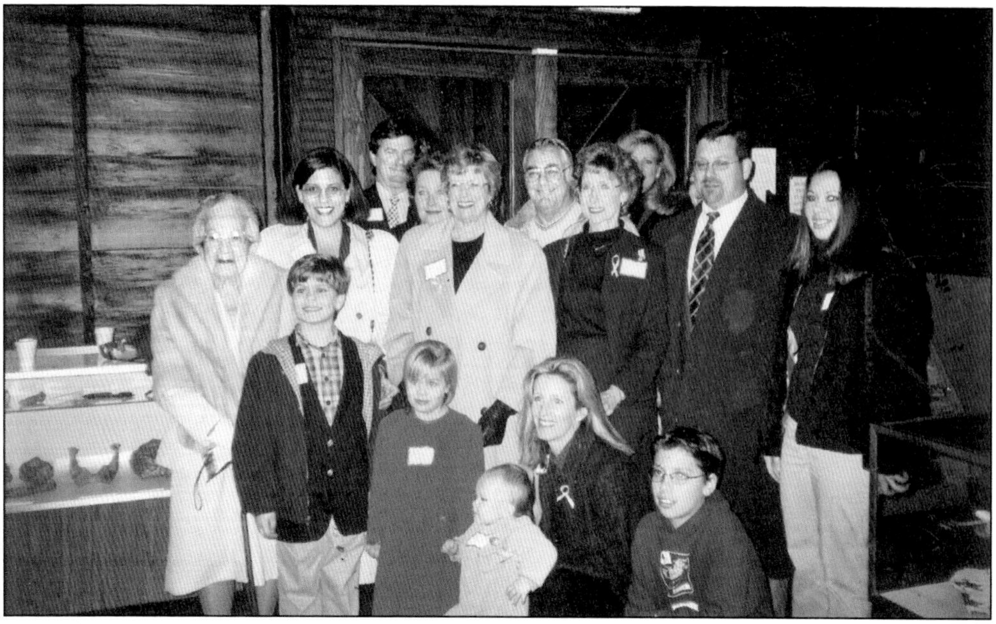

In her honor, Elin Oak Becker's family attended the grand opening at the Mulberry Phosphate Museum in October 1986. Elin worked for the Florida Phosphate Council and assumed the awesome task of raising funds (private and grants) to provide the museum with a state-of-the-art educational facility. Elin succombed to cancer in 1999, knowing many had and would continue to enjoy the fruit of her labor. The museum's first director was Gary Hacking. (MPM)

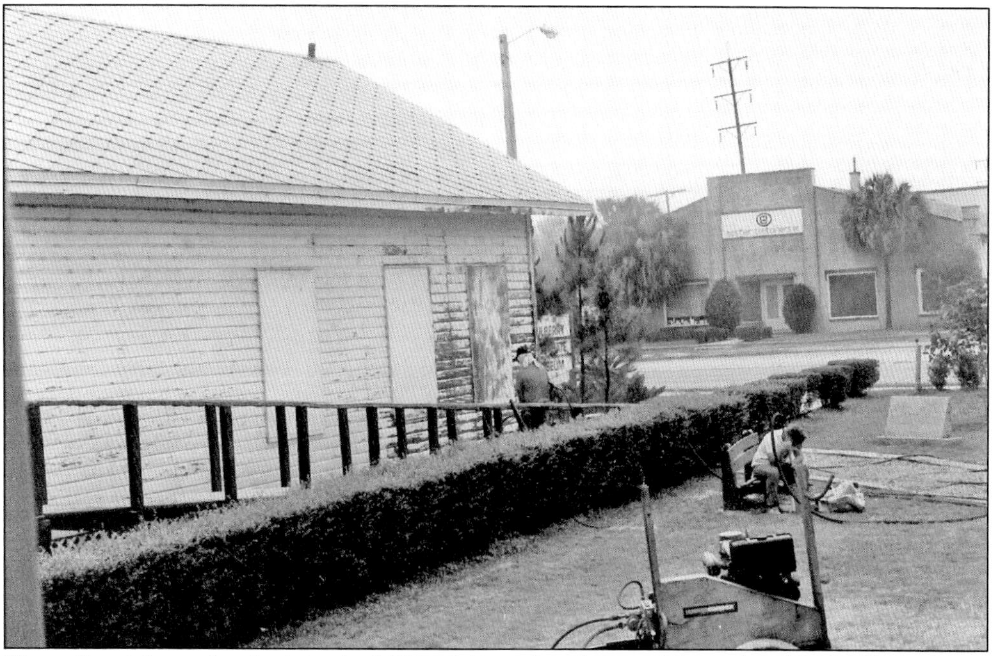

The railroad depot that had, in the 1800s, delivered packages addressed to "the Mulberry Tree" was restored and used as a museum. The pressure washing was done by the fire department, which was a volunteer organization until the 1970s. Across the street is Master Container, a factory supplying Styrofoam cups throughout the world since 1969. (MPM.)

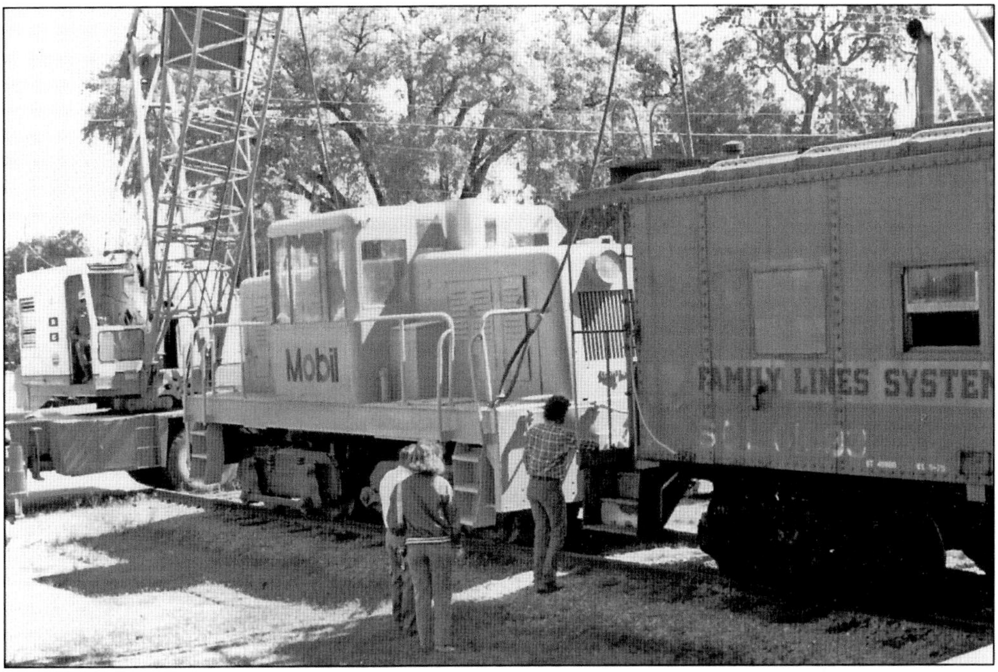

A real-life engine, four boxcars, and a caboose used by the mines were donated to the museum. The caboose displays how the brakeman and switchman worked. The boxcars were converted into two air-conditioned classrooms/meeting rooms, available for use by public organizations. (MPM.)

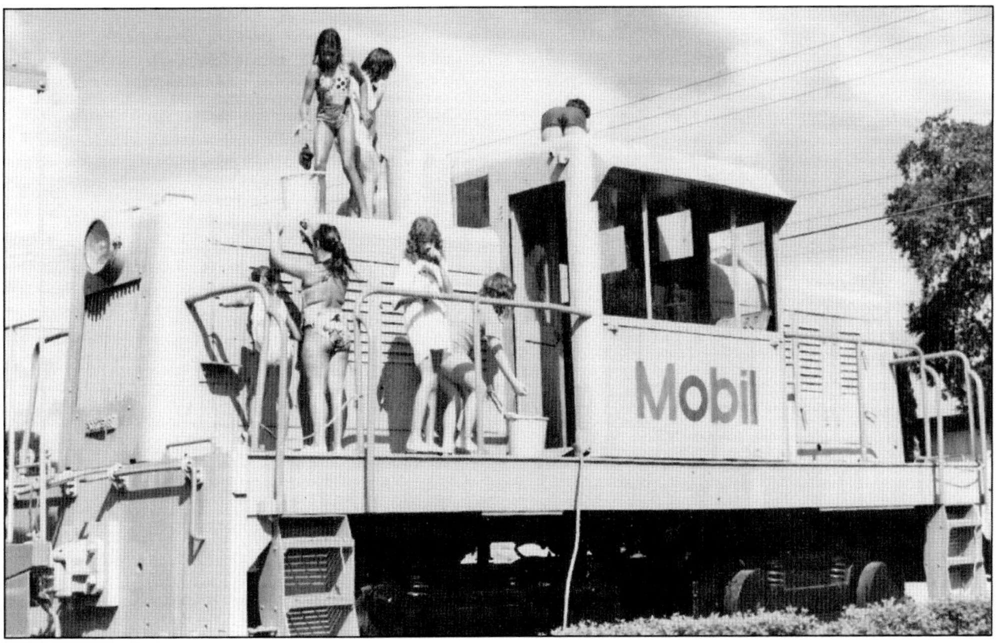

The local Girl Scout troop volunteered to wash the engine and caboose in preparation for the opening ceremony of the Mulberry Phosphate Museum. The story is told that this engine was used in World War II, and the bullet holes are still visible. Collectors visiting the museum to verify the engine number said that, after the war, the engine was returned to its owner and used in the mining industry. When Mobil retired the engine, it was donated to the museum. (MPM.)

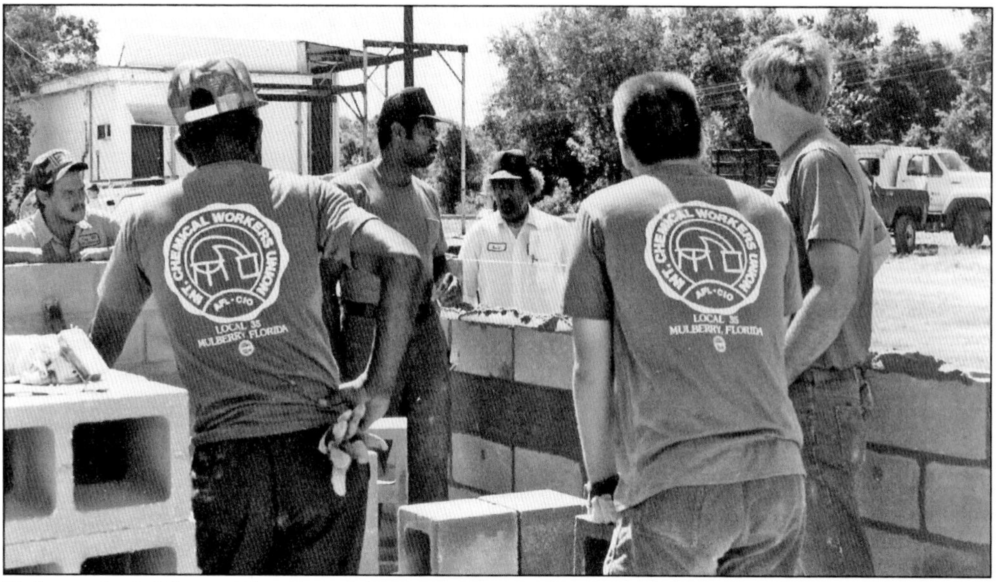

To bring the Mulberry Phosphate Museum into compliance with building codes and regulations, facilities were added for men's and women's private use. The workers in this picture are unidentified except for the gentleman in the white shirt who is David Glover, supervisor of maintenance for the City of Mulberry. The others are volunteers from the local International Chemical Worker Union No. 35. (MPM.)

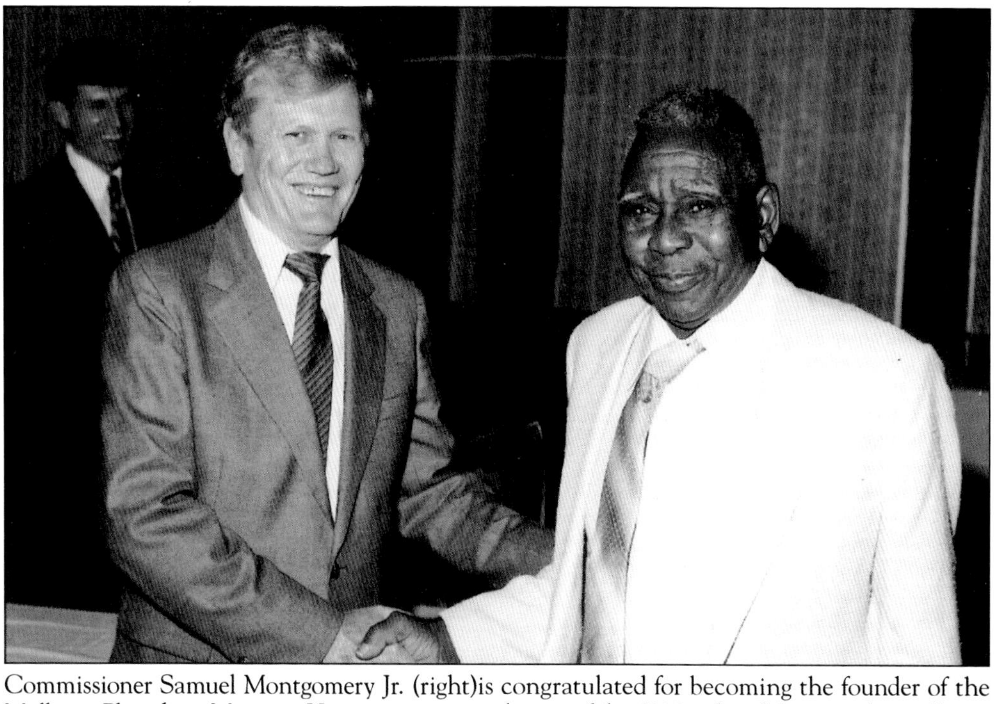

Commissioner Samuel Montgomery Jr. (right)is congratulated for becoming the founder of the Mulberry Phosphate Museum. He set into motion the use of the 1899 railroad depot as the Mulberry Phosphate Museum and encouraged the city to purchase the private fossil collection owned by Joe Larned since 1972, the collections from the old museum in Bartow, and others. These purchases expanded the city's own collection. Lou Haag became the first curator. (Montgomery family.)

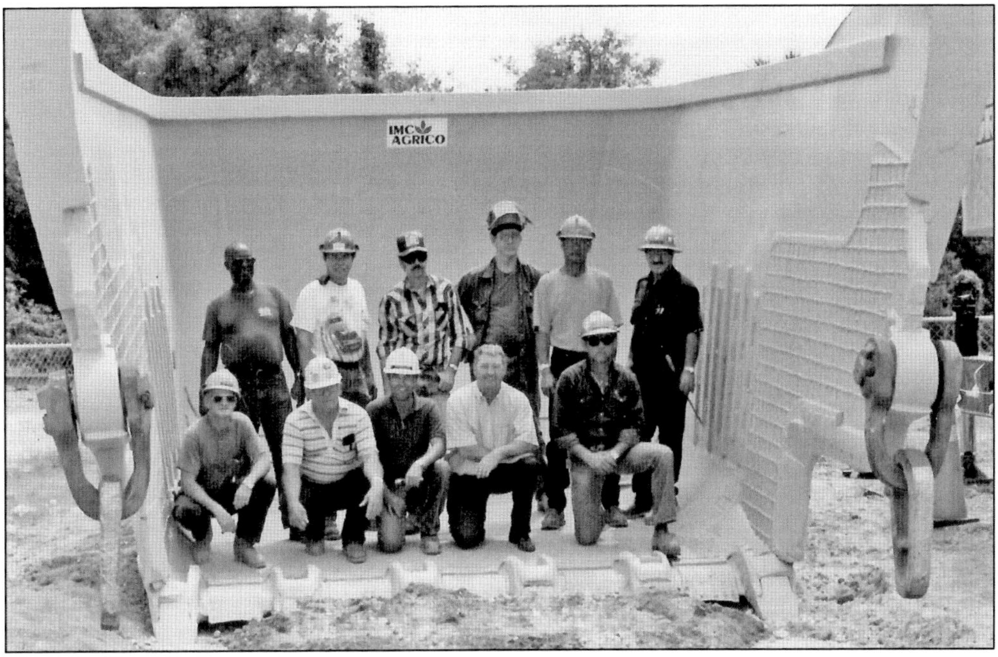

With assistance of Larry Isaac in 1994, International Minerals and Chemical Company-Agrico (IMC-Agrico) donated to the museum a dragline bucket that was used in the digging part of the mining process. Manufactured in 1965, the bucket was used to move more than a half billion tons of material. The bucket was used at IMC-Agrico Bradley Junction, Hanesworth mines, and retired in 1987. (MPM.)

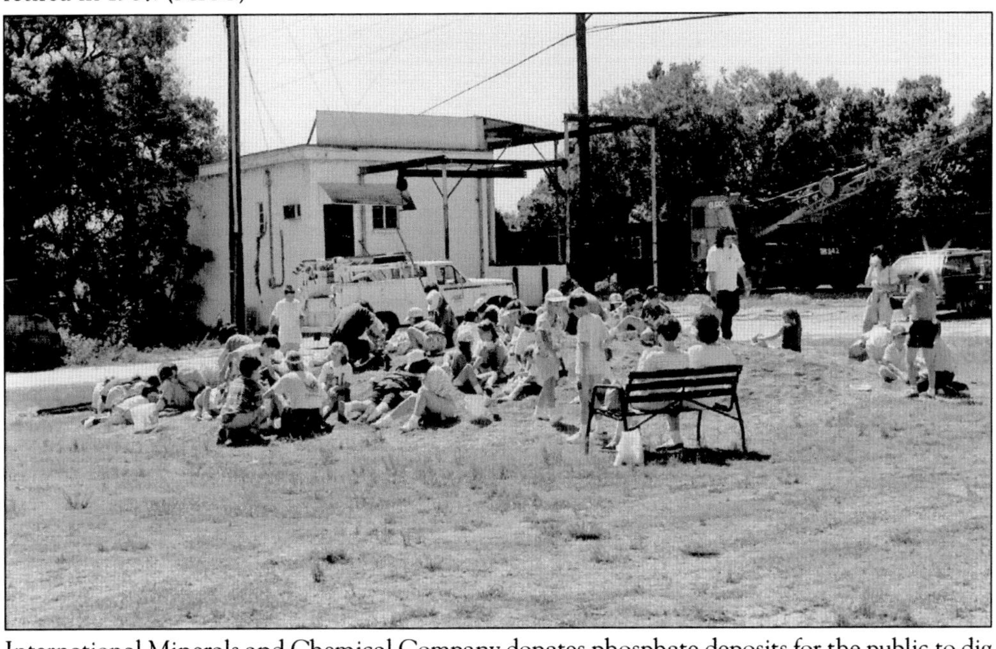

International Minerals and Chemical Company donates phosphate deposits for the public to dig through at the museum. Fossils such as, but not limited to, the teeth of great white sharks, bull and tiger sharks, a stingray mouth plate, horses, gators, ribs of sea cows, and vertebras of other sea creatures can be found in the deposits. (MPM.)

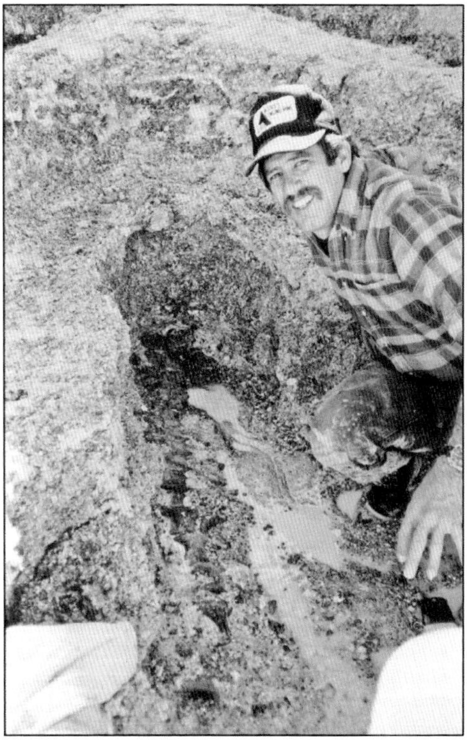

In the 1990s, International Minerals and Chemical Company, Kingsford Mine, was mining for phosphate when Frank Garcia came upon a rare 20th-century find: the fossils of a prehistoric animal. They immediately stopped mining in the area and called in an anthropologist to verify, identify, and remove the remains. (MPM.)

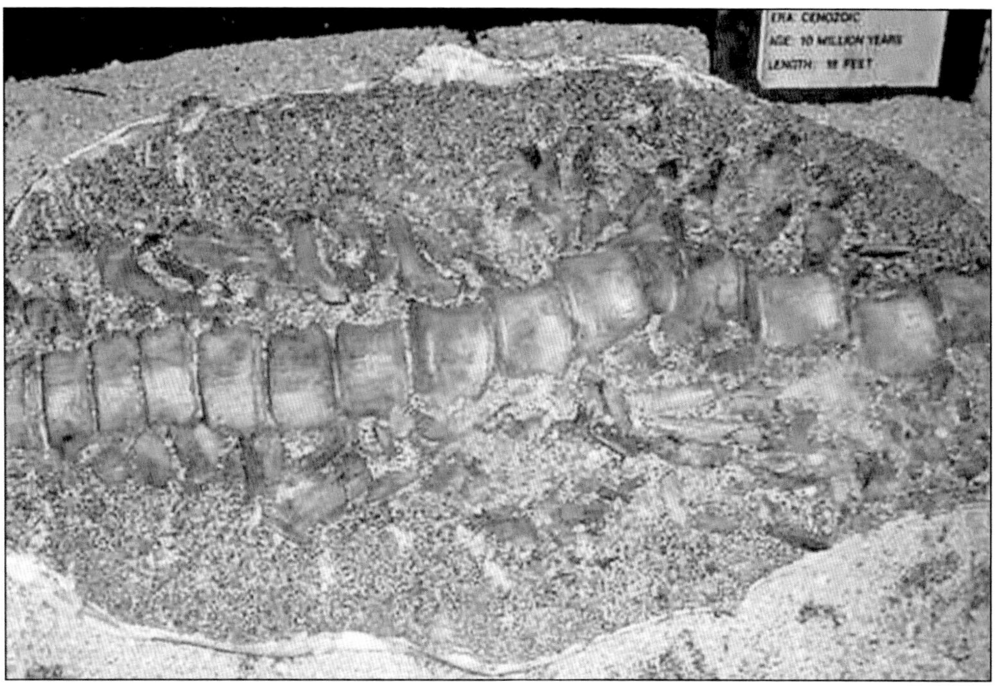

The finding on IMC's site was the fossil remains of a baleen whale. This mammal existed during the Cretaceous age and was approximately 10 million years old. The remains were carefully removed and donated to the Mulberry Phosphate Museum. All 10 feet of the baleen whale are on display at the museum. (Stephanie L. Dukes.)

Life-size replicas and paintings of prehistoric animals by the artist Henry de Reus were obtained from the museum in Bartow, Florida, which was closed. Here is the city's museum director, Gary Hacking, and an unidentified Mosaic Mine representative. Social studies teachers around Polk and Hillsborough Counties are encouraged to plan field trips to the museum. (MPM.)

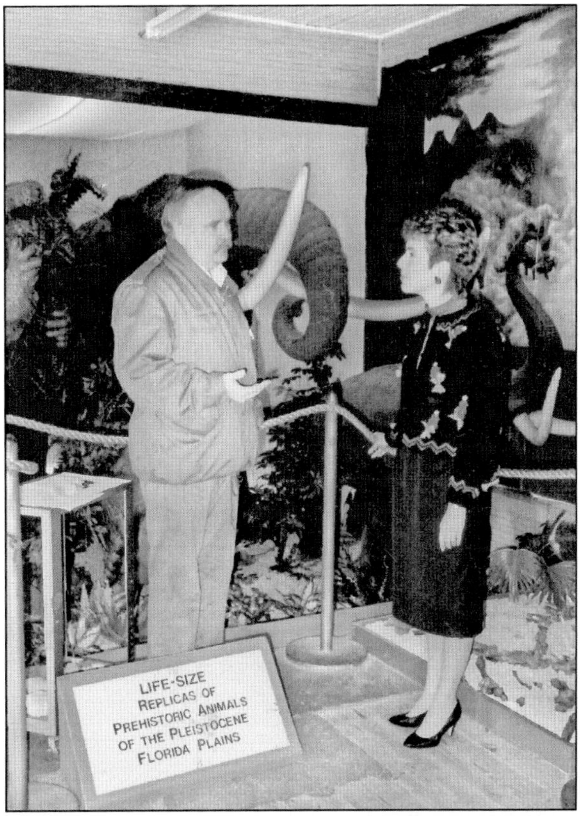

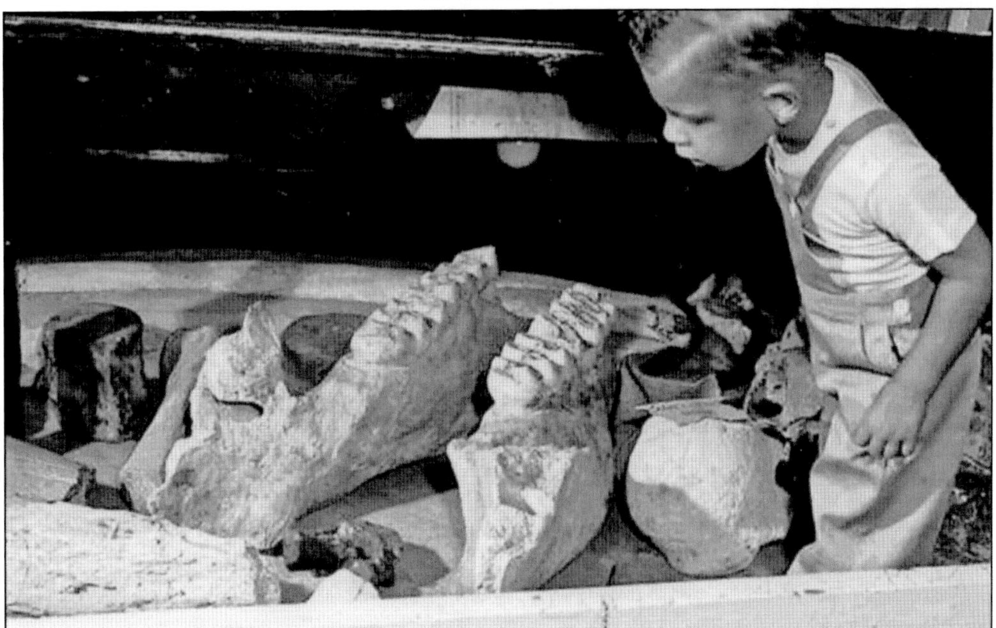

This unidentified young boy is pictured in the 1980s examining the fossil teeth of a prehistoric animal. Curiosity tempted the young child to climb into the exhibit for a closer look to make sure the teeth were real. (SLAF.)

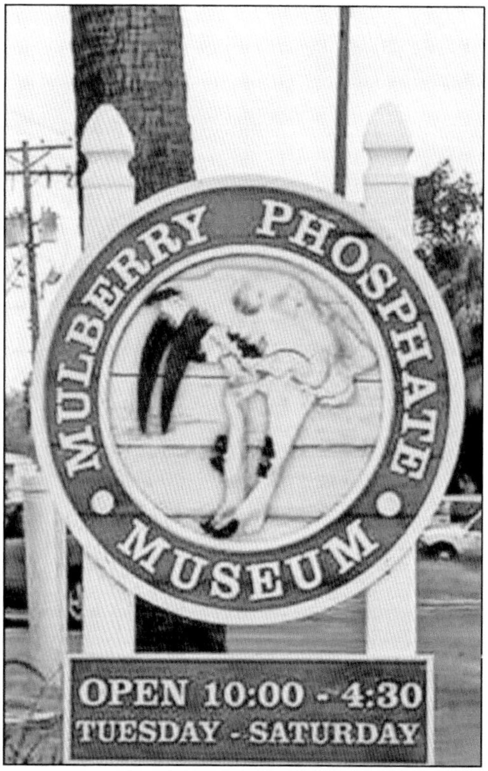

The Mulberry Phosphate Museum is open free to the public. Donations are accepted and appreciated. This sign displays the fossil skull of a Smilodon, the largest of the saber-toothed cats first seen 1.6 million years ago and last seen about 11,000 years ago during the Ice Age . City officials and the museum curator, Lewetta "Lou" Haag, invite visitors and locals alike to stop in and see the fossils that remain from when Florida emerged from the primeval sea. This is a glimpse of prehistoric Florida. (Stephanie L. Dukes.)

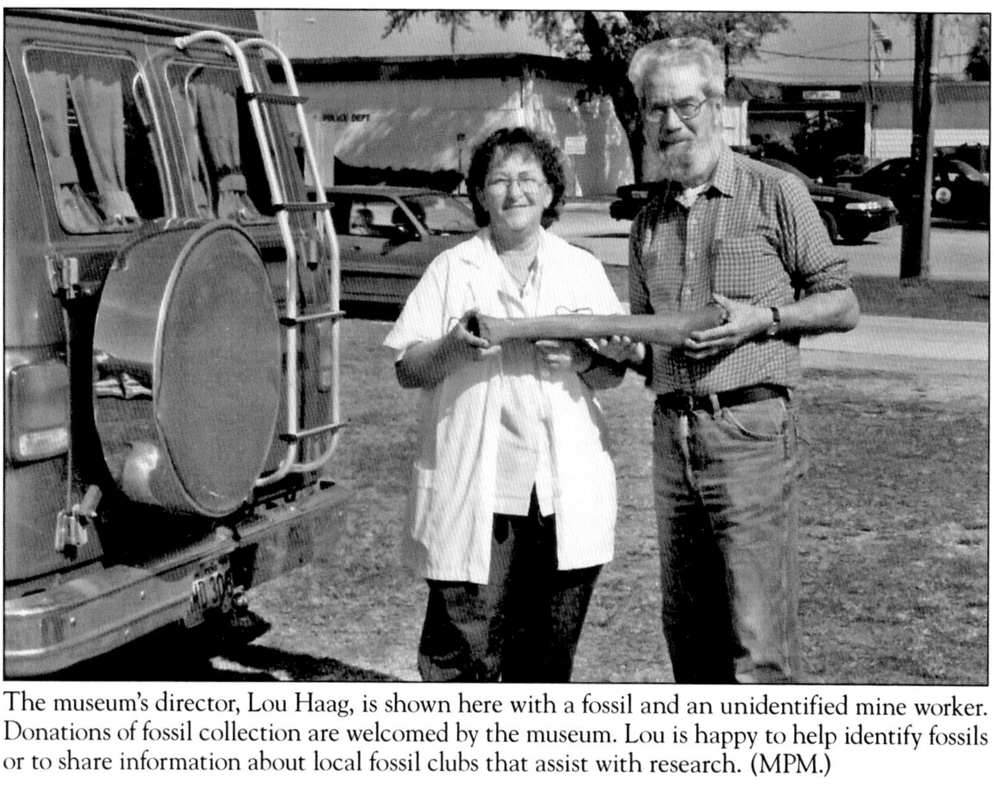

The museum's director, Lou Haag, is shown here with a fossil and an unidentified mine worker. Donations of fossil collection are welcomed by the museum. Lou is happy to help identify fossils or to share information about local fossil clubs that assist with research. (MPM.)

Two

PHOSPHATE MINING

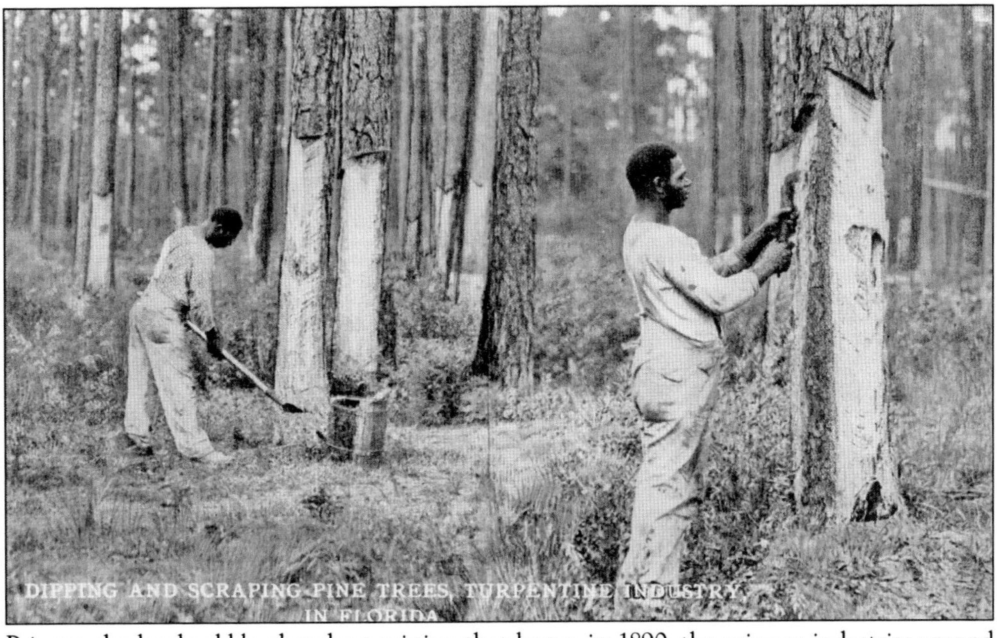

Prior to the land-pebble phosphate mining that began in 1890, the primary industries around Mulberry were farming, lumber, naval stores, and, to a lesser extent, citrus. At that time, the largest citrus groves were in northern Florida but would later move south following the severe freeze of 1894–1895. Here workers are harvesting pine tree resin to be distilled into turpentine. Growth of the mining industry could be seen in the change of companies' names relative to a change of ownership and/or joint venture. For instance, the U.S. Agricultural Corporation was renamed the International Agricultural Corporation (IAC) in 1901. The IAC entered the Florida phosphate mining industry in November 1909 by purchasing the Prairie Pebble Phosphate Company (PPPC). The IAC was renamed the International Minerals and Chemical Corporation (IMC) in December 1941. The IMC-Agrico Company was a joint venture, formed in July 1993, between IMC Fertilizer and Freeport-McMoRan Resource Partners, LP. (RF.)

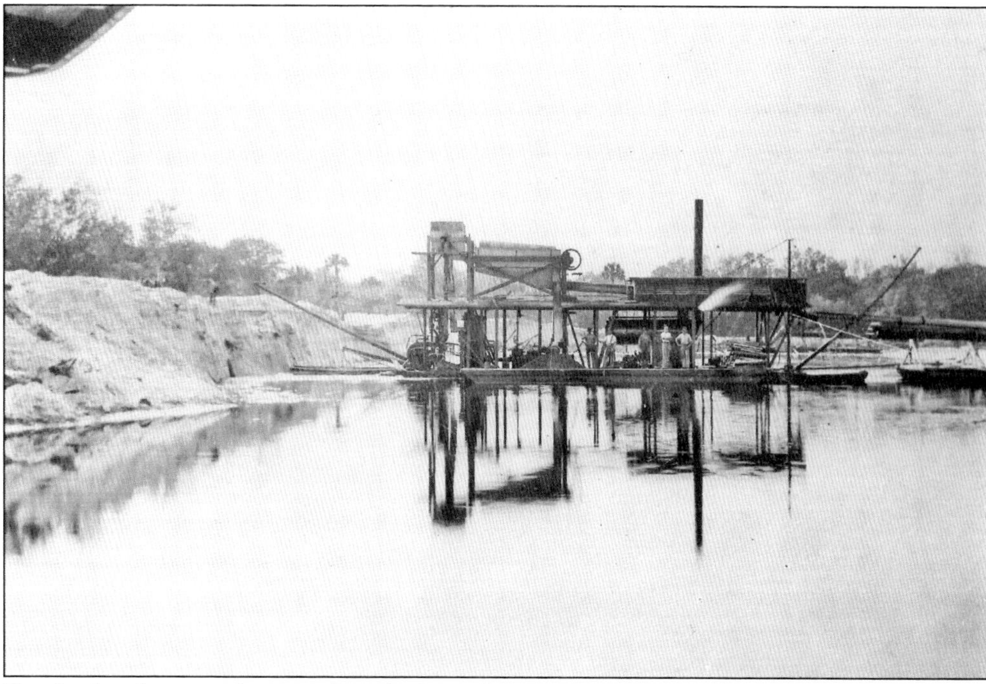

Florida phosphate was first mined on the Peace River in 1888. Suction dredges were used to collect the phosphate ore from the banks and bottom of the river. The phosphate slurry is pumped to the box on top of the dredge, where it is washed with water to remove much of the sand. The remaining phosphate is dumped into a barge at the aft end of the dredge. (RF.)

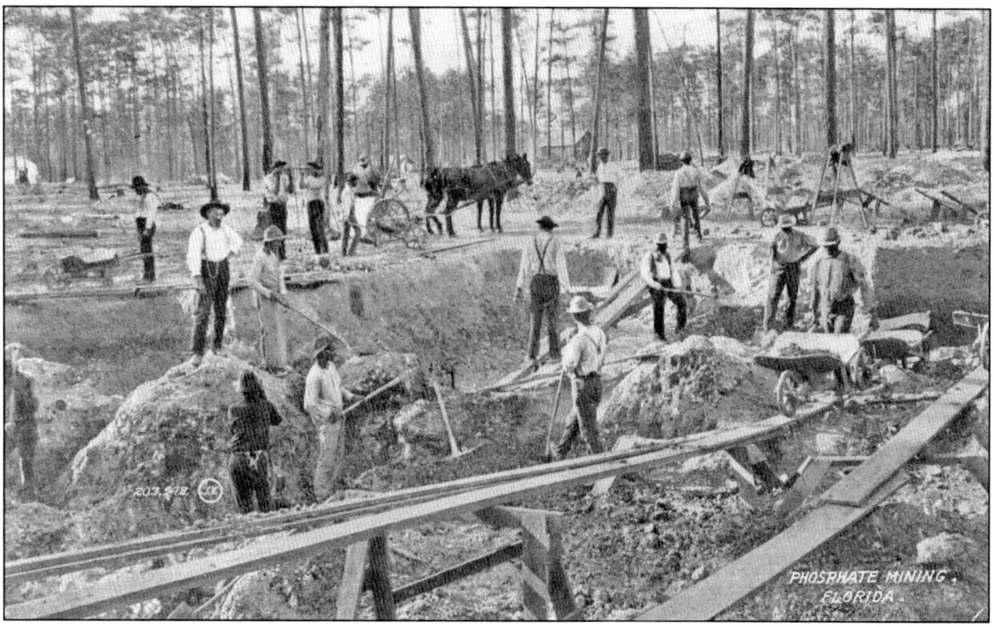

Both hard rock phosphate in north Florida and land-pebble phosphate in Bone Valley were initially mined by pick and shovel, which soon gave way to more efficient methods, such as a mule and scraper. The mining of the land-pebble phosphate, covered only by a 15- to 30-foot-deep layer of sand and clay, proved far easier and cheaper than hard rock mining. (RF.)

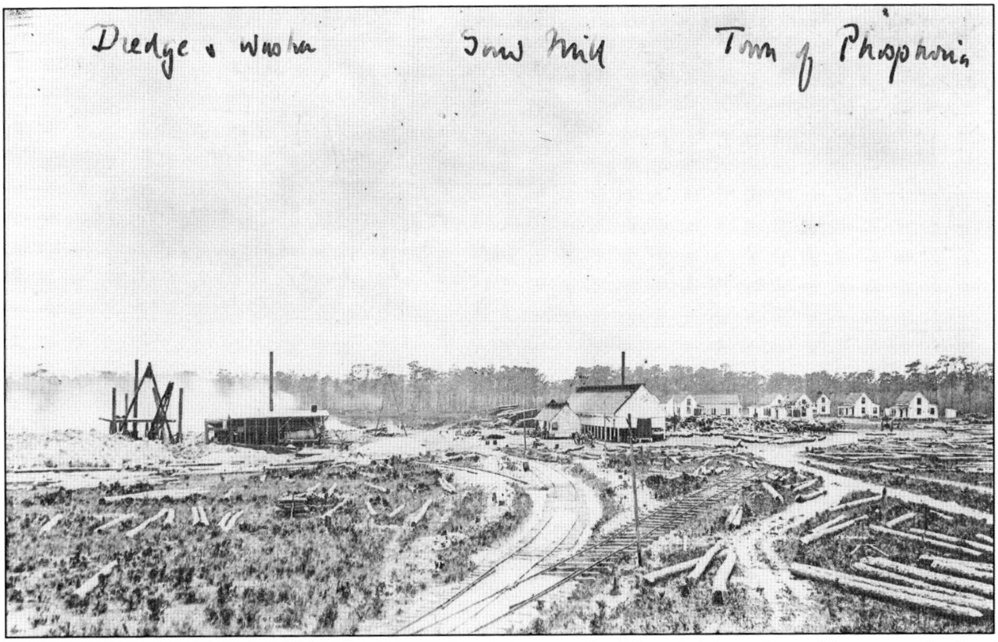

One of the earliest land-pebble mining companies was the Florida Phosphate Company, Ltd. of London, located at Phosphoria, approximately seven miles southeast of Mulberry. Here are the mining operations on the left, the saw mill in the center, and the company village of Phosphoria on the right. Phosphoria had a post office from October 1891 until May 1908. (RF.)

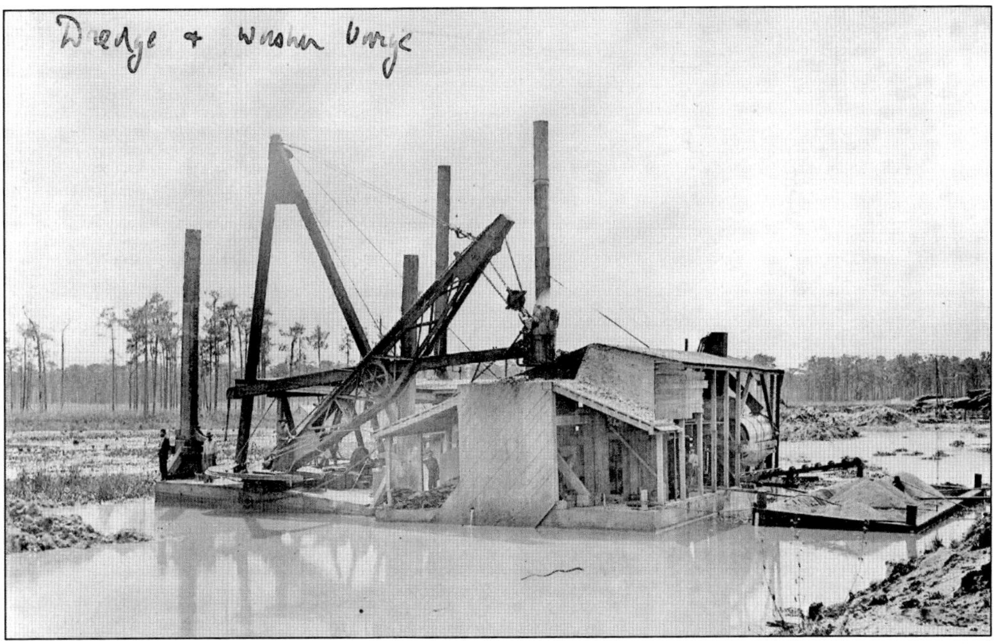

The first mining at Phosphoria was done with a suction dredge, used also to mine river-pebble phosphate. While a big improvement over the pick and shovel and mule and scraper, dredging required miners to keep enough water in the pit to float the dredge. If the water became too shallow, the expensive dredge could break its back. (RF.)

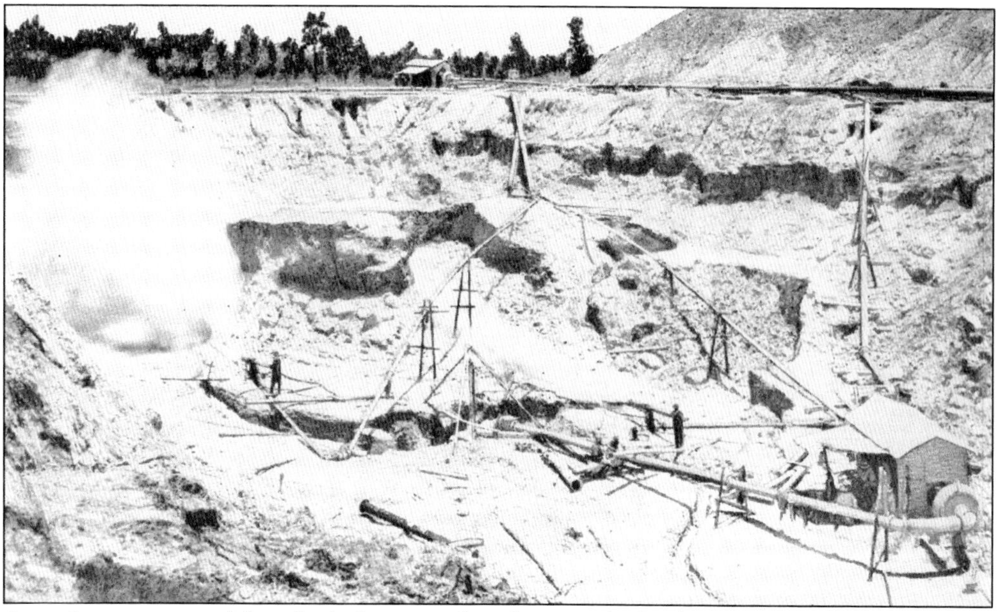

A much more successful method of mining phosphate was hydraulic mining. Water was directed at the phosphate matrix by high-pressure nozzles called water giants. Using the centrifugal pump in the "pit car," the phosphate slurry was pumped to the nearby washer. While very efficient, this method of mining was quite dangerous to the mining crew in the pit. (RF.)

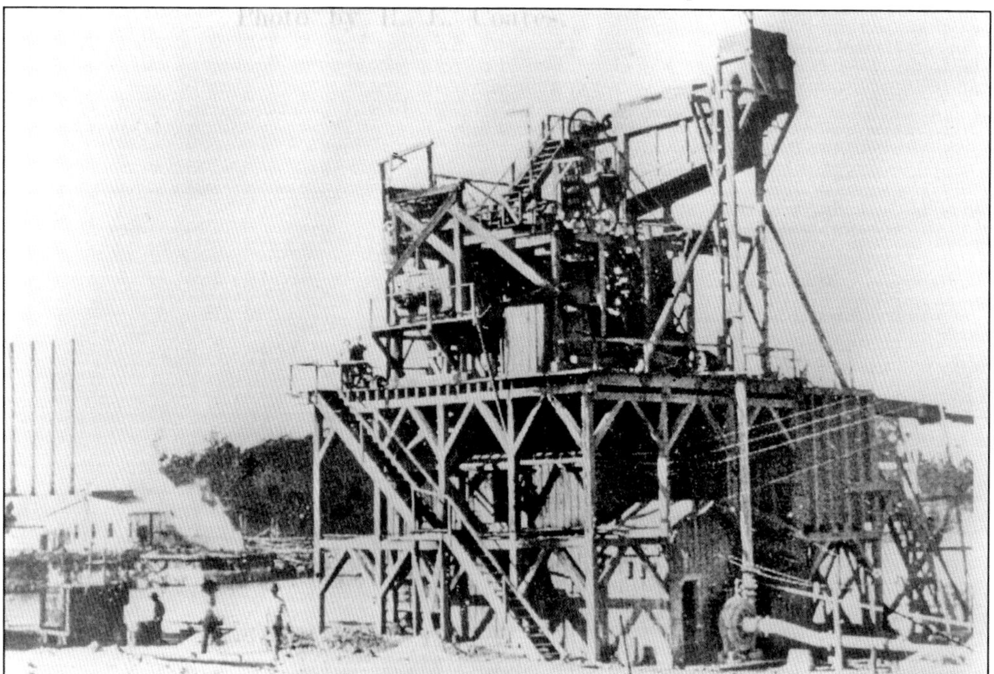

The Florida Mining Company, started in 1907 by Harry L. Pierce, was located just southeast of Mulberry on the north prong of the Alafia River. The early washers, such as those shown here, were built of wood so they could be easily torn down and relocated. They washed most of the sand and clay from the phosphate but also lost much of the small-grained phosphate. (RF.)

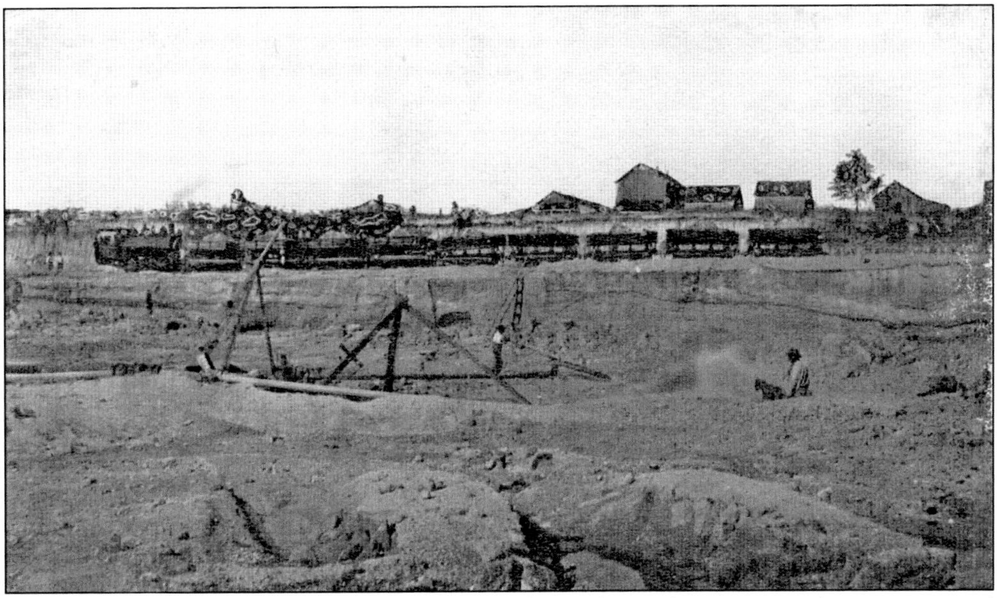

This early photograph of phosphate mining near Mulberry shows a locomotive pushing open-topped cars of wet phosphate rock from the washer to the temporary storage site. The wooden hopper cars could be dumped to the side. When required, the wet rock would be carried to the dryers, which would reduce the moisture content to less than two percent. (RF.)

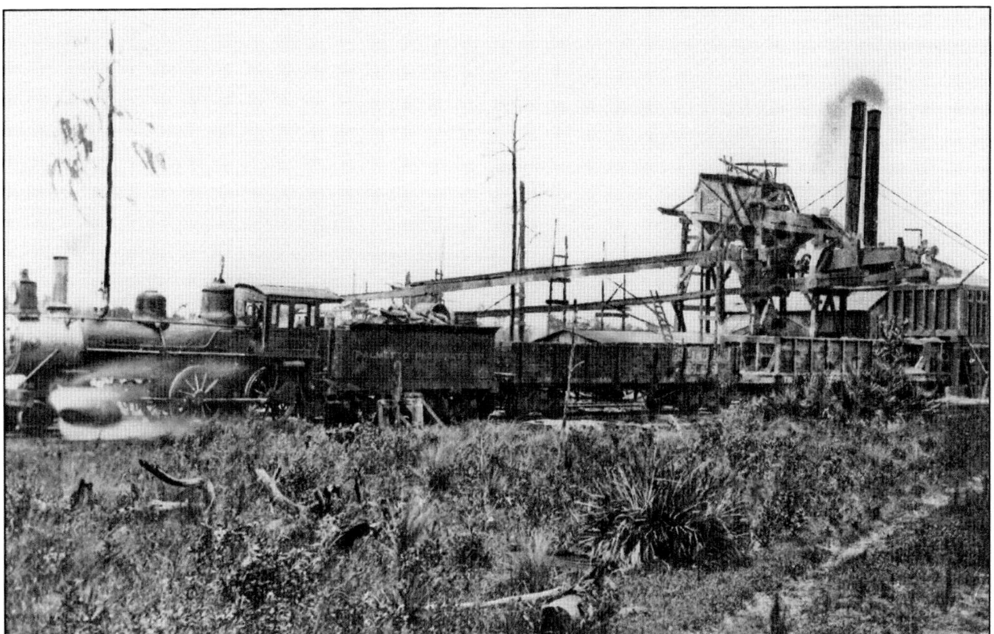

The Palmetto Phosphate Company was founded by Christopher Gustavus Memminger in July 1893. It was located at Tiger Bay, which was approximately 13 miles southwest of Mulberry. Shown here is the steam-powered washer, with an old locomotive pulling hoppers of wet rock to the dryer. The Palmetto Phosphate Company was subsequently purchased by the American Agricultural Chemical Company in November 1911. (RF.)

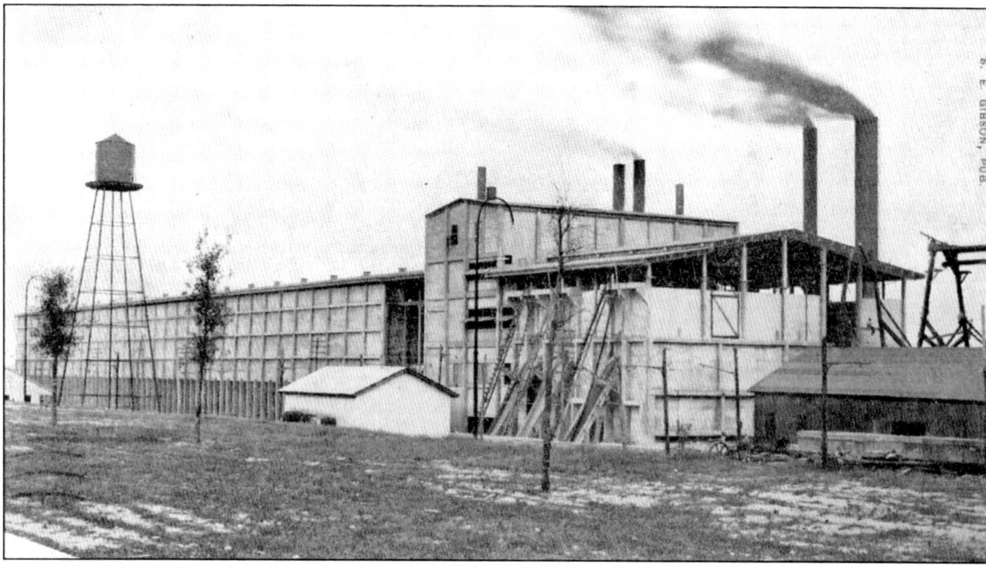

After Joseph Hull made a fortune in mining phosphate on the Peace River, he came to Mulberry and started the Prairie Pebble Phosphate Company, located at Prairie, about one mile northwest of Mulberry. He aggressively expanded the company by purchasing smaller companies nearby. In 1909, he sold the company to the International Agricultural Corporation, which is the ancestor of the Mosaic Company, currently the largest phosphate mining company in Florida. (RF.)

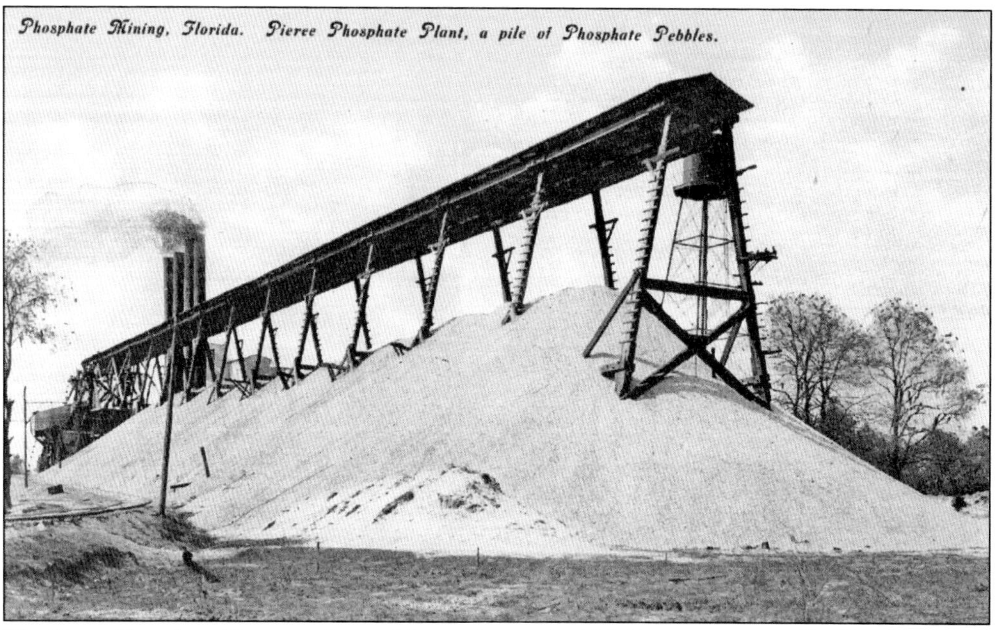

The Pierce Phosphate Company, located four miles south of Mulberry, was started by Harry L. Pierce in early 1906. In October of the same year, he sold the company to the American Agricultural Chemical Company, the second largest fertilizer company in the United States. Here is the wet rock storage site with the dryers and dry bins in the background. (RF.)

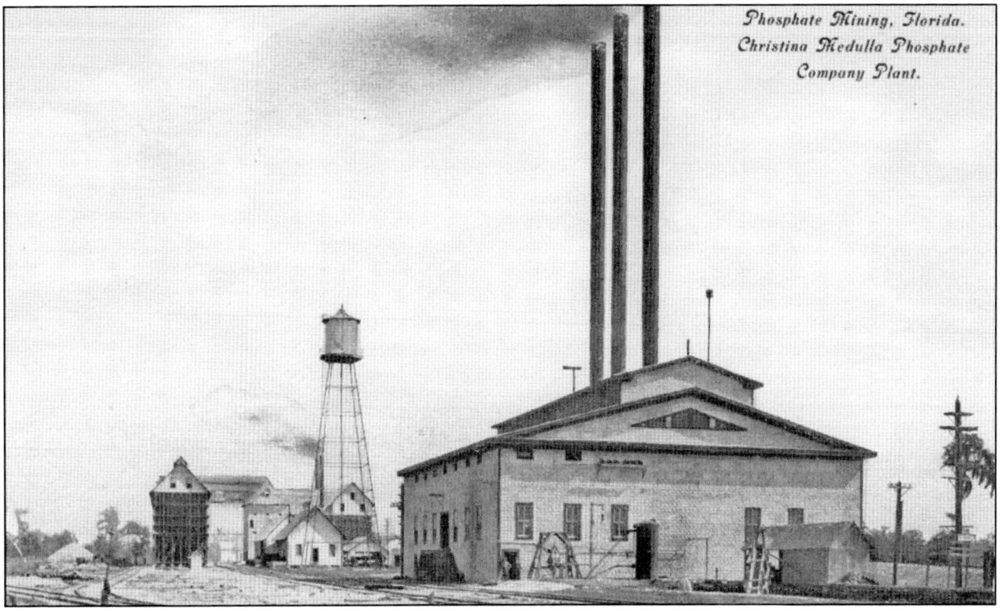

The Medulla Phosphate Company was started by Christopher Gustavus Memminger in September 1907 and was located three and a half miles north of Mulberry. Memminger named the site of his plant and workers' village Christina after his only daughter, Christine. Shown here are the power plant in the foreground and the drying plant and dry bin in the background. The company was sold to the Phosphate Mining Company in January 1910. (RF.)

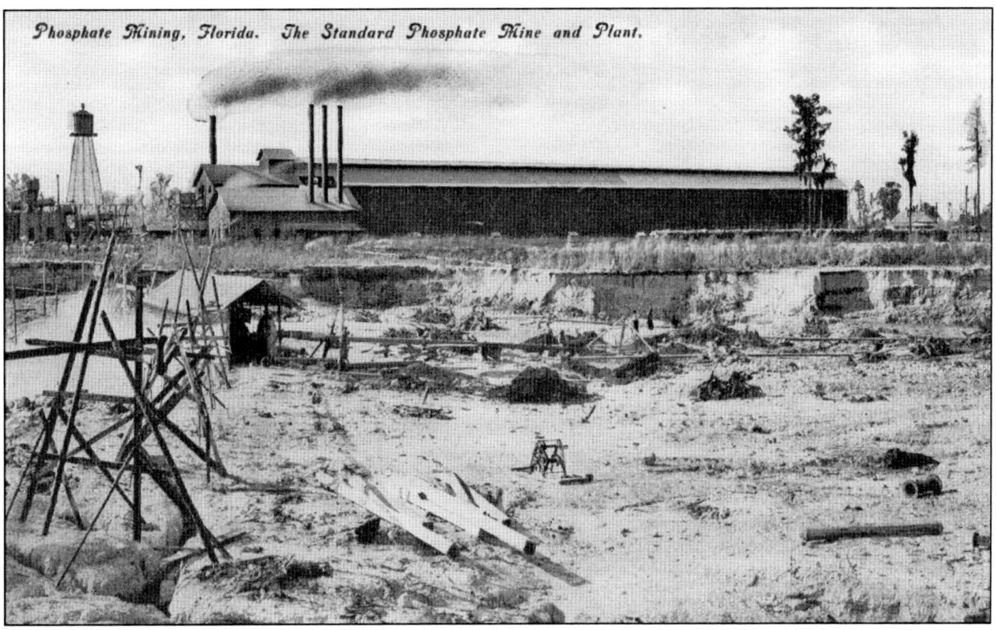

The Standard Phosphate Company was started in 1891 and was located just north of the Medulla Phosphate Company. It was acquired by a French company, the Societe Anonyme des Phosphates de Florida, which named the site of the plant Tancrede, after Paul Tancrede, one of the company's officers. Here is a little of the desolation caused by the open cast, or strip, mining for phosphate. (RF.)

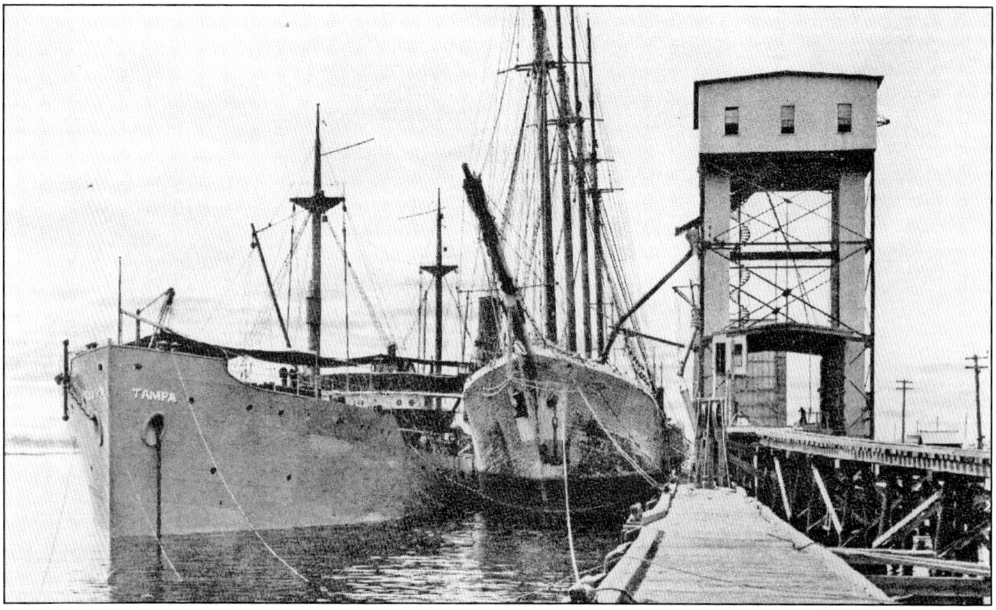

Until the late 1940s, almost all of the mined phosphate from around Mulberry was shipped to plants on the Eastern Seaboard for rendering into fertilizer. The first phosphate shipping terminals were at Port Tampa and later at the Port of Tampa. Long trains of phosphate, called phosphate drags, carried the ore to the loading docks, where hoppers loaded the phosphate into ships. (RF.)

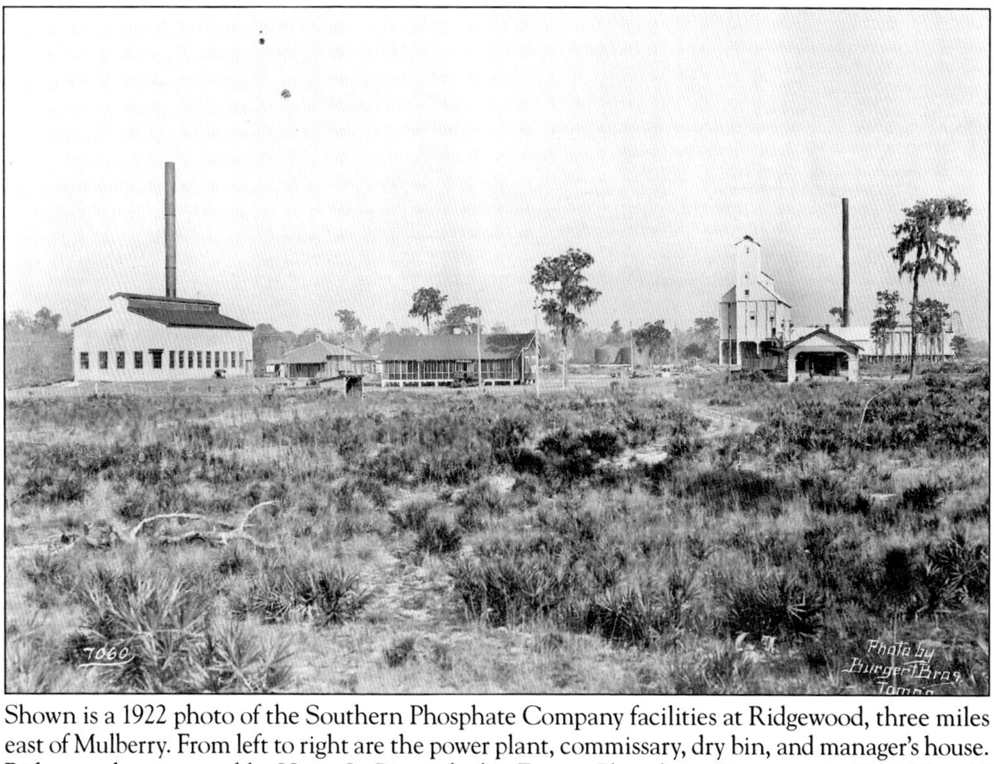

Shown is a 1922 photo of the Southern Phosphate Company facilities at Ridgewood, three miles east of Mulberry. From left to right are the power plant, commissary, dry bin, and manager's house. Ridgewood was started by Harry L. Pierce for his Export Phosphate Company in 1912. He sold the Export Phosphate Company to the Southern Phosphate Company in 1919. (RF.)

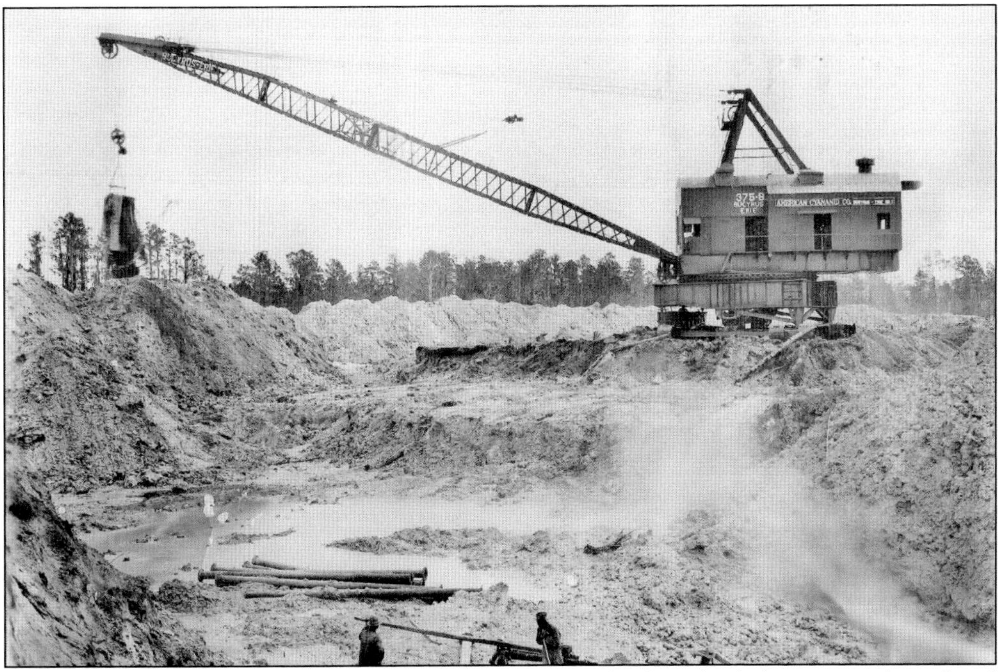

By the time this photograph was taken in 1930, electric draglines had almost entirely replaced steam shovels and steam draglines. This Bucyrus-Erie 375-B crawler dragline, introduced the previous year, could carry a 10-cubic-yard bucket. Here the American Cyanamid Company mines its property at Sydney, west of Mulberry and just inside Hillsborough County. (RF.)

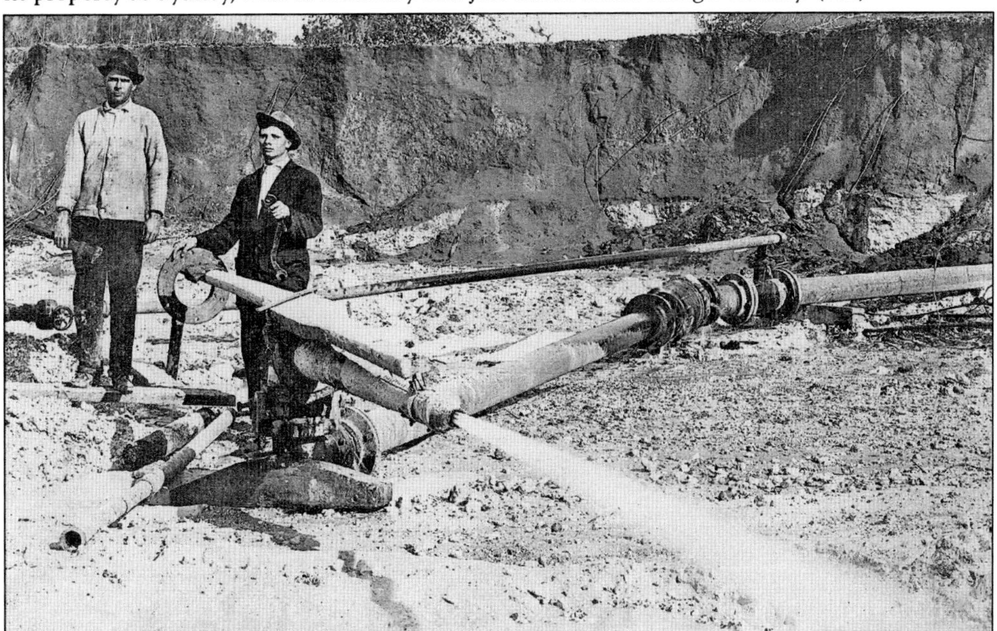

Charles Arthur "Cat" Thomas went to work for the American Agricultural Chemical Company in 1937 as a carpenter. He later got a job as operator of a hydraulic giant mining phosphate. In this photograph, taken about 1940, Thomas is on the right controlling the direction of the jet. The crude controls can clearly be seen. (RF.)

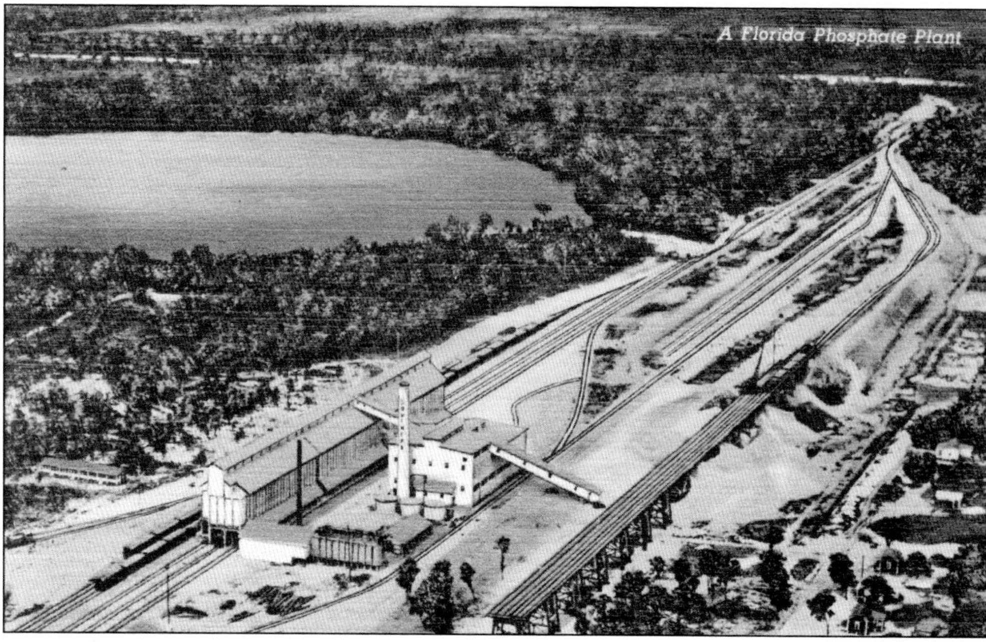

Here is the greatly expanded plant of the Southern Phosphate Company at Ridgewood, c. 1945. The dry bin seen in a previous photograph can be seen to be much larger. Behind the plant is Bonny Lake, a favorite recreation spot for many families in the Mulberry area. Unfortunately, the lake was later destroyed when W. R. Grace, the successor company to the Southern Phosphate Corporation, mined the area for phosphate. (RF.)

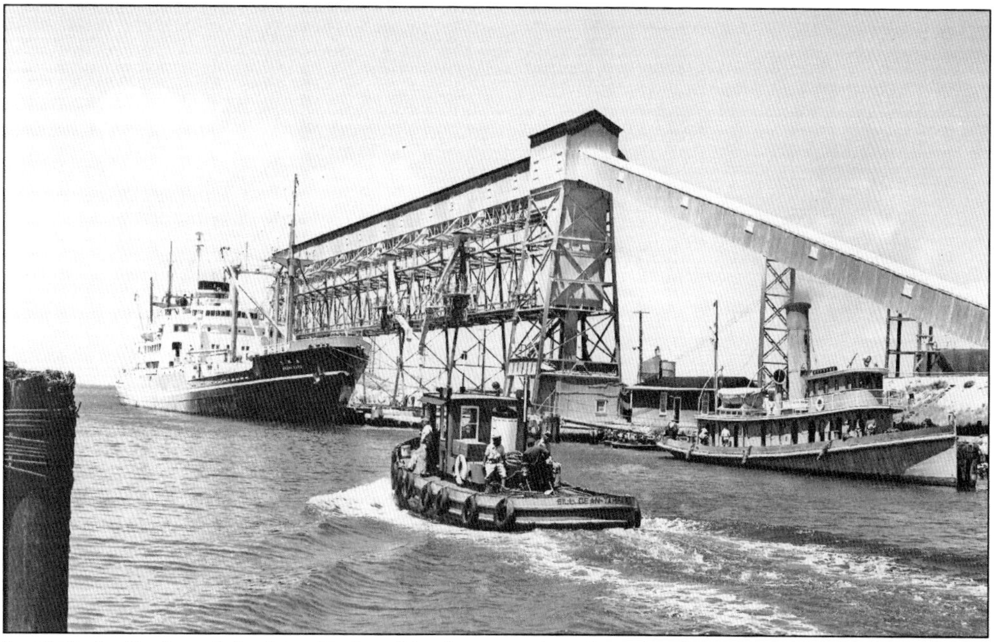

In 1947, the Seaboard Air Line Railroad built a new phosphate loading terminal at Seddon Island in the Port of Tampa. It was capable of loading 1,500 tons of phosphate rock per hour. This facility supplemented the terminals at Port Tampa and Boca Grande, also owned by the Seaboard Air Line Railroad. (RF.)

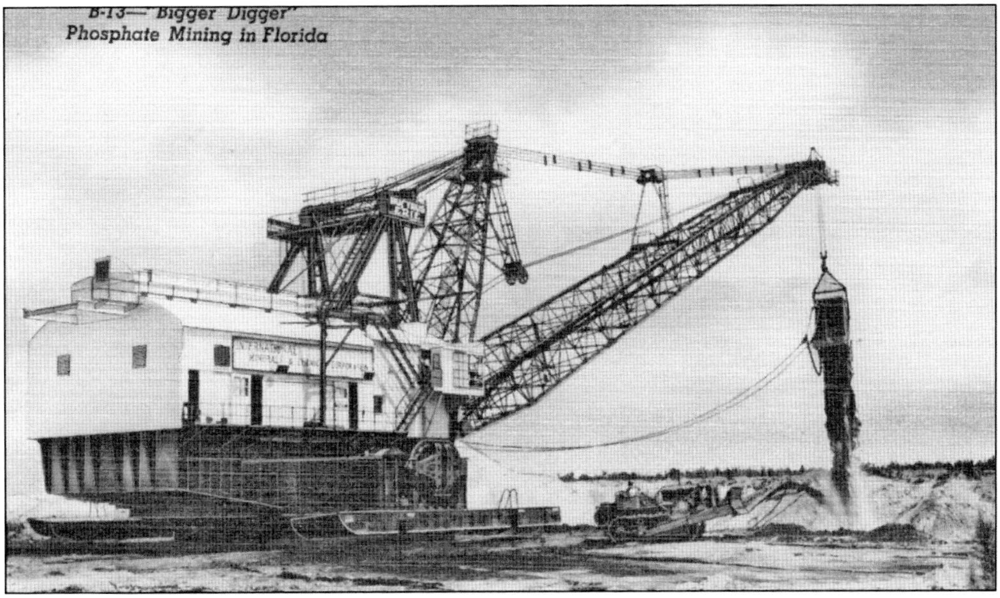

Draglines became ever larger and more powerful, and their bucket sizes likewise increased. In 1944, the Bucyrus-Erie Company introduced the 1150-B dragline, the largest in the world at that time. This 1,200-ton machine had a 215-foot boom and a 21.4-cubic-yard bucket. The International Minerals and Chemical Corporation, formerly the International Agricultural Corporation, purchased one in 1946. They promptly named it the Bigger Digger.

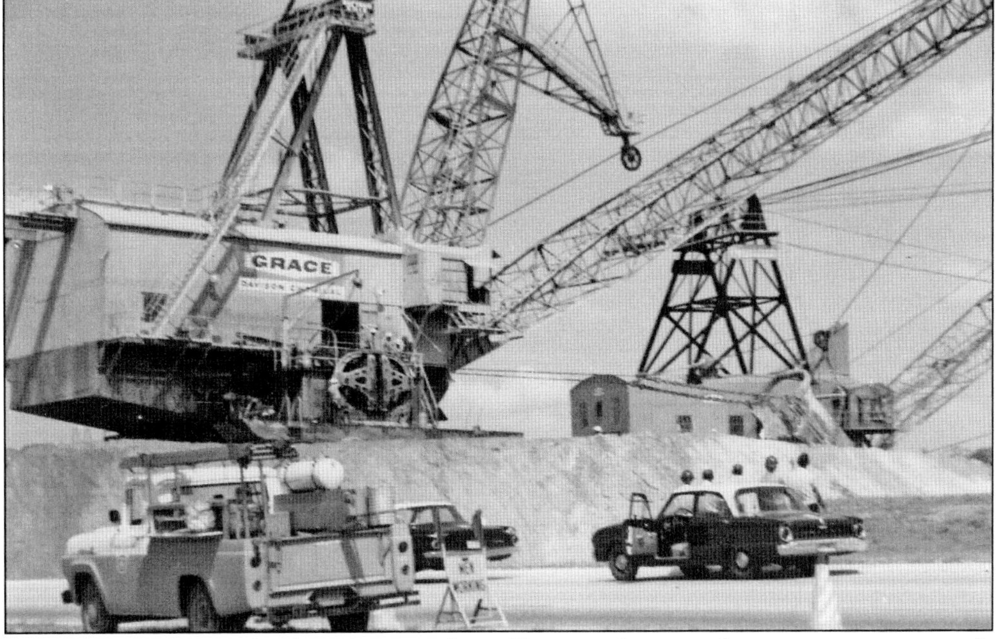

Since the 1930s, most draglines have used a walking mechanism of two pontoons to provide mobility, with walking speeds of typically 0.15 miles per hour. In the mid-1960s, the W. R. Grace Company had to move two draglines south of their Ridgewood complex, east of Mulberry. Here are the two draglines backing over Highway 60, which has been buffered by a large mound of sand. (RF.)

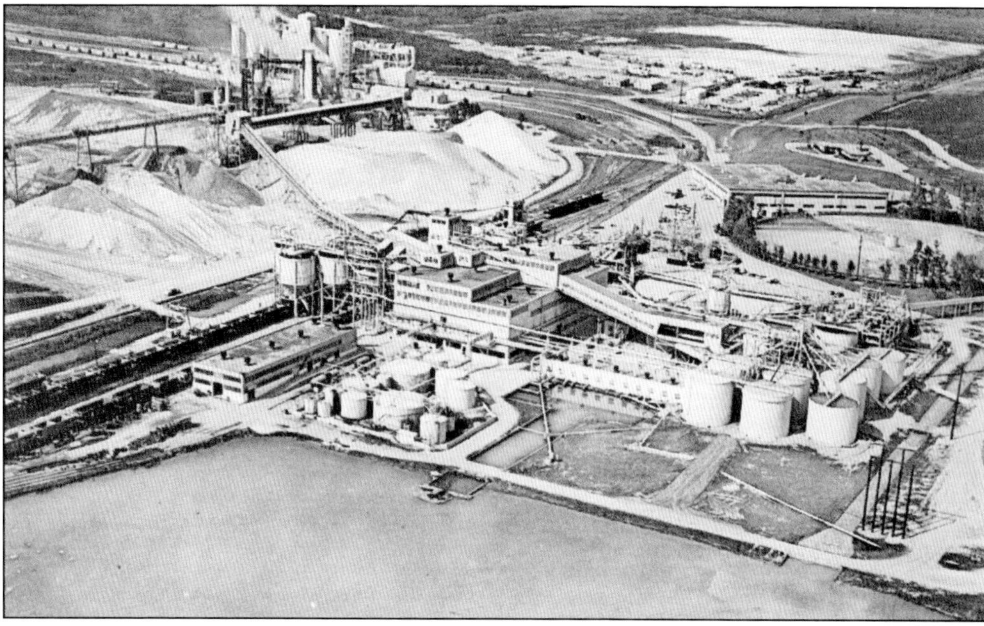

In March 1948, the International Minerals and Chemical Corporation (IMC) opened its Noralyn mine, located about eight miles south-southeast of Mulberry. With a production capacity of 1.5 million tons of phosphate per year, it was, at the time, the largest phosphate mine in the world. IMC named this mine after the mother of the company president, Louis Ware. (RF.)

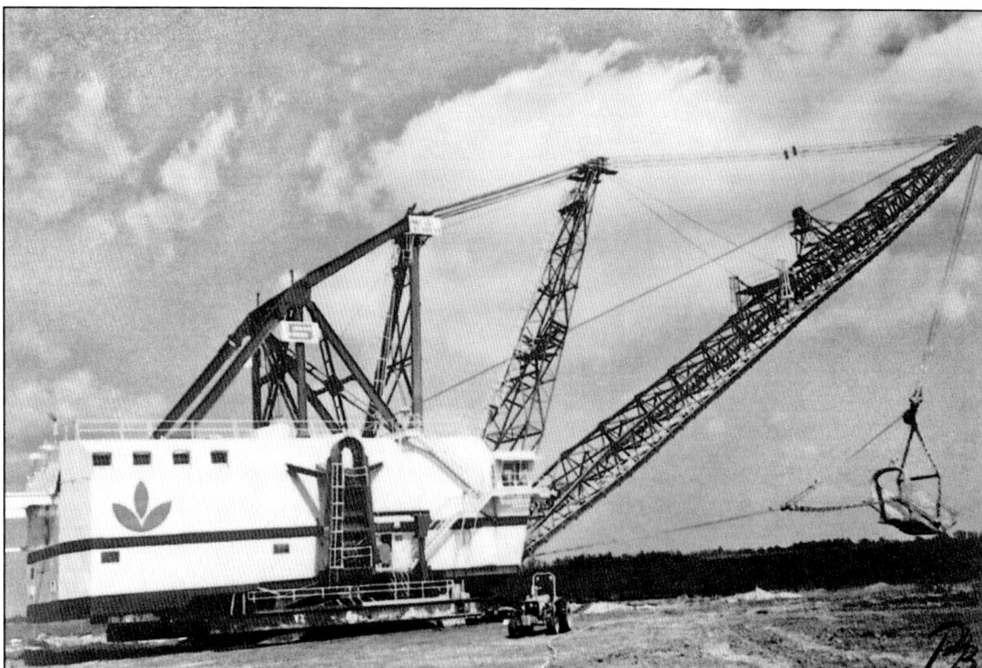

By the early 1990s, draglines in Bone Valley were huge. Typical was this P&H dragline, operated by the IMC-Agrico Company. This dragline weighed 1800 tons and carried a bucket with a capacity of 36 cubic yards. The IMC-Agrico Company was a joint venture between the IMC Fertilizer Group, Inc. and several other companies. (RF.)

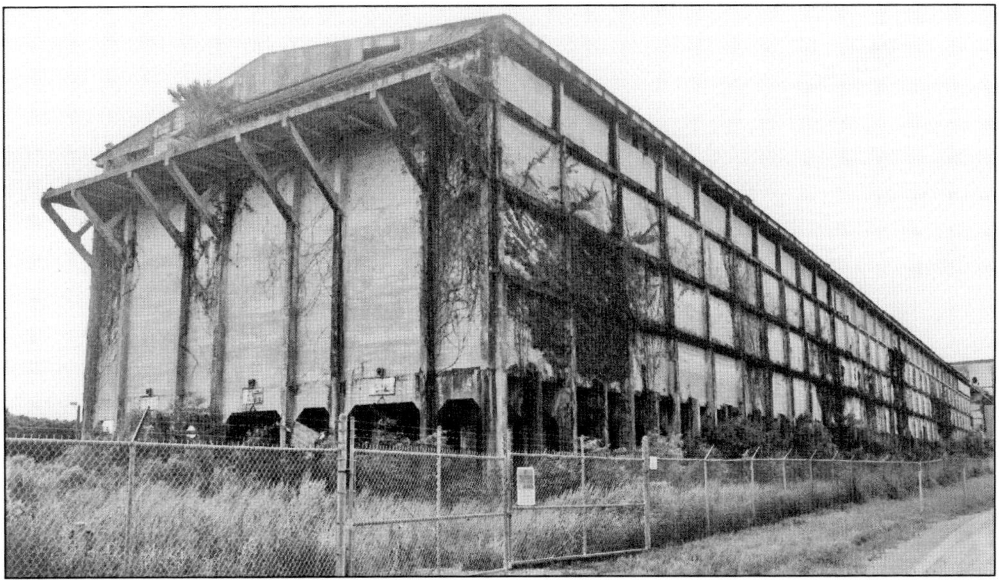

The phosphate deposits in Polk County had, for the most part, been mined out by 2007. While most of the mining had moved south, the processing plants remained around Mulberry. There are few reminders of the many companies that mined in Bone Valley, sadly. Shown here is the derelict dry bin of the Prairie Pebble Phosphate Company seen in a previous photograph. It sits on the outskirts of Mulberry. (RF.)

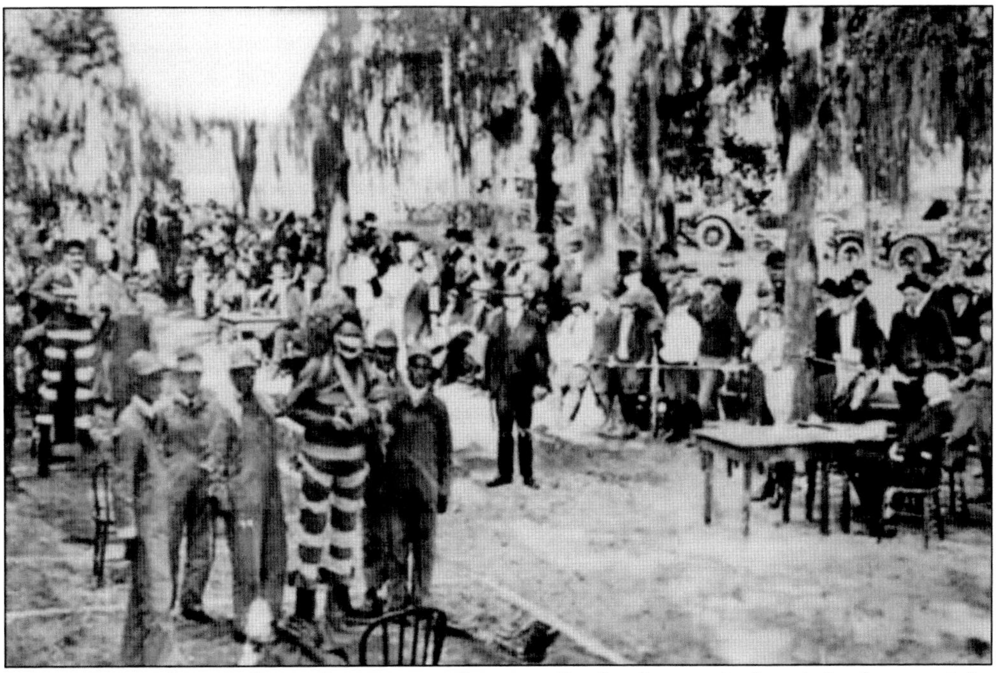

To improve employee safety and increase productivity, Burdett Loomis Jr. founded a chapter of the Joseph A. Holmes Safety Association at Pierce in 1922. Shown is the first Intra-Company First Aid Contest, held at Pierce on March 10, 1923. The winners are the team from the American Agricultural Chemical Company. Held annually for many years, the spirited competitions were popular with residents of the various company towns. (Raymond L. Driver.)

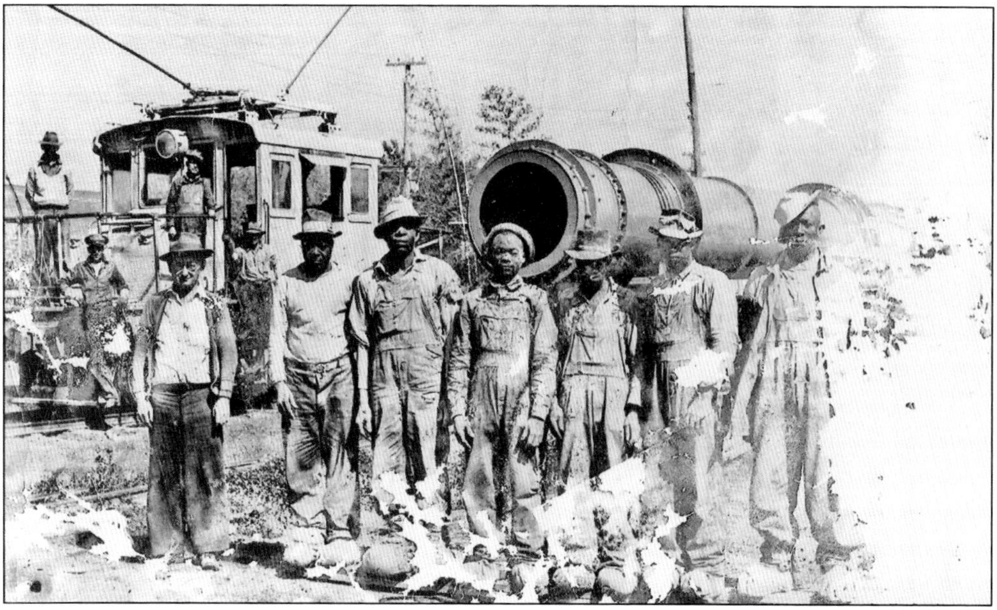

It is noted that this dryer shell for dryer unit No. 15 arrived by electric locomotive at 11:00 a.m. on April 4, 1942. The men are listed left to right with years of employment: (standing in the foreground) yardmaster Jack Sheets, 16; Gen. Jackson Jones, 22; Wayman Smith, 8.5; Arthur Carr, 6.5; Wash Williams, 39.5; Ollie Anderson, 3; Isom Helper, 17; and Alexander Franklin, 20; (on the locomotive) Walter Johnson, 1.3; Bill Caraker, 9; Roscoe Johnson, 18; Archie Moore, 8.5. (Essie N. Helper Morgan.)

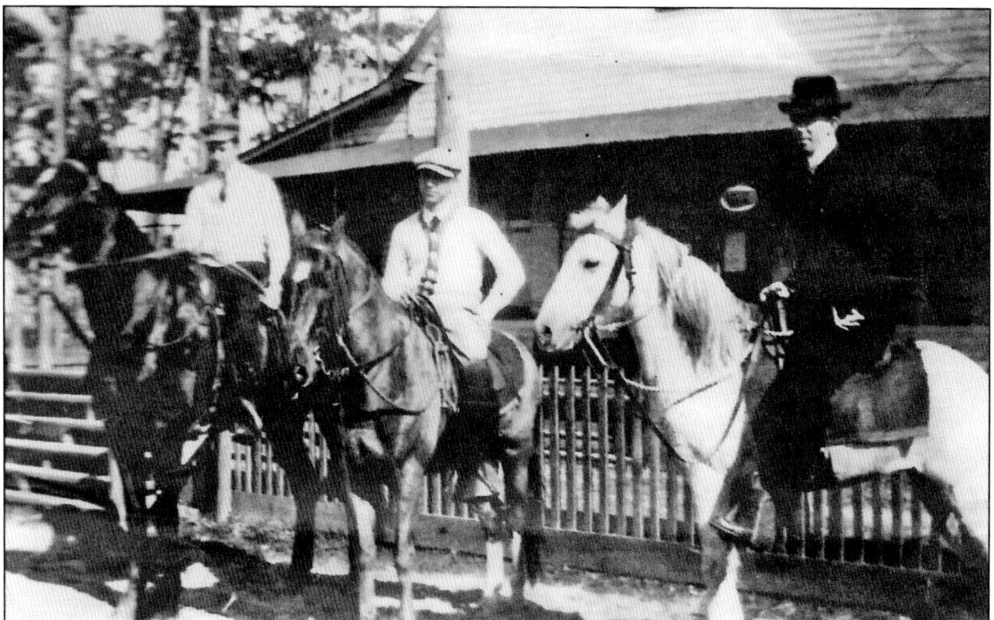

The unidentified men on horses are in front of the Phosphate Mining Company's commissary at Nichols, Florida. Tokens provided by mine employers were used by workers to purchase everyday household and personal items at the commissary. Town merchants soon started accepting the tokens as a strategy for capitalizing on this growing buying power. (MBS.)

Three

Communities Become a Town

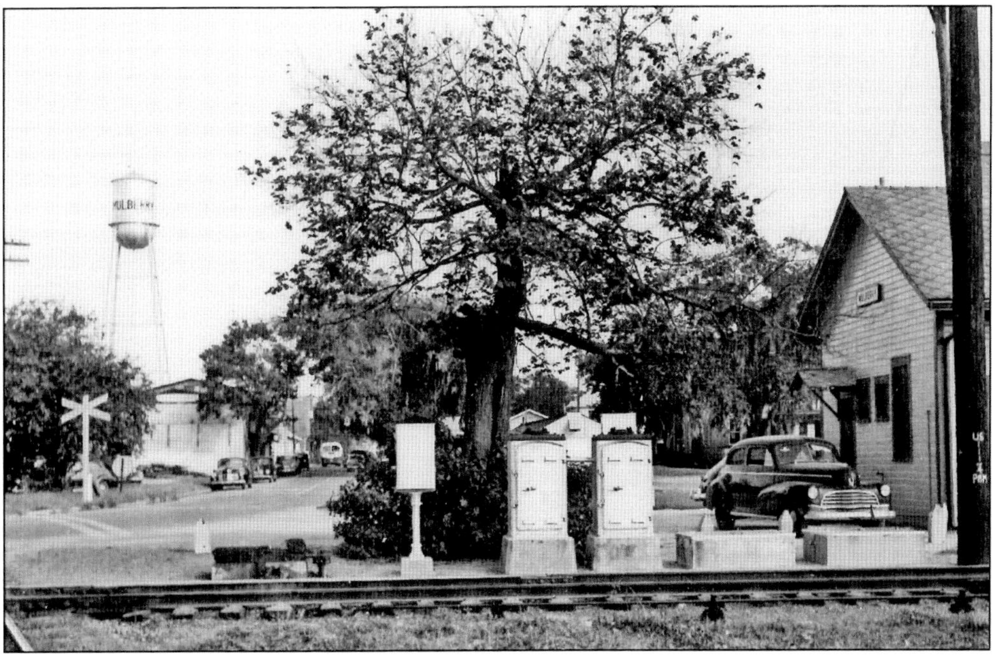

Mulberry was incorporated in February 1901. The first settlers can be traced back to 1840s. Shown in the foreground of this 1950s photograph is the water tower featuring the name of the city. Take a good look at the railroad crossing sign, the historic mulberry tree after which the town was named, and the railroad depot that is now the Mulberry Phosphate Museum. This photograph may have been taken by Alva C. Pipkin as the car looks as if it is Pipkin's father's car. This photograph is also similar to one that was published in the Mulberry yearbook, the *Ledger*, and the *Mulberry Press*. Pipkin was a correspondent for these publications. (Howard Wiggs/MBS.)

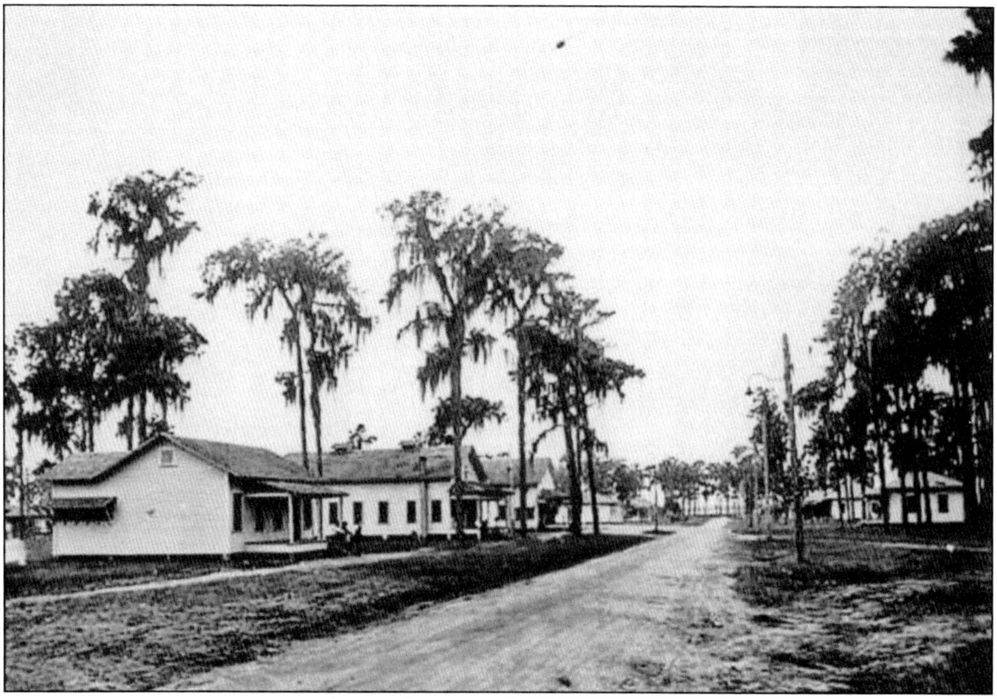

As people migrated to the frontier area, mining companies developed company towns to supply transportation, medical care, shopping, education, and housing. An African American author for the Federal Writers' Project (1935) gave this description of the African American quarters: "Mostly comfortably furnished homes . . . well-equipped schoolrooms . . . and automobiles of the latest makes." Rising company cost for these communities and the development of towns such as Mulberry in close proximity of the mines encouraged companies to offer their employees an opportunity to purchase one of the provided houses and to resettle by moving the house to an adjourning town. (SLAF.)

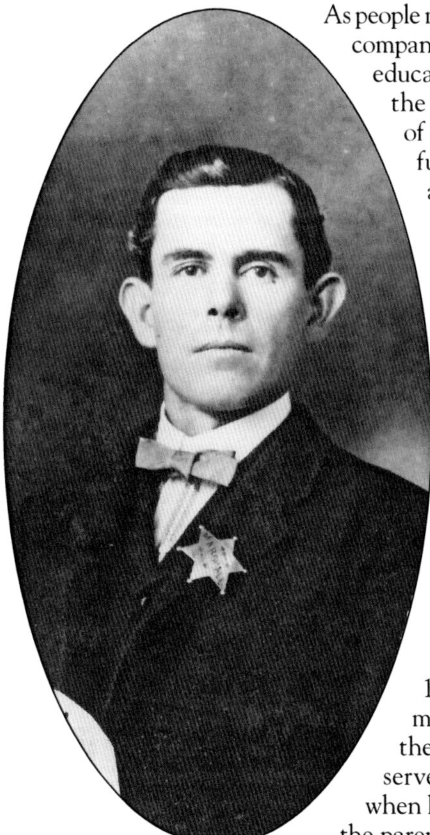

William Clement Sprott (1874–1953) was born in Savannah, Georgia. Arriving in Mulberry in the late 1890s, he worked as a carpenter in the mines. Sprott married Anna Laura Bargesser on March 17, 1900, and the same year, he started a livery stable business. Sprott served as city marshal from 1908 until January 12, 1910, when he was shot twice by a hired assassin. The Sprotts were the parents of one son and seven daughters.

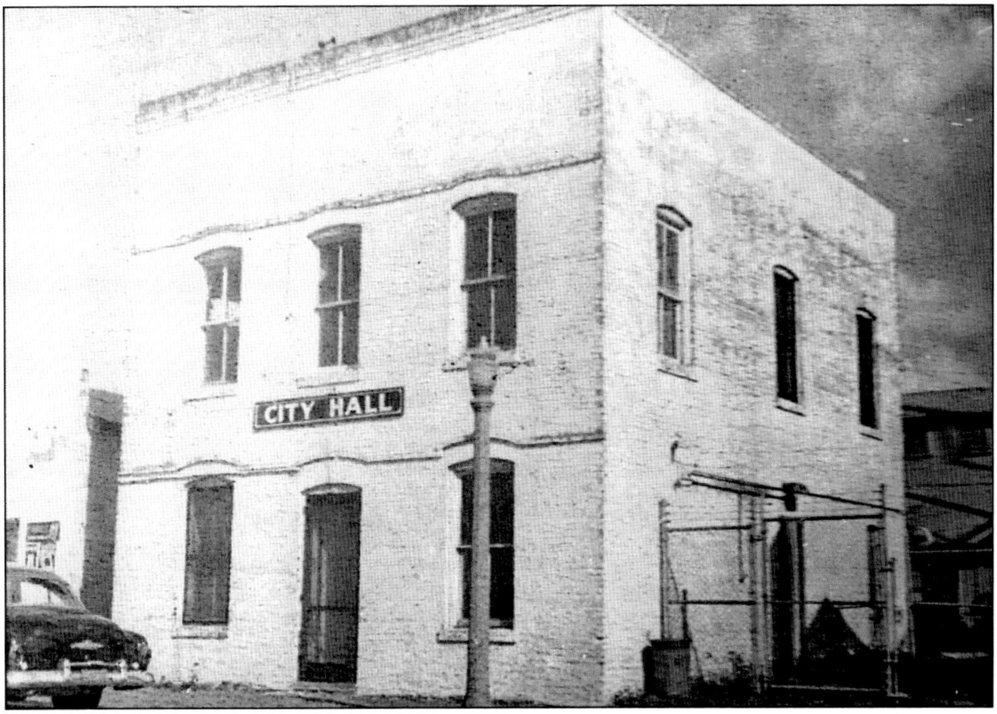

In 1909, this brick structure was built to be the city hall. The jail was located on the first floor. Legend has it that two African Americans were arrested for drunkenness and, later that night, the old wooden city hall burned down; some say the prisoners started the fire to keep warm, some say to escape. No jailer was present, and the prisoners were never found. (Henrie H. Sparkman/MBS.)

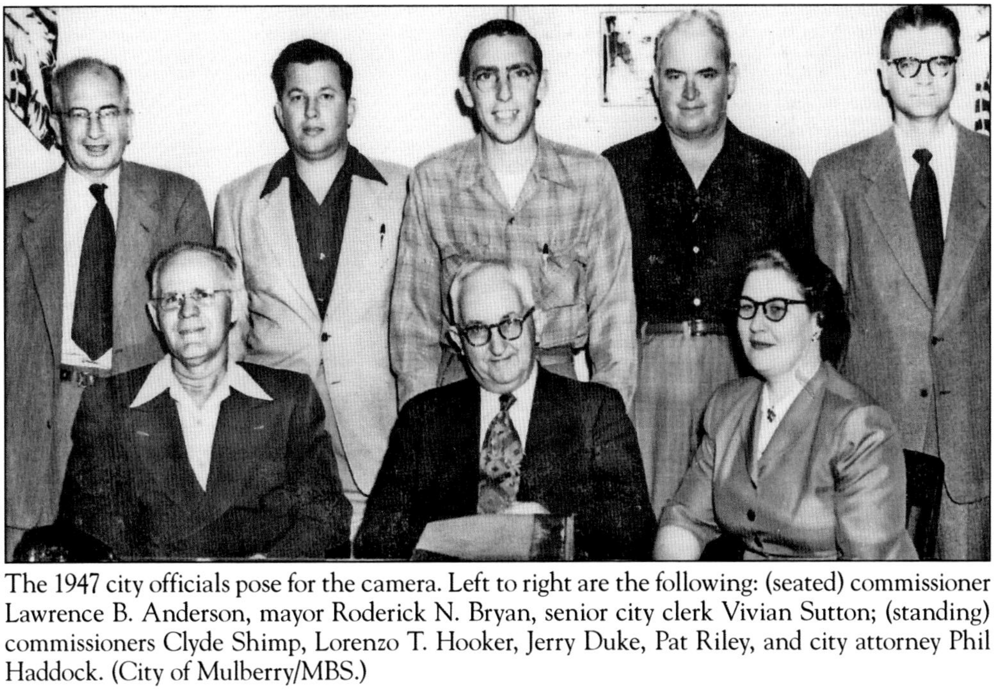

The 1947 city officials pose for the camera. Left to right are the following: (seated) commissioner Lawrence B. Anderson, mayor Roderick N. Bryan, senior city clerk Vivian Sutton; (standing) commissioners Clyde Shimp, Lorenzo T. Hooker, Jerry Duke, Pat Riley, and city attorney Phil Haddock. (City of Mulberry/MBS.)

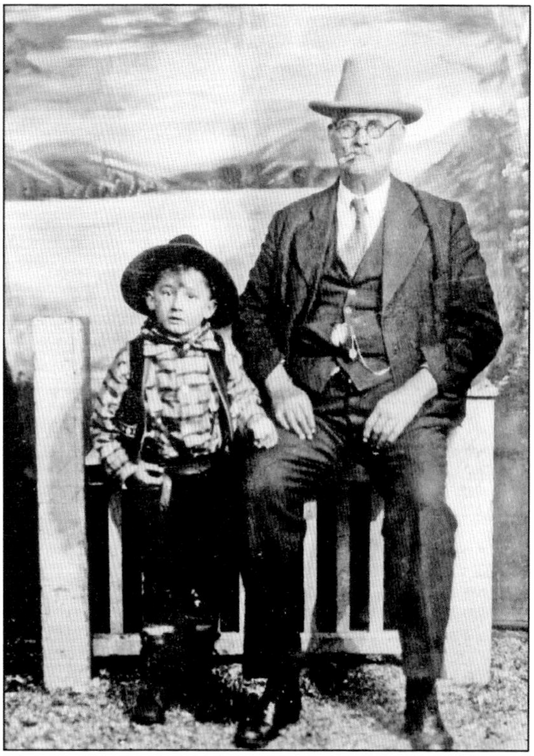

Four-year-old William Benjamin Hunt, son of Henry and Annie Louise Lee Hunt, is shown with his grandfather, city marshal D. Hunt, who was born in North Carolina and moved to Medulla to establish a turpentine business in the early 1930s. He married Lulu Sapp, they had one child, Henry Benjamin, and then they moved to Mulberry. City marshal D. Hunt once owned all of the land along Drane Field Road. (Annie Louise Lee Hunt/MBS.)

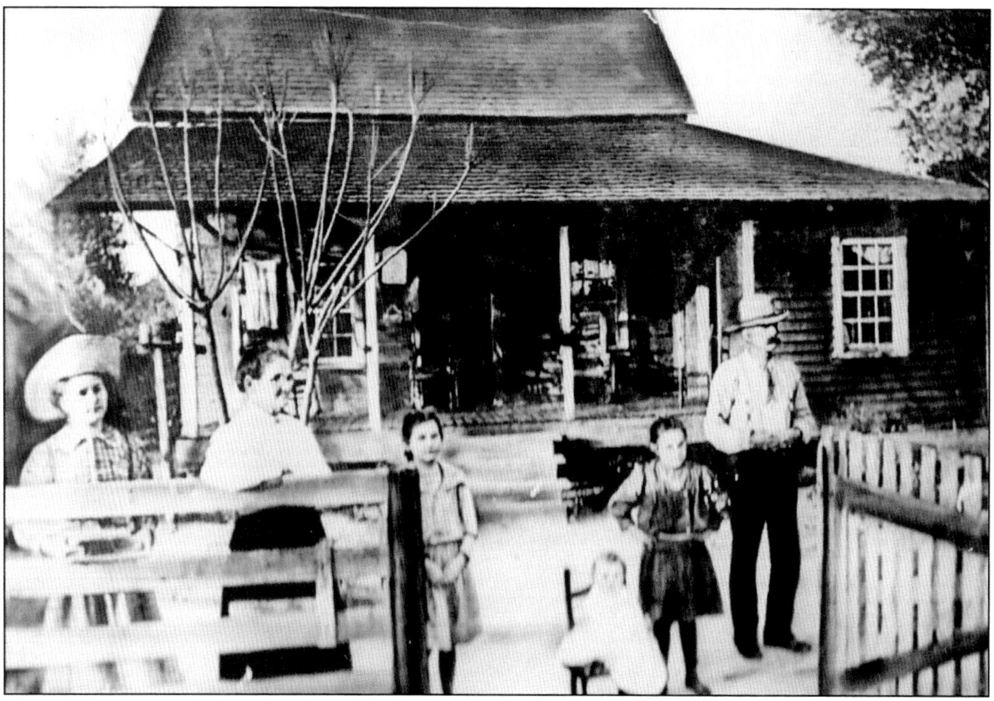

James and Letitia Harvey Shuman homesteaded in 1867 in the Brewster area. Pictured here are, from left to right, Myrtle Shuman Moore, Julie Shuman, Lorena Whatley, two unidentified children, and George Shuman. (Ernestine Alderman Stavely/MBS.)

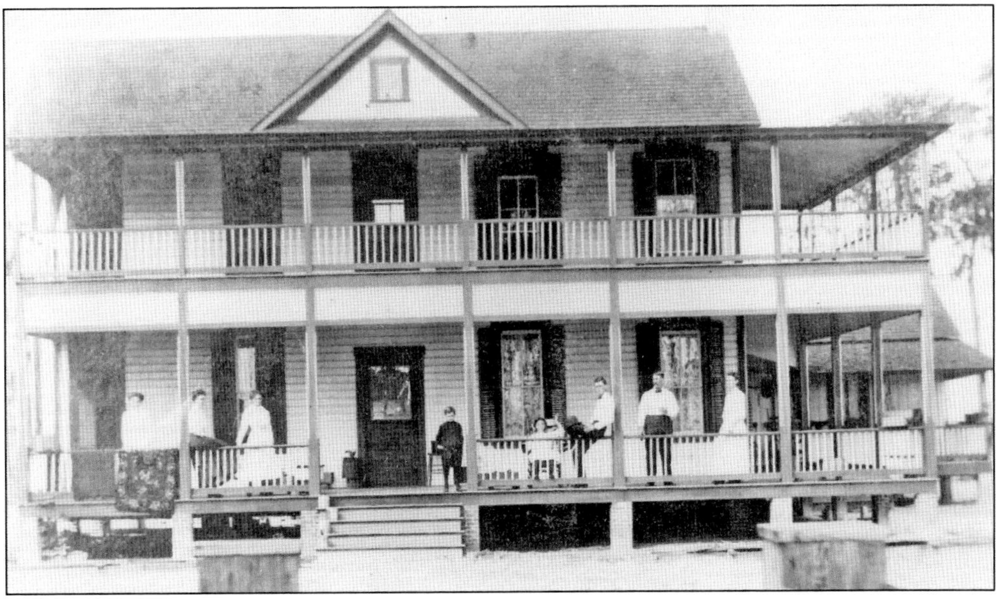

Joseph O. Whidden (1865–1918) and Callie Jane Branch (1868–1955) married on September 12, 1889. Whidden was a president of the Bank of Bradley, owned a mercantile store, and served as a teacher in Bradley. Whidden also owned a wood camp in Phillippi where this picture was taken of their home. The wood camp supplied the railroad and mines with wood. The Whiddens had five children: Vernon Whidden, Onzelo Whidden, Effie Whidden (Kilpatrick), Zella Whidden (Driskell), Annie Whidden (Gratham). (Evalyn Kilpatrick Stephens/MBS.)

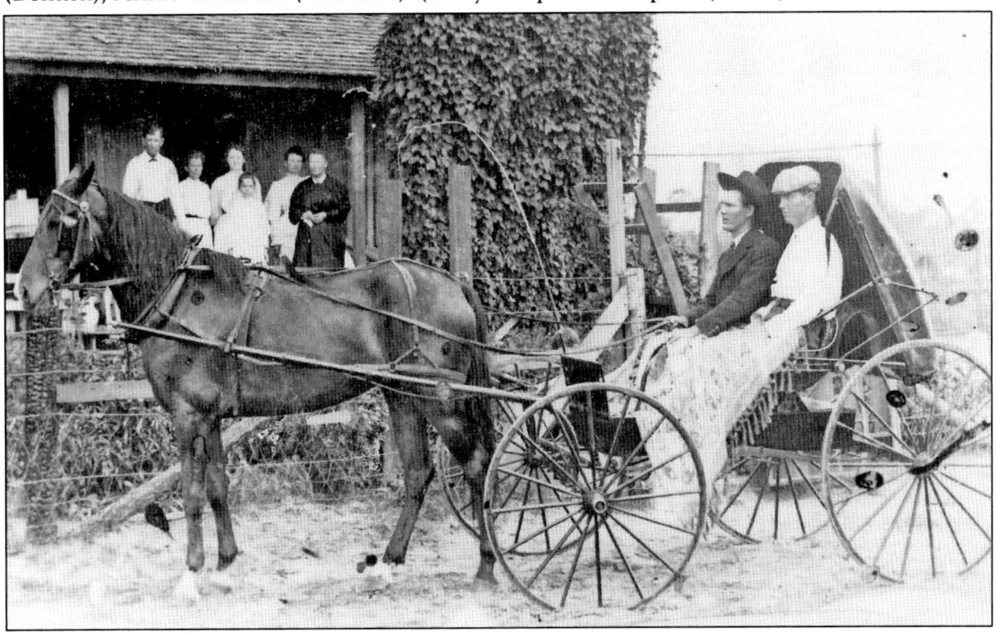

The gentleman riding in the buggy wearing the black suit is John F. Kilpatrick (1875–1952). Others in the picture are unidentified. Kilpatrick married Effie Whidden (1892–1975) on February 26, 1911. Seven children were born to this union: Carter, John, Evalyn (Stephens), Nell (Turner), Bob, Patricia (Holleman), and Mickey. John and Effie are buried in the Mt. Olive Primitive Baptist Church Cemetery, which was constituted in 1881. (Evalyn Kilpatrick Stephens/MBS.)

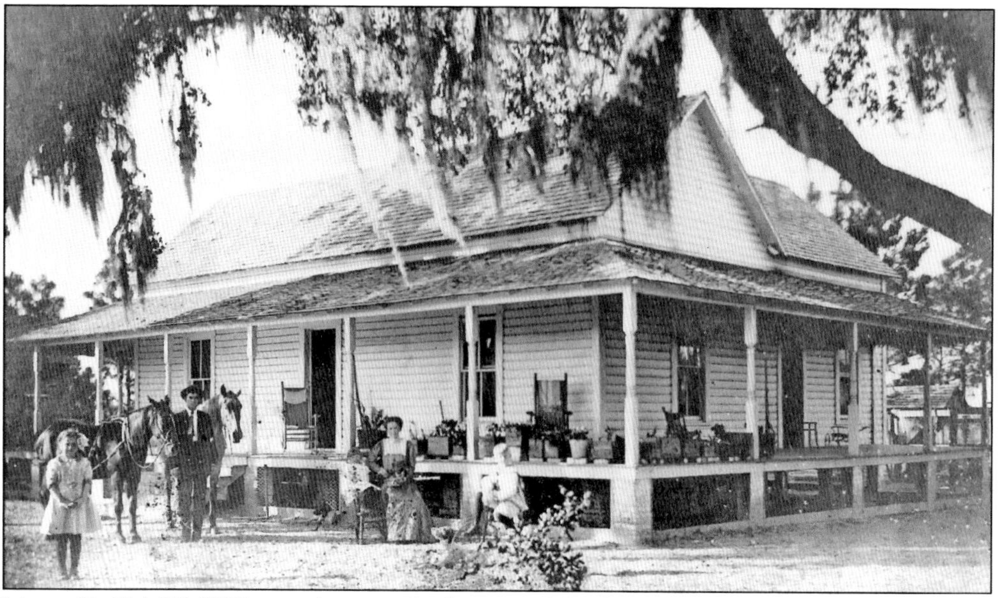

Mayor Carl M. "Kid" Ellis was born in this house on March 17, 1912. He was mayor of Mulberry for 32 consecutive years, from 1958 to 1990. His parents, William Martin and Mary Maude Newsome Ellis, built the house during 1906–1907 for about $800. This 1908 picture is of Carl's relatives; from left to right are cousin Blanche Ellis Austin, father William Sr., sister Laura Mae, mother Mary Newsome, and brother William "Bill" Jr. (MBS.)

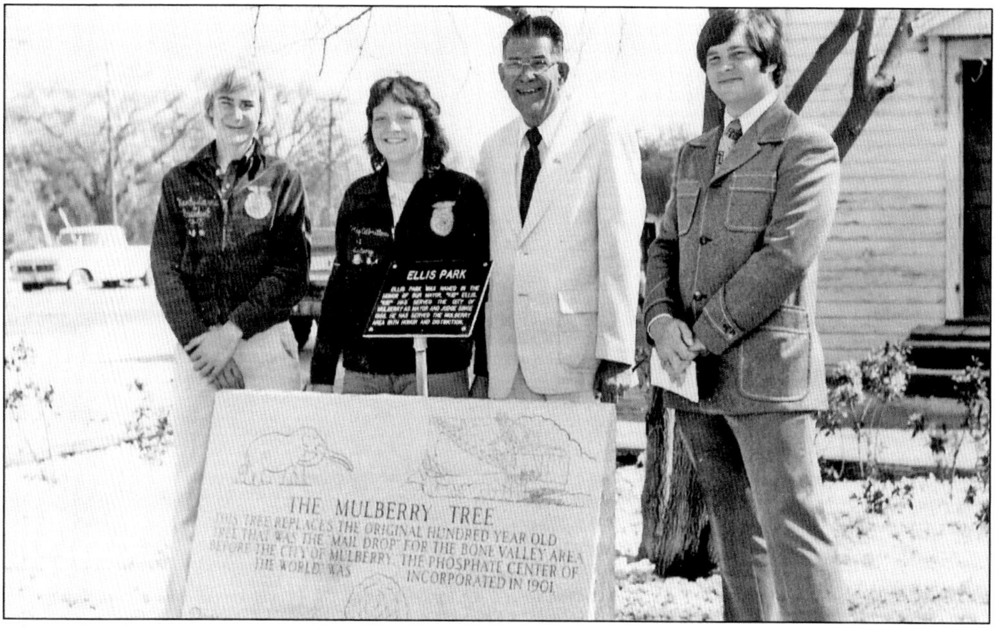

The City of Mulberry honored Mayor Carl "Kid" Ellis by dedicating this park located at the Mulberry Phosphate Museum on February 12, 1976. Standing with the mayor are Future Farmers of America members Marty Davis, Kathy Albritton, and city manager James O'Conner. Former mayors include Thomas M. Reynolds, Harold Clark, Frank R. Miller, Dr. Hugh K. Murphy, Dr. Claude C. Pearce, Carl A. French, Augustus G. Long, Henry M. Clark, Willard L. Jenkins, E. R. Caldwell, J. Gayle Brown, and Roderick N. Bryan Sr.

Ruby Sprott McConn Burdette Moses (1906–2005) was city clerk from 1953 until 1969. This 1930 picture includes Ruby's children, from left to right, four-year-old Jean Anne, Ruby, two-year-old Patrick Jefferson Jr., and five-year-old George Lincoln. Ruby outlived three husbands. In 1924, she married Patrick Jefferson McConn, who died in 1928 from diabetic coma. Then she married Charles Burdette in 1934, and they had three children: Charlotte, Ruth Geraldine, and David. Charles died in a 1951 car accident. In 1957, Ruby married Willard Moses, who died in 1983. (Ruby Moses/MBS.)

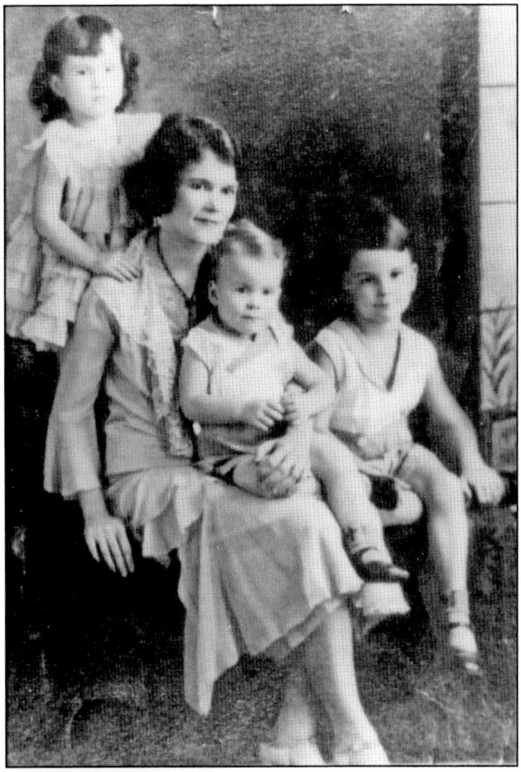

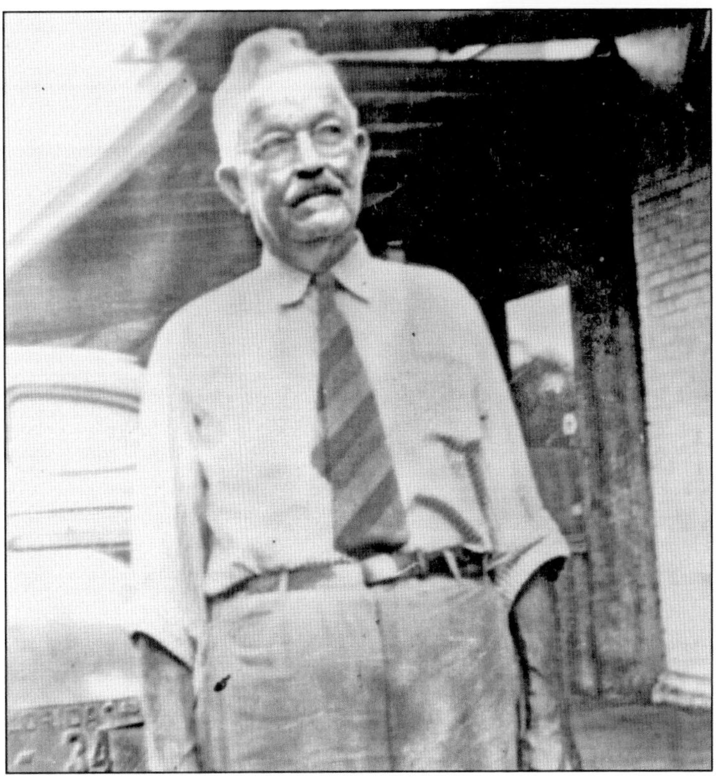

Henry Clark was mayor of Mulberry from 1874 to 1955. He was the father of Inez Clark Harned and the grandfather of Henrie Harned Sparkman and George Thomas Harned Jr. (Henrie H. Sparkman/MBS.)

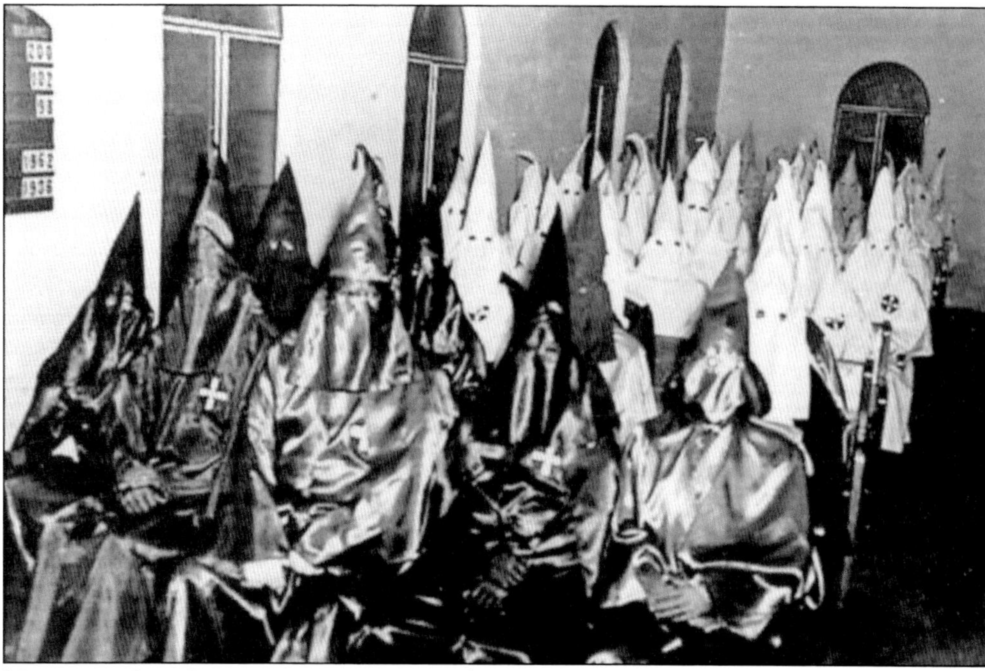

Meetings such as this one were common as African American mining employees moved into the neighboring developing towns. This photograph of the Ku Klux Klan at East Side Baptist Church of Mulberry was taken on December 30, 1956. Group members such as these saw themselves as the keepers of the law: judge, jury, and executioner. (SLAF.)

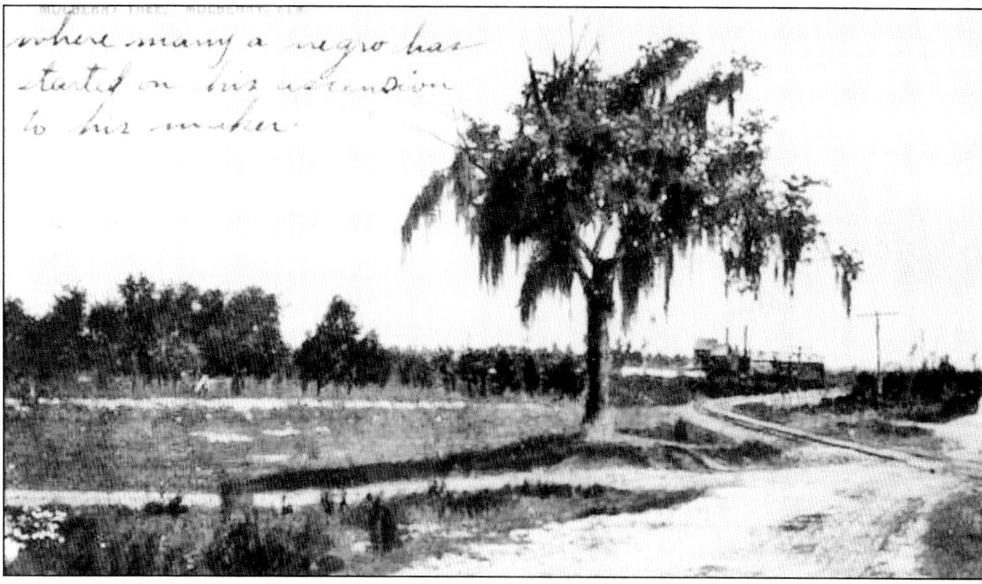

This postcard of the historic mulberry tree with a handwritten note ("where many a negro has started on his ascension to his maker") is where a lynching was held in Mulberry. This same tree is where the railroad would drop off packages and passengers for the Mulberry area. The tree stopped growing and stood bare for years. Some say that when Mulberry changed her ways and started giving the African American community equal treatment, the tree began to flourish again. (SLAF.)

Earl "Chucky" Smith Jr., the son of Earl and Martha Smith, was raised in Medulla, Florida. His family roots were in Nichols, Florida, and he graduated from Lakeland High School (LHS) in 1969. The first African American to become a member of the LHS band (as a trombone player), he attended Bethune Cookman College for two years and served 26 years in the Lakeland Fire Department. He humbly served through the ranks as a firefighter, rescue truck driver, and training inspector. He retired in 2007 as a fire inspector/investigator. Married to Mary, he is the father of three and is brother to Shirley, Janice, Cornelius "Niecie," Gene "Toby," and Gwendolyn "Cookie." (The Smith family.)

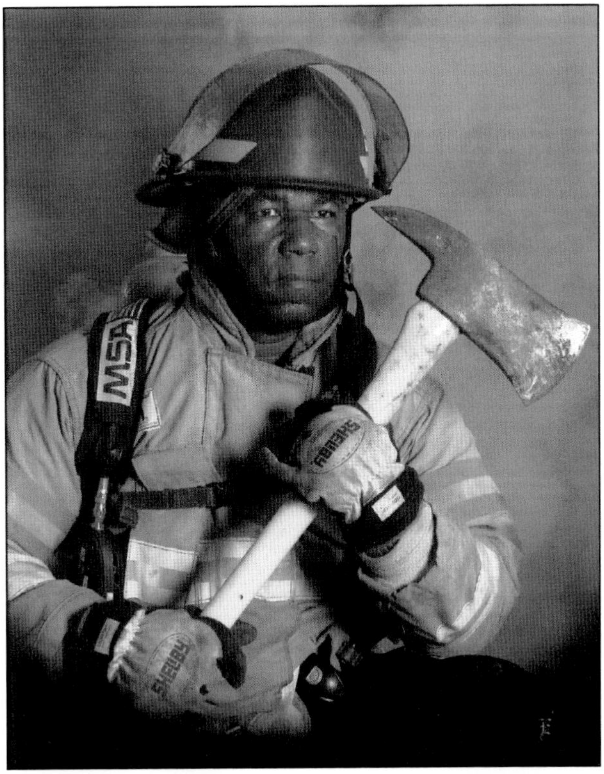

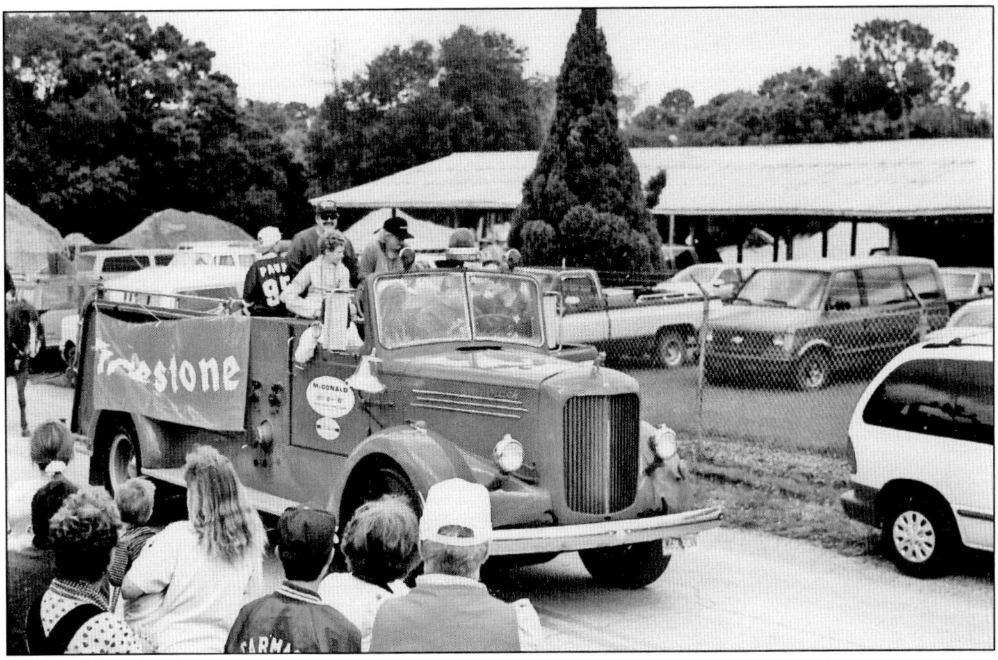

The fire department of Mulberry was a volunteer organization for years. Mulberry Phosphate Museum director Lou Haag was once a member of this fine group of men and women. The vehicle shown here is a 1959 truck once used to fight fires and save businesses' and private citizens' property. (MCC.)

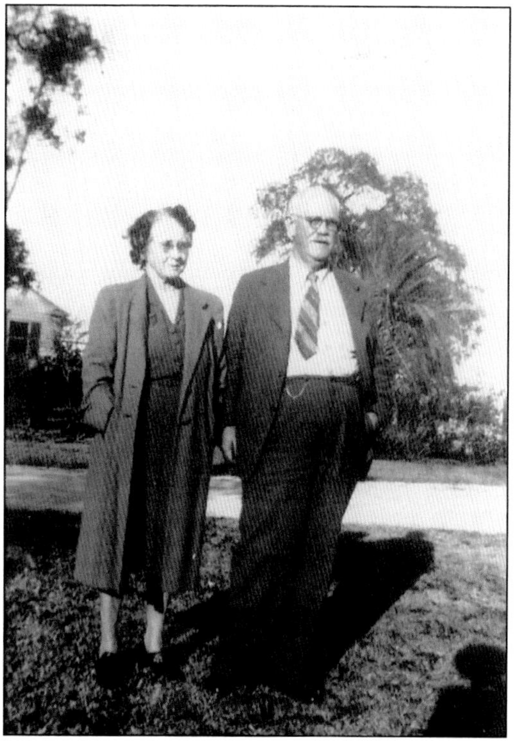

This is a photograph of Dr. Claude Clifford Pearce and his wife, Nettie Lenora Whitaker Pearce. Dr. Pearce came to the area as the company doctor for International Agriculture Phosphate Company. He also owned Pearce Drug Store, was a member of the local school board, served as a city council member, and was mayor of Mulberry. The public library of Mulberry was named in 1953 after Dr. Pearce to honor his contributions to this community. (SLAF.)

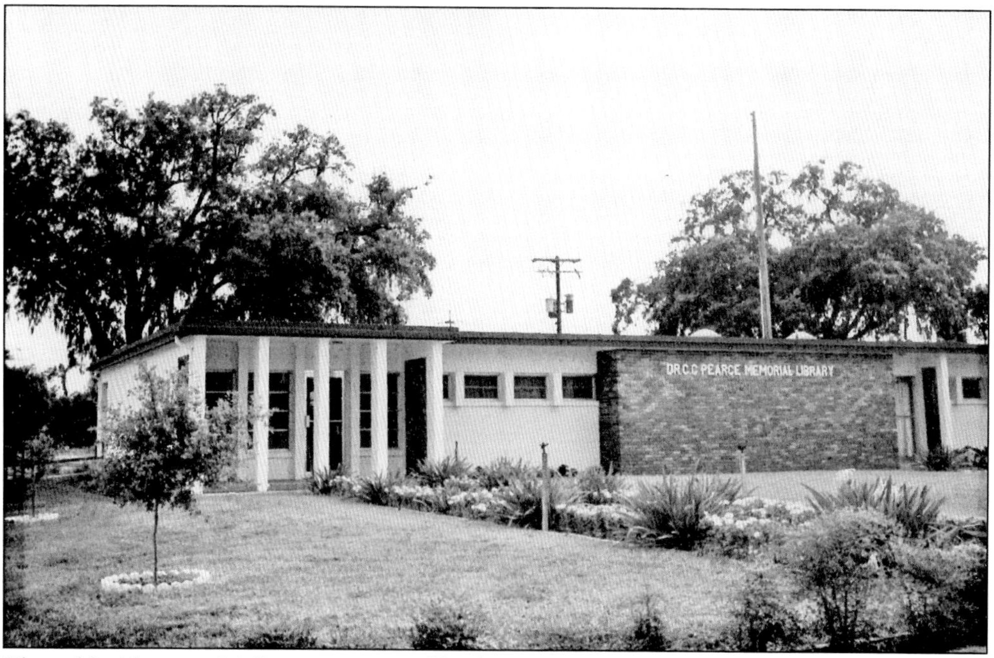

The public library in Mulberry was started by the town's women's club in 1949. The first location was the second floor of the old city hall (1950–1960). The library then moved to a location on Highway 37, just one block south of Highway 60. The current location of the library is next door to city hall on Highway 60, the former location of the Mulberry branch of the Polk County Health Department. (Dr. Claude Clifford Pearce Memorial Library.)

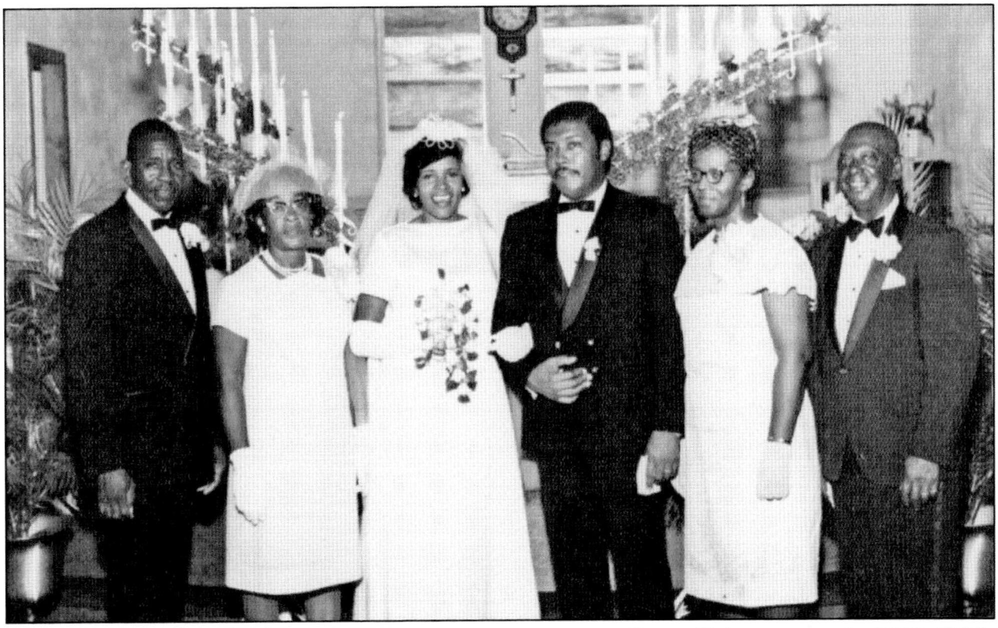

Mulberry's first elected African American city commissioner, Samuel Montgomery Jr. (1917–1984), is shown here at left on July 5, 1969, with, from left to right, his wife, Mollie Dockins (1914–1995); daughter Juanita; son-in-law James W. Helper; the groom's stepparents, Essie N. Helper Morgan and John Morgan. Samuel was born in Valrico, Florida, and started working for International Minerals and Chemical Corporation in 1958. Not pictured are the Montgomerys' daughters, Carol, Valeria, and Maxine. (Essie N. Helper Morgan.)

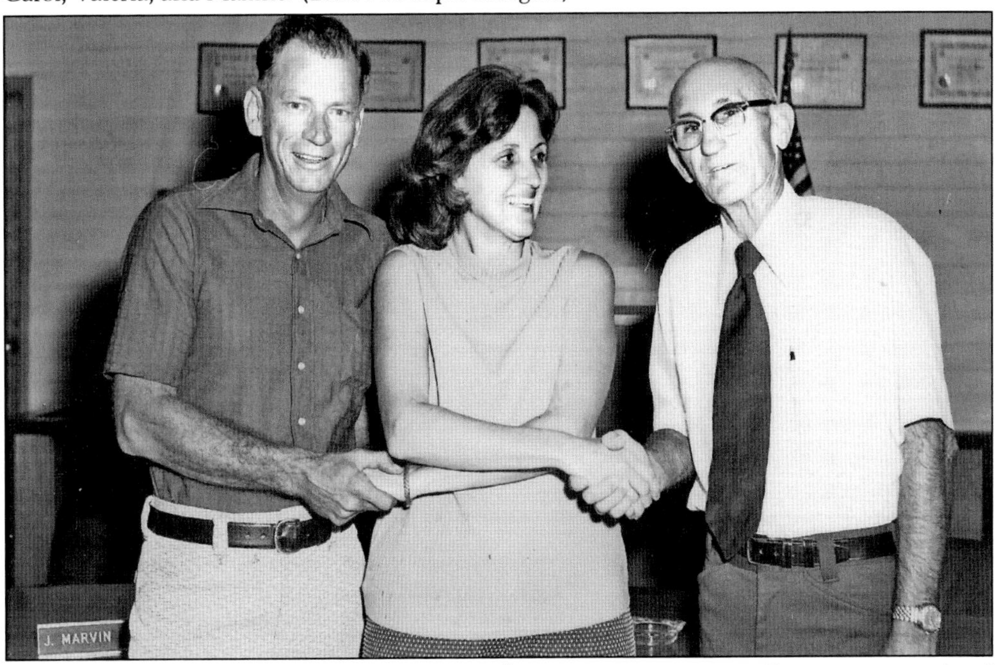

Janie Eason was the first woman to serve as a Mulberry city commissioner. Eason is congratulated by fellow commissioners Max Howard (on the left) and Dick Hawkins. The Janie Eason Park was named in her honor. (Geneva Richardson/Mulberry Historical Society.)

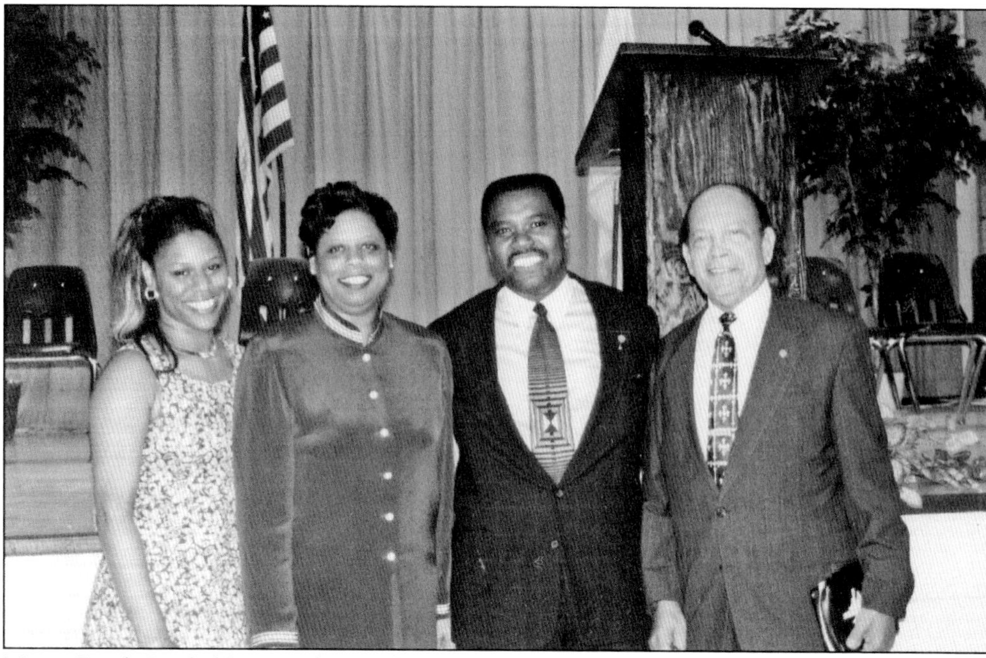

Mayor Frank Satchel Jr. served as Mulberry's first African American mayor from 1990 to 2000. Satchel is honored to be the first African American to be named Polk County's Teacher of the Year (1975), city commissioner (1974), and high honors graduate (1966). Pictured here from left to right are Satchel's daughter Fraenda; his wife, Dr. Brenda Brown; Mayor Satchel; and his father, Rev. Frank Satchel Sr. Richie, the mayor's son, is not pictured. (MCC.)

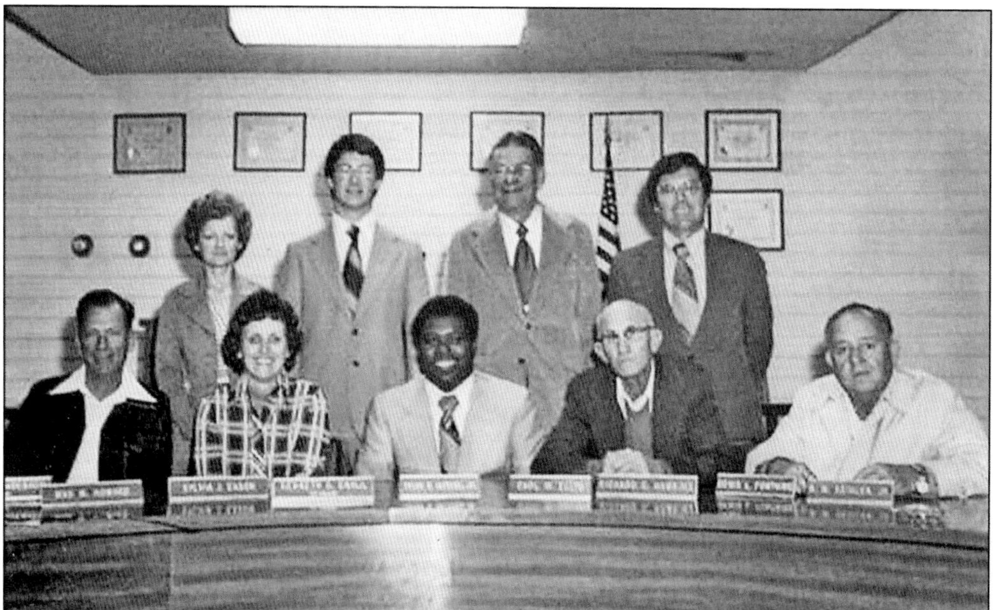

City officials take time to pose for a photograph. From left to right are the following: (seated) Max Howard, Jamie Eason, mayor Frank Satchel Jr., Richard Hawkins, and Arthur M. Seigler; (standing) city clerk ? Madebach, city manager Kenneth Small, former mayor Carl Ellis, and Denis Fontaine. (Mulberry City Hall.)

Mayor Sam McLaughlin was born on July 11, 1931, in Plant City. He married Lou Driggers of Mulberry and became the father of Karen and Sammie McLaughlin IV. McLaughlin served as mayor of Mulberry from 2000 until 2002 and as city commissioner from April 2005 until June 2005 and was an active member of the Mulberry Kiwanis Club, the Fraternal Order of Free and Accepted Masons, and the Mulberry Historical Society until his untimely death on September 8, 2007. (The *Mulberry Press*.)

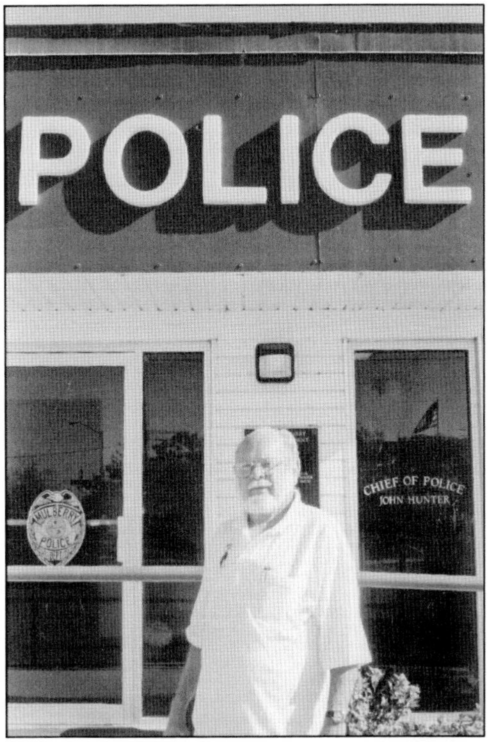

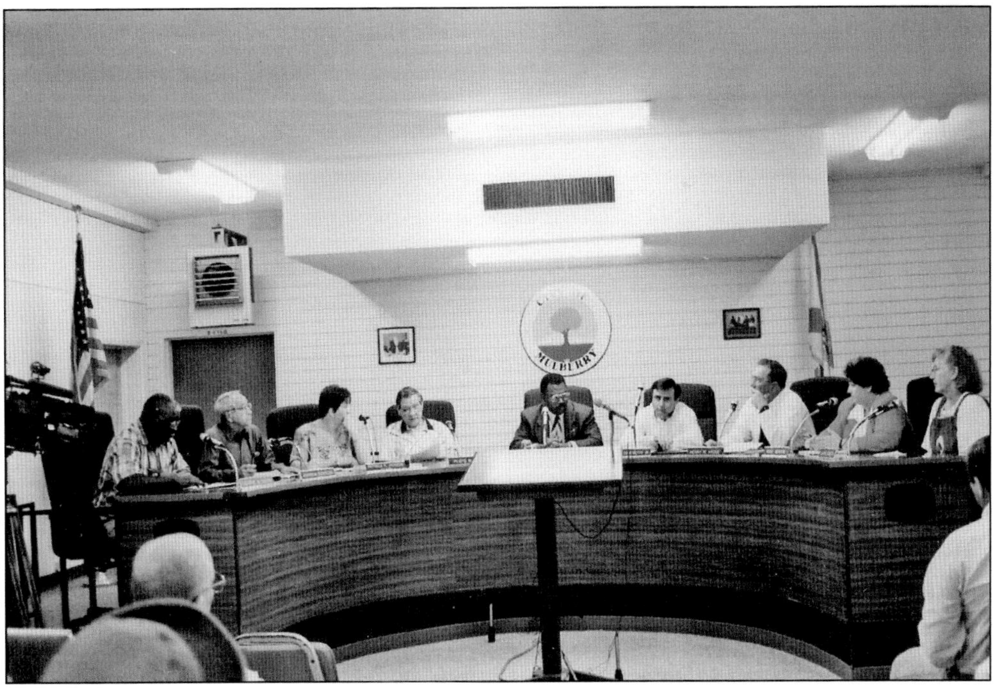

A city's board of commissioners should reflect the gender and ethnicity of its citizens. This 1990s photograph shows, from left to right, commissioners Johnnie Smith, Andrew Scrocca, city clerk Patricia Jackson, Floyd Woods, mayor Frank Satchel Jr., attorney Frank Comtaretto, Henry M. Hague, Vicky Beaver, and Janie Eason. (The *Mulberry Press*.)

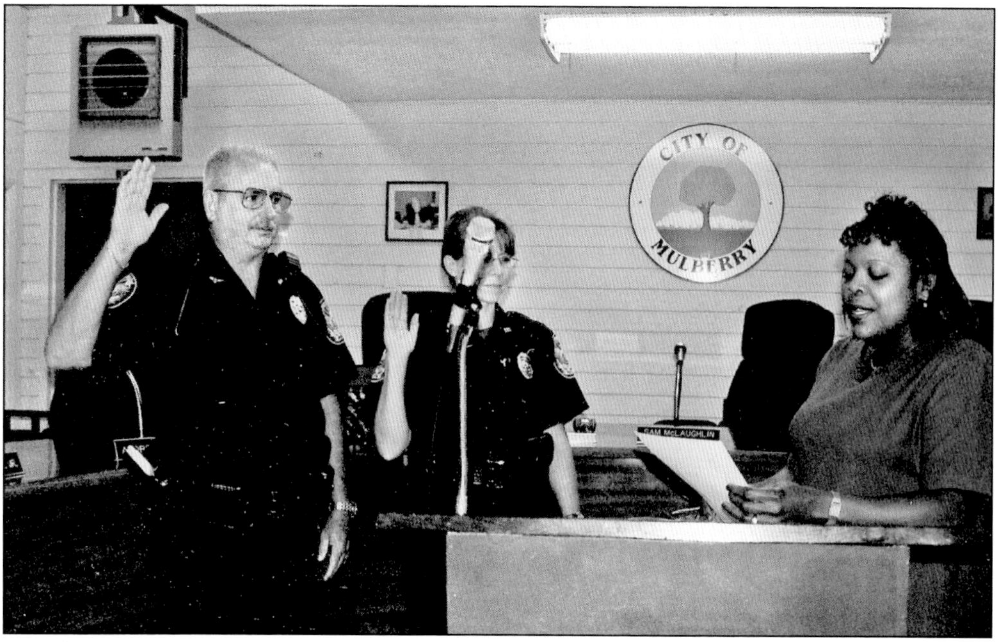

City clerk Vanessa Baker gives the oath of office to new officers of the Mulberry Police department. Baker worked part-time as a receptionist in 1980 as part of the Cooperative Business Education (CBE) program at Mulberry High School. She started full-time in 1981 and advanced to city clerk on September 8, 2000. Among others who previously held the clerk's position are Eldridge Saxton Whidden, Vivian Sutton, Ruby Moses, Earline Sampley, ? Madebach, and Patricia Jackson. (The *Mulberry Press*.)

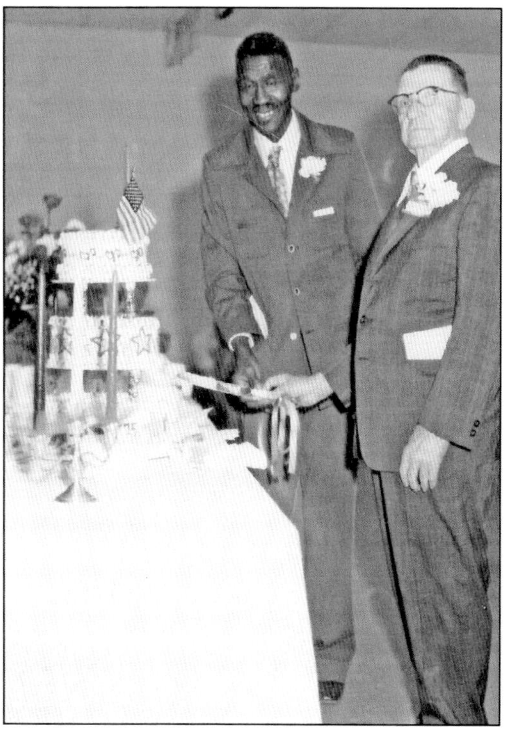

Eddie Woodard (left) and Oscar Moore represented the pioneer families of Mulberry on February 13, 1976, by cutting the city's 75th birthday cake. Moore was recognized as the citizen living in Mulberry for the longest amount of time, 81 years. Woodard worked for 47 years for International Minerals and Chemical Corporation. (MBS/Mulberry Historical Society.)

Four

ENTREPRENEURSHIP

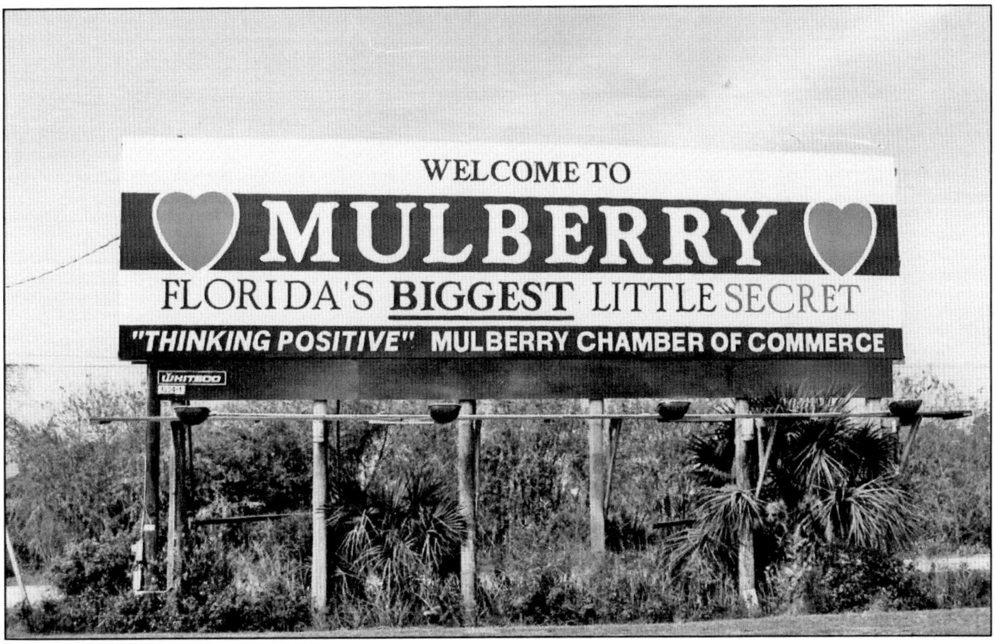

The Mulberry Chamber of Commerce was organized in March 1959 with 65 members. The first president was John W. Alderman, and the chamber meeting was held in city hall. In 1950, the fourth annual phosphate official program booklet states that "Mulberry has produced two millionaires that lived and raised a family in its limits. Began with very little, played no stock market. No other town in the United States our size can say this." This effort is due to a strong chamber of commerce. One of the latest members to join is the mega-store, Wal-Mart. Some of the other landmark businesses are John Thomas Barber Shop, Johnny Mitchell's Café, Western Auto, McDonald's, Thirftway, Barbara's Coffee Shop, Rexall Pharmacy, Mulberry Pharmacy, and E. J's Bar-B-Que. (MCC.)

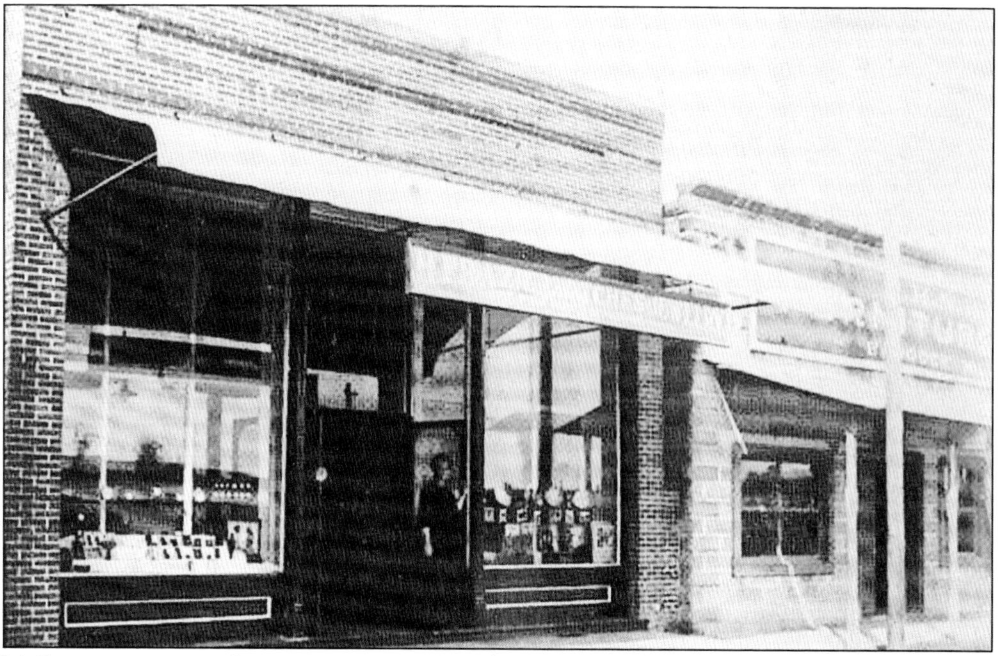

Mulberry incorporated into a town in 1901. This is a 1908 photograph of H. Frazier, Watches and Jewelry Fine Watch Repairing on the left and H. S. Badcock Furniture Store on the right. Henry Stanhope Badcock sold this store to his son Wogan for $9,000. Today the Badcock and More Company has been in business for more than 100 years and have more than 320 stores. (SLAF.)

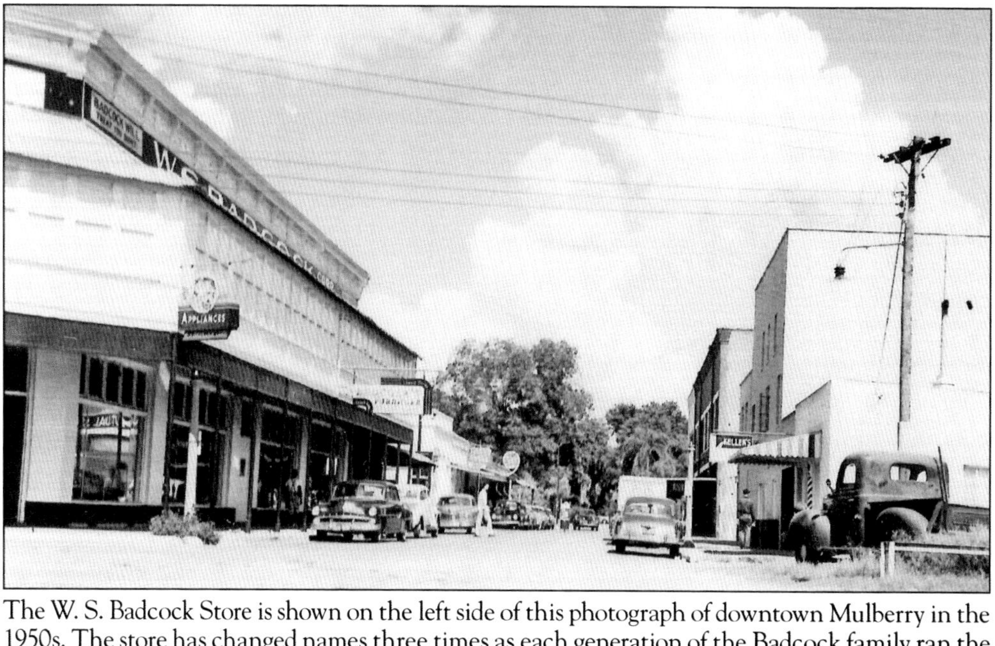

The W. S. Badcock Store is shown on the left side of this photograph of downtown Mulberry in the 1950s. The store has changed names three times as each generation of the Badcock family ran the business: first the name was H. S. Badcock, then W. S. Badcock Corporation, and now Badcock Furnishing Centers and Badcock and More Stores. On the right are the Mulberry Barber Shop, Keller's Dry Cleaners, and the Union Hall, formerly The Theatre. (Howard Wiggs/MBS.)

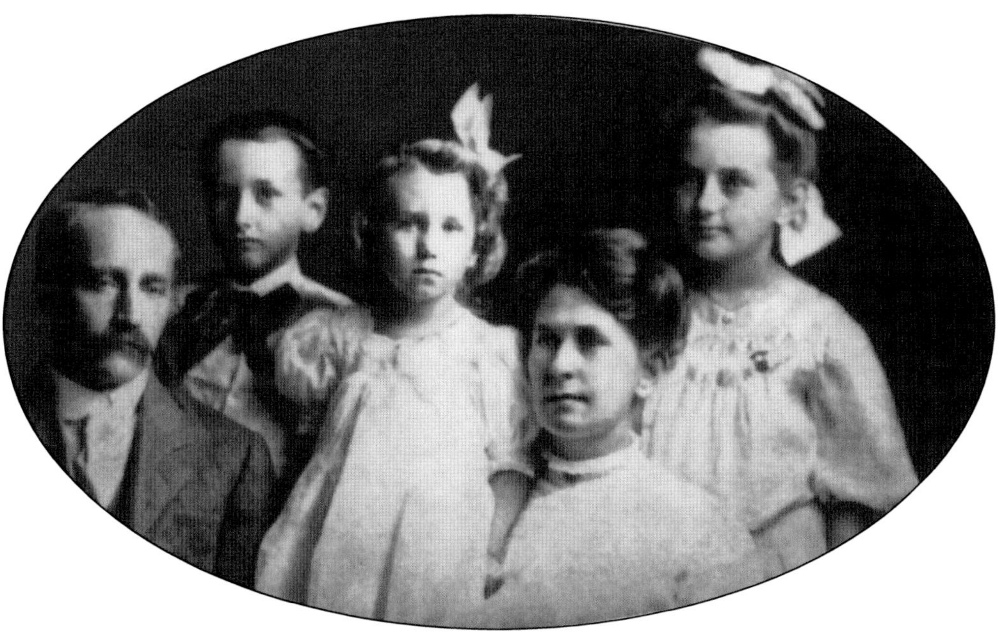

Born in Fleckney, Leicestershire, England, in a rectory on October 7, 1867, the 7th of 12 children, Henry Stanhope Badcock (whose parents were Rev. Thomas and Emily Ford Smith Badcock) came to America at the age of 21. Henry migrated from New York to Florida, where he met Hattie Omah Vaugh. They married on August 3, 1896, and pictured from left to right with them are their three children: Wogan, Omah, and Emily. (MBS.)

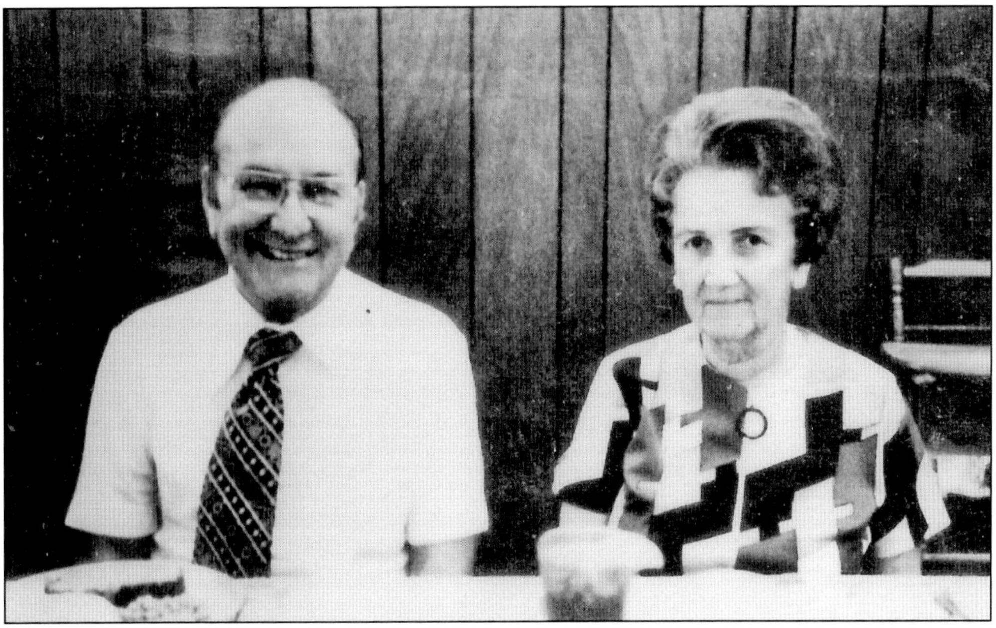

Wogan Stanhope Sr. and Evelyn Clark Badcock are shown here. Wogan Jr. was born in the rear of the store in the family's living quarters. The Badcock's legacy of strong business values and philanthropy has been passed on to their children, Evelyn Marie, Maida Frances, and Wogan Jr. In June 1976, the baseball park at Mulberry's youth complex was name in Wogan Sr.'s honor. (Evelyn Badcock/MBS.)

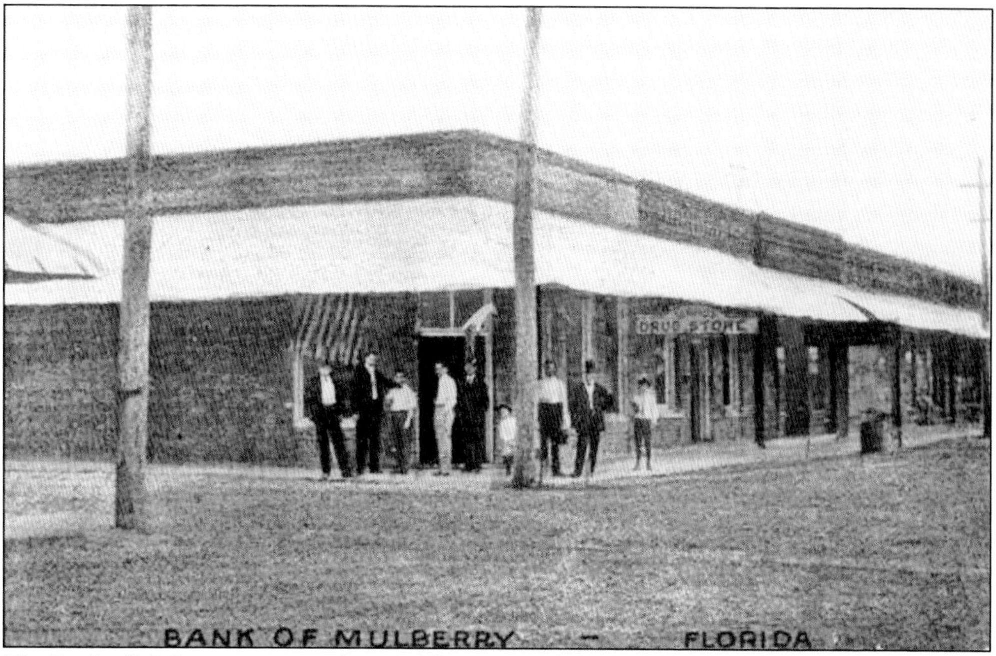

The Bank of Mulberry was started in 1907 by Levi Nathaniel Pipkin (1866–1953). Pipkin was part of a Florida and Georgia pioneering family originally hailing from Scotland and Ireland. Levi's parents were Nathan and Margaret Elizabeth Hart. He married Florence Beulah Proctor, and they raised six children: Juanita, Luther, Thelma, Eunice, Bernice, and Ruth Elizabeth. (SLAF.)

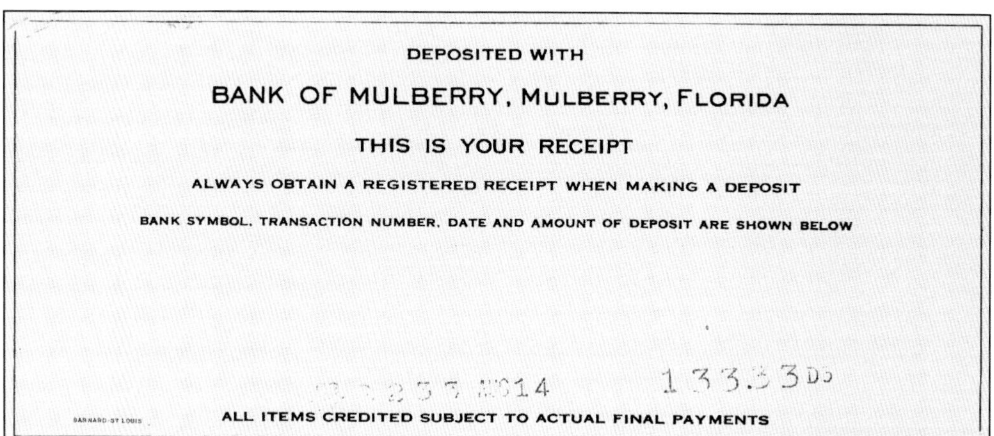

DEPOSITED WITH

BANK OF MULBERRY, MULBERRY, FLORIDA

THIS IS YOUR RECEIPT

ALWAYS OBTAIN A REGISTERED RECEIPT WHEN MAKING A DEPOSIT

BANK SYMBOL, TRANSACTION NUMBER, DATE AND AMOUNT OF DEPOSIT ARE SHOWN BELOW

133.33

BARNARD-ST LOUIS ALL ITEMS CREDITED SUBJECT TO ACTUAL FINAL PAYMENTS

This is a bank deposit receipt of Isom and Essie Helper dated August 14, 1959. The amount of $133.33 was a year's wages for some teachers during this time. Such low salaries encouraged the Helpers to become business owners. (Essie N. Helper Morgan.)

Son of Isom Sr. and Bessie Wheeler Helper, Isom Helper Jr.'s second marriage was to Essie Marie Nelson in 1941, and to this union, six children were born: David, Nila, Isom III, Sharon, Larry, and Lauren. Isom II, who worked at International Minerals and Chemical for 22 years, used his salary to invest in his own businesses as a landlord and an owner of a neighborhood convenience store and funeral home. (Essie N. Helper Morgan.)

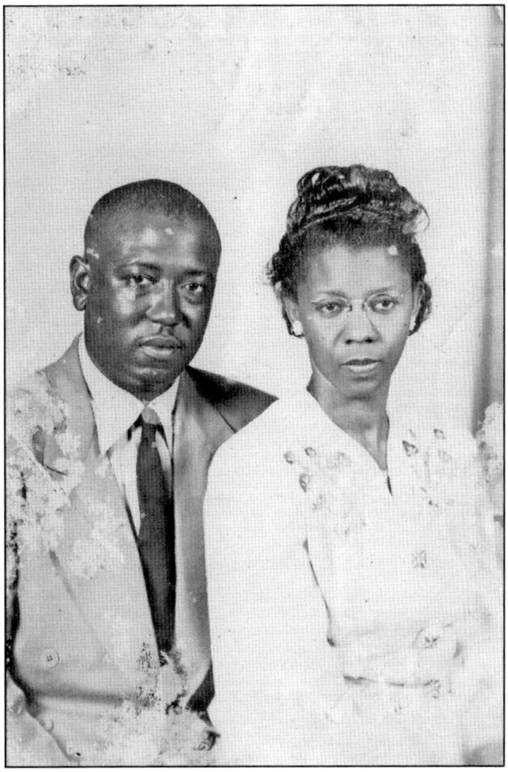

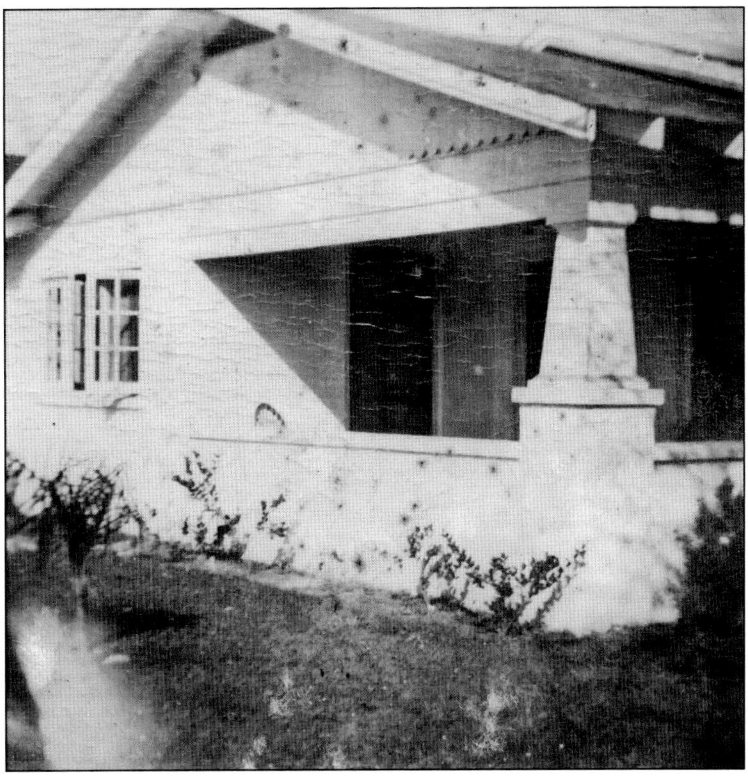

In 1949, Isom and Essie Helper bought bricks each pay period until they had a sufficient amount to construct this home at 105 Northwest Fifth Avenue. In 1958, they placed an addition onto the house for their business, Johnson Funeral Home and Ambulance Service. The name was changed in 1958 to Lewis Funeral Home and Ambulance Service. (Essie N. Helper Morgan.)

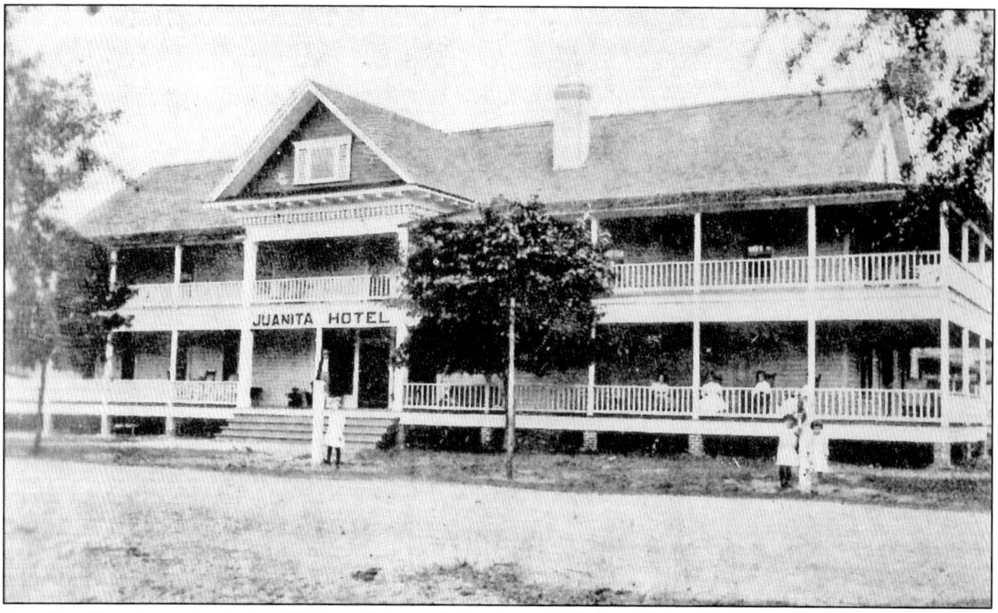

Juanita Hotel was built in 1901 and demolished in 1950. In 1910, the Levi N. Pipkin store was moved to make the hotel's annex. Woodrow Johnson worked at the hotel every morning before walking to school at Union Academy in Bartow. Johnson became the first African American male to graduate high school from the Mulberry area. In 1985, this became the site of Tampa Electric Company. (MBS.)

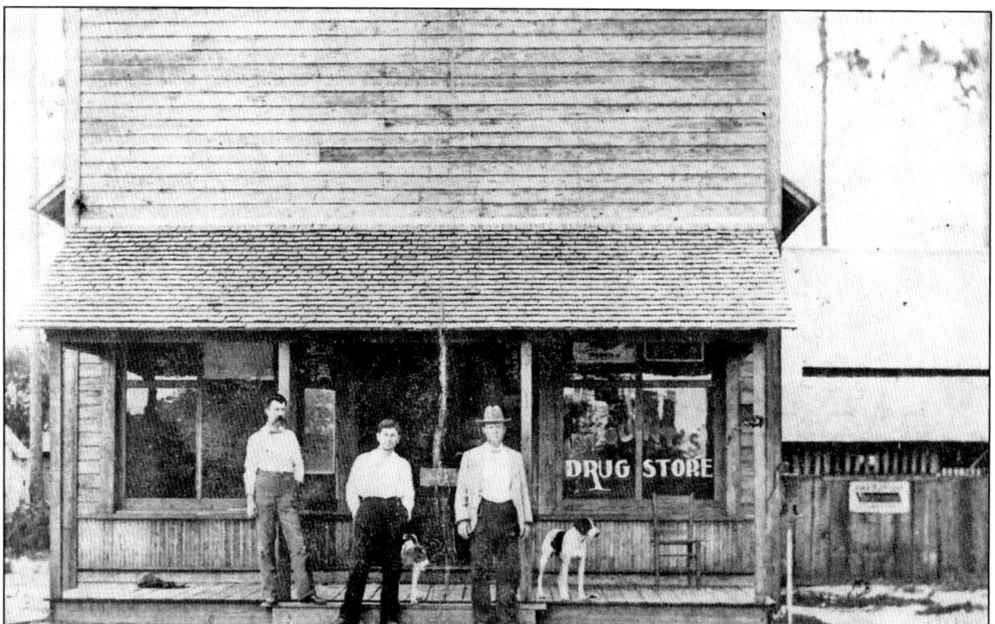

In about 1851, the Blount family consisting of 20 members and 12 slaves moved to this area and established a homestead just east of Mulberry. The most notable of the group are Reading and Riley Blount and Strety Parker. In 1856, the family constructed a private fort, Fort Blount, which was used by federal troops during the Seminole Wars and by Florida volunteers during the Civil War. (Addie Overstreet Grenshaw/MBS.)

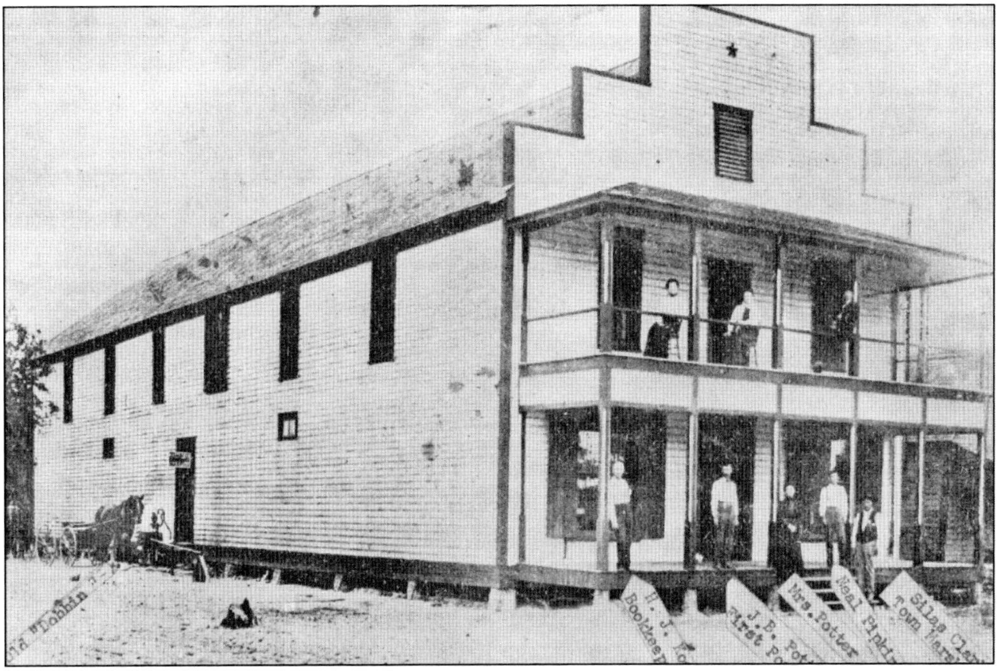

This is the Levi N. Pipkin General Store, founded in 1894 as the first major business in Mulberry. H. J. Koerner was the bookkeeper, and the town marshal, Silas Clark, was always stopping in for a little chat. Pipkins lead a group to bring the railway from Bartow to Mulberry, which the group later sold to Seaboard Air Line. The post office, established on May 11, 1900, was located in the rear of the store, and John B. Potter was its first postmaster. (SLAF.)

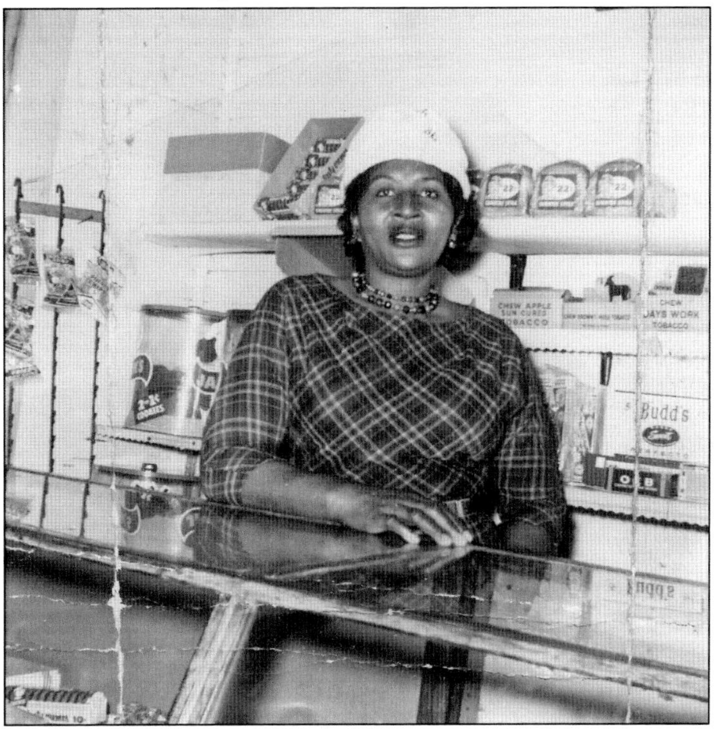

Edith Cromartie Brown was born on January 15, 1921, the first daughter of Thomas and Bernice Cromartie. Edith married William Brown and joined with Henderson McColough to purchase Mr. Vicker's Store, which McColough and the Browns operated until their health no longer allowed it. Among the other items, notice the two-for-a-penny cookies. (Sandra Brown.)

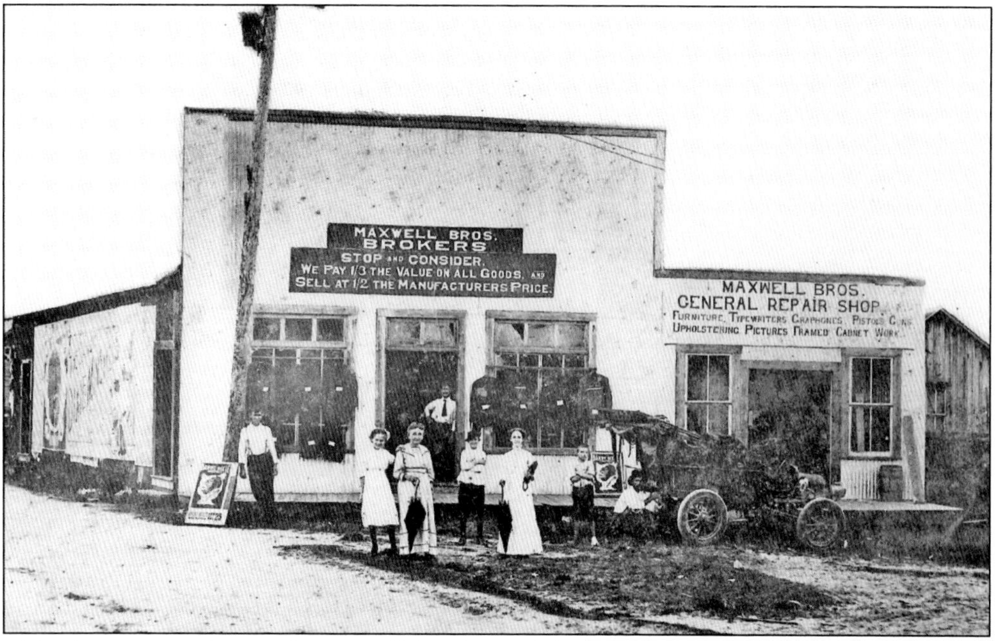

This picture was taken in the early 1900s. Behind this building was a Chinese laundry. The persons shown are unidentified. Members of the Maxwell family included Ludlow W. Maxwell, born *c.* 1838; wife Addie Records, born *c.* 1844; daughter Mabel Maxwell, born *c.* 1884; Mabel's daughter, Bertha, born *c.* 1905. Frank Maxwell, born *c.* 1879, was married to Ethel, born *c.* 1889, and they had one son, Pruice L., born *c.* 1909. (Addie Overstreet Crenshaw/MBS.)

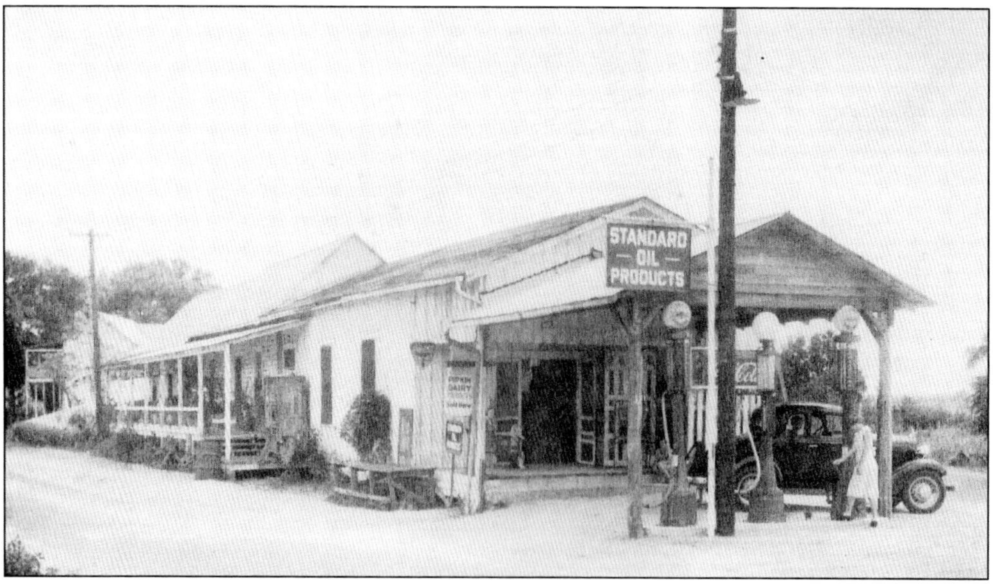

This store was owned by Thomas L. and Stella Brandt around 1925–1940. The Brandt family moved from Virginia and lived in the house directly behind the store. The family includes five girls and one boy: Judith (Feeny), Catherine (Sheppard), Nancy (Steinke), Samuel Robert, Stella (Dabry), Jane (King), Anna (Flanagan), and Elsa (Meigher). Stella remembers her mother using an apple cart as a crib for her. Notice the sign on the door promoting Pipkin's dairy products. (Stella Brandt Darby.)

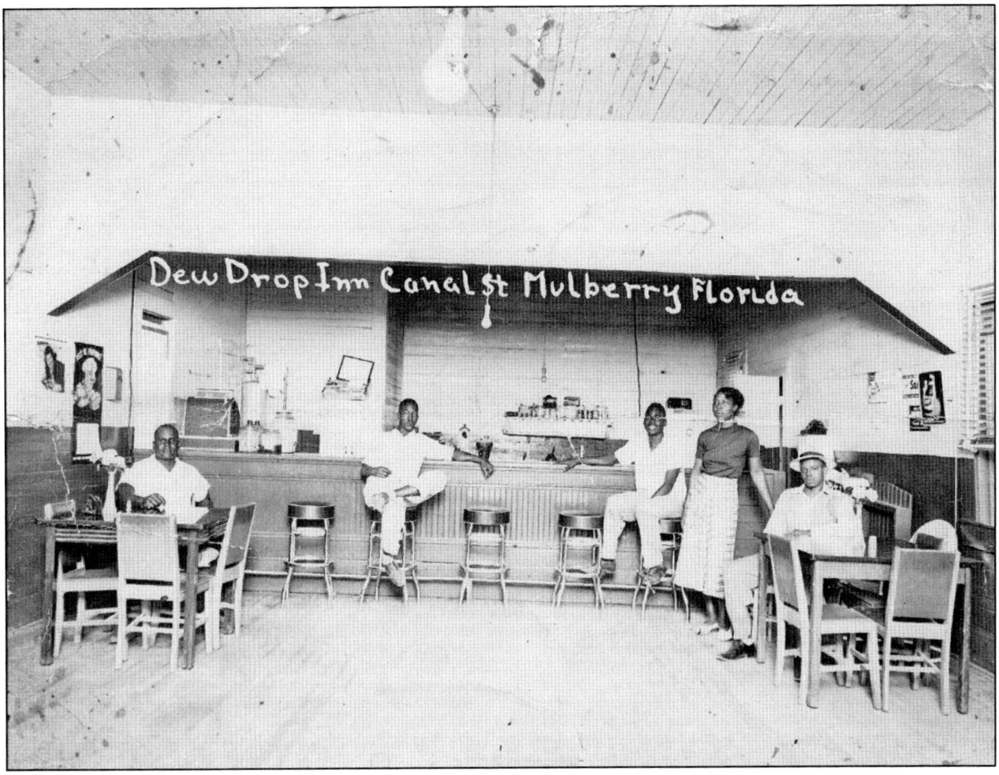

The Dew Drop Inn was owned by Robert Lawrence and was the main hang-out for those in the African American community of Mulberry. This picture was taken about 1939. Leisurely relaxing from left to right are Robert Lawrence, unidentified, Al Green, Nila B. Brown, and unidentified. The business was located at the corner of Canal Street and Southwest Fourth Avenue. It provided to its customers convenience items such as cold drinks, snacks, thick hamburgers, and jukebox music. (Reunea Boyd Bigham.)

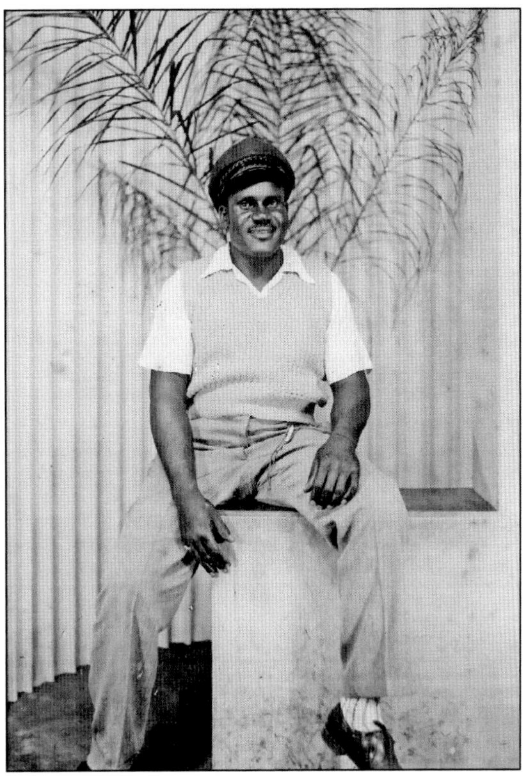

Robert Lawrence was born on September 10, 1908, in Pike County, Alabama, to Mr. and Mrs. Dan Lawrence. Robert moved to Mulberry and started a taxi cab business and a café known as the Dew Drop Inn, which later was changed to the Blue Chip Café. Lawrence departed this life on May 14, 1974. (Reunea Boyd Bigham.)

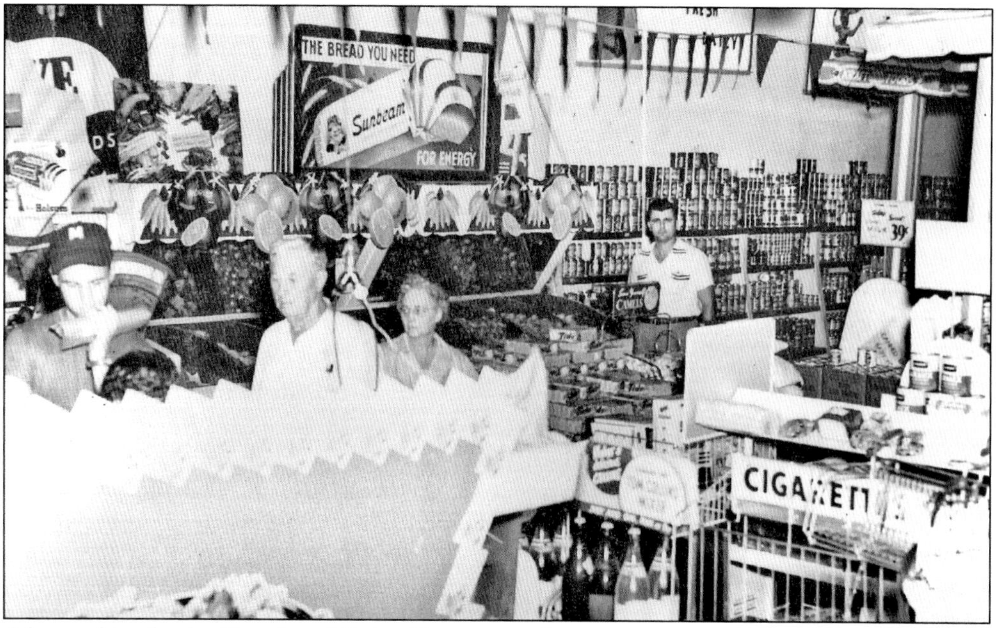

After working for the Phosphate Mining Company at the commissary since 1911, Leonard Caldwell partnered with Douglas S. Waters, J. Walker Keel, the International Agricultural Company, and Roderick N. "Judge" Bryan on March 4, 1924, to open the Mutual Stores. Caldwell was general manager, and Bryan was secretary and treasurer. Caldwell became president and manager of the Mutual Stores in 1927. (Dick Hawkins/MBS.)

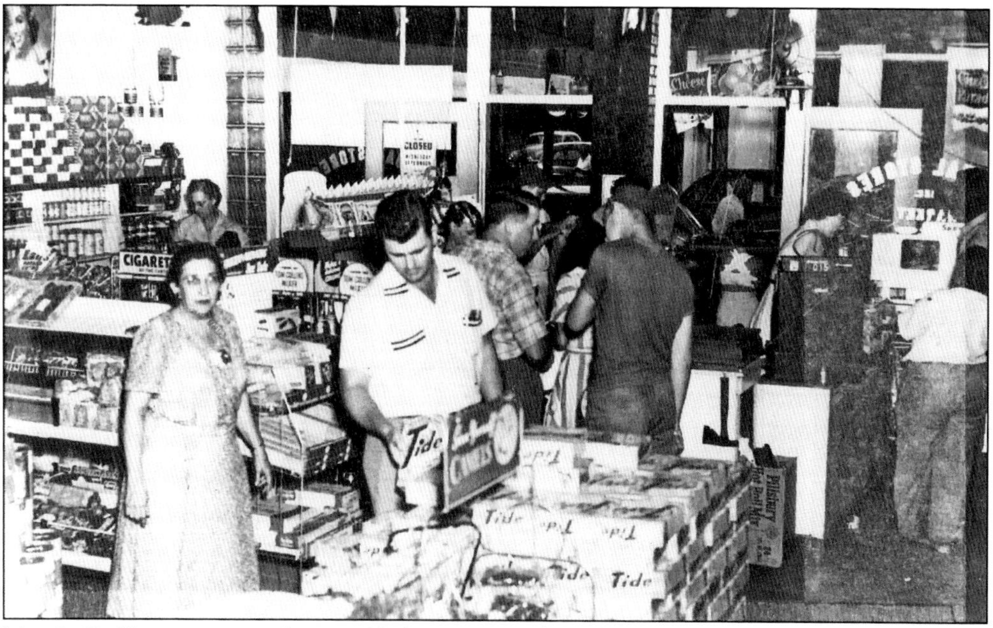

Mrs. L. R. Hunter was in charge of ladies' wear and goods at the Mutual Stores. H. W. Rawls starting working there in 1927, and W. J. Martin started in 1925. A 13¢ sale was held in honor of the Mutual Stores' 13th anniversary in 1937. Judge Bryan was also in charge of the credit for the stores. Bricks were sold when the Mutual Stores building was demolished in the 1980s. (Dick Hawkins/MBS.)

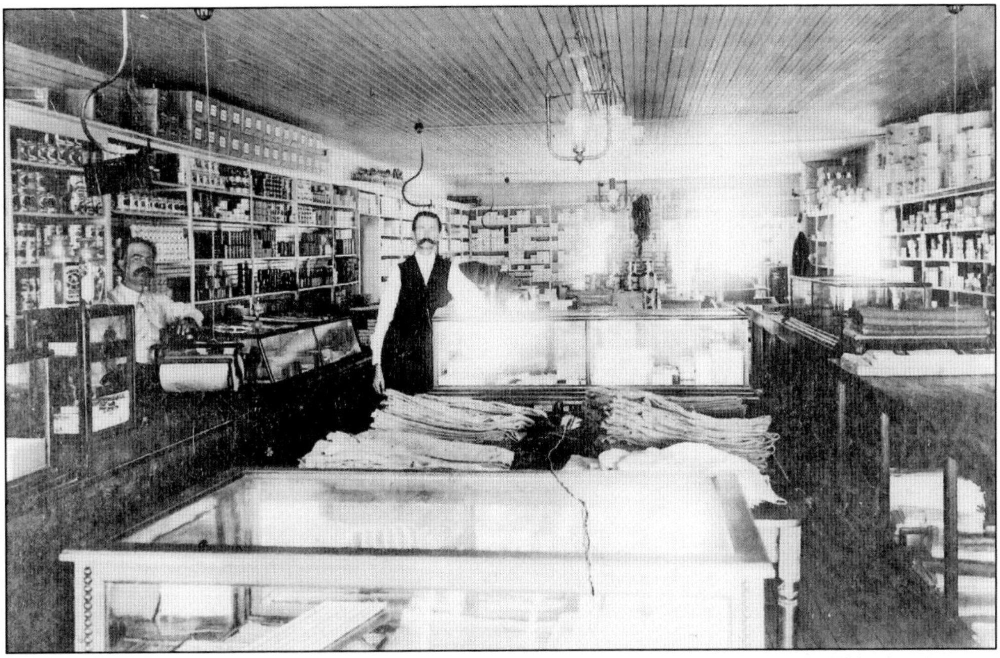

Whidden and Whidden Mercantile Store represents the partnership between Eldridge Saxton "E. S." Whidden (1870–1929) and his brother Joseph O. Whidden. E. S. Whidden was a school teacher, school board member, and manager of Land Pebble Phosphate Company Commissary before starting this company in 1904 until 1920. E. S. Whidden was also a county commissioner, justice of peace, and a Mulberry city clerk before his death in 1929. (Florence Whidden Speight/MBS.)

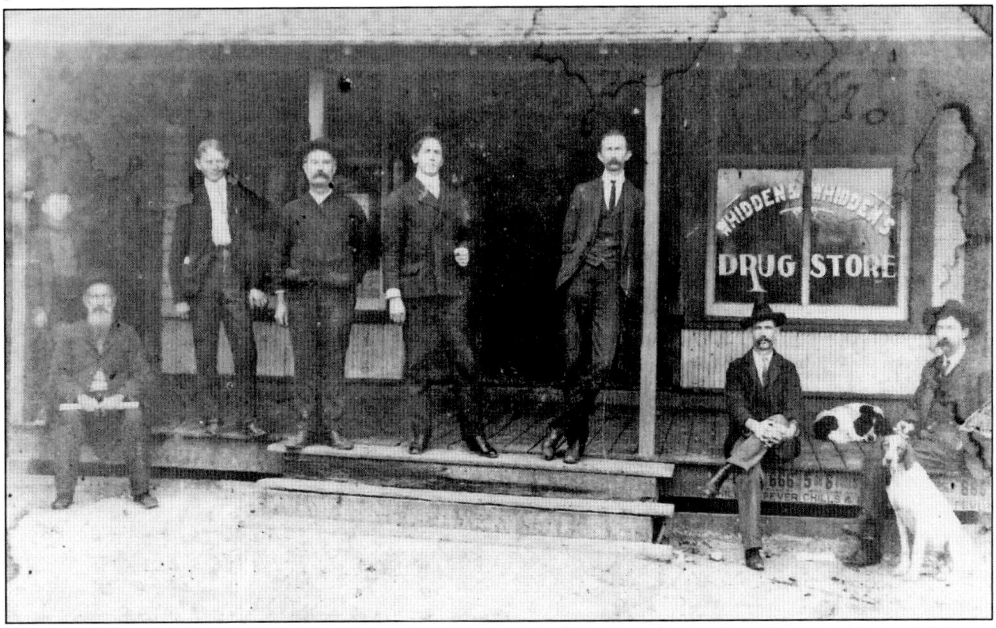

In 1898, Eldridge Saxton Whidden married Susan Holland, and together they had five children: Mont Julian, Stella (Scarboro), Earl, Florence (Speight), and Eve (Bornman). The parents of the Whidden children, 13 in all, were pioneer Floridians Bennett and Emily Durrance Whidden. Bennett was a veteran of the Seminole Wars and the Civil War. (MBS.)

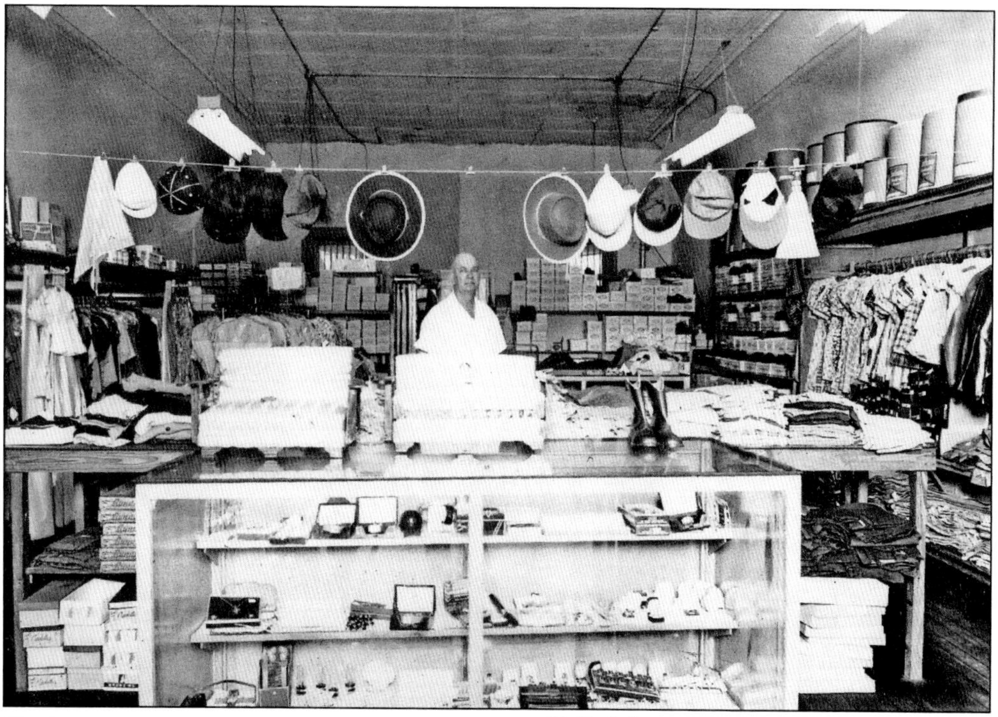

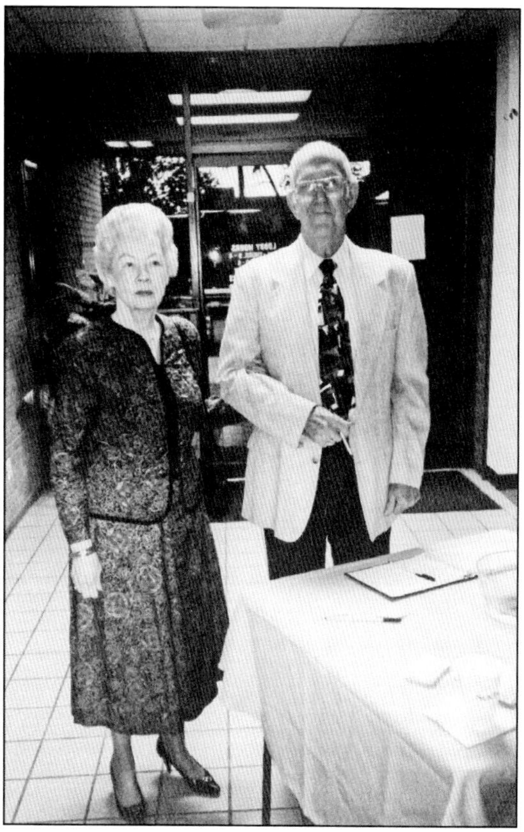

E. P. Osborne Store owned and operated the Jot'em down store. Because of the excellent wages and the continuous stream of employment, Mulberry residents had many to spend creating the demand for more than one store to shop. Not to mention the population of Mulberry was well over 2,500 people. Even during the Depression, most workers of the phosphate industry did not suffer for a lack of basic needs, food, clothing, and shelter. (Mrs. E. P. Osborne Sr./MBS.)

John and Maida Kilpatrick operated the Maida's Modern Shop for more than 30 years. The shop was name for Wogan Badcock Sr.'s daughter, Maida. The shop carried apparel for the entire family and provided personal service to its customers. The first location was in the Mulberry Shopping Center on Second Avenue Northeast along with the Rexall Drug Store, and the second was on North Canal Street (Highway 37). (MCC.)

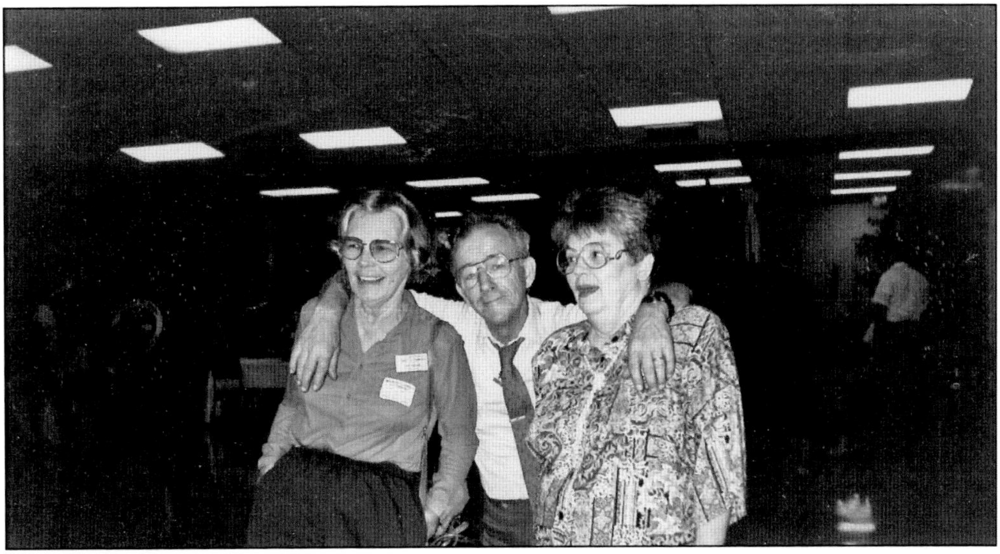

Doss Flower Shop was opened in 1955 by Leola Doss, one of three siblings: (from left to right) Leola Doss, Bill Brogan, and Katrina Heim. The business has always been on Main Street (now Badcock Boulevard): in 1960, it moved from the 200 block, next door to Keller's Cleaners, to one block east and across the street to its present location, 111 West Badcock Boulevard, in a *c.* 1909 red brick building, one of the oldest of its kind still standing in Mulberry. (MCC.)

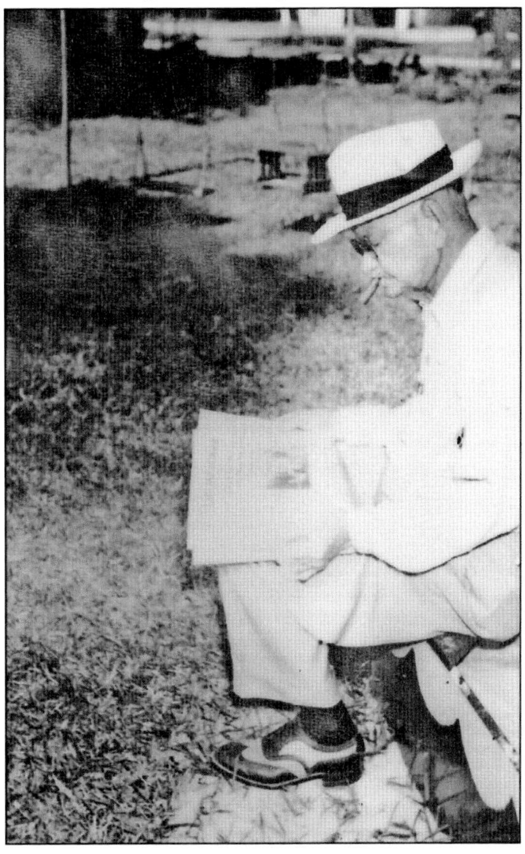

In 1926, Dr. Velpean Ragsdale, the son of physician Dr. Milton Ragsdale, arrived in Pierce, Florida, as the company doctor for American Agricultural Corporation and soon became the community doctor. He married Edna Ball in 1912 and achieved the rank of major while serving in the U.S. Army during World War I from 1915 until he was discharged in 1918. (Katheryn Ragsdale/MBS.)

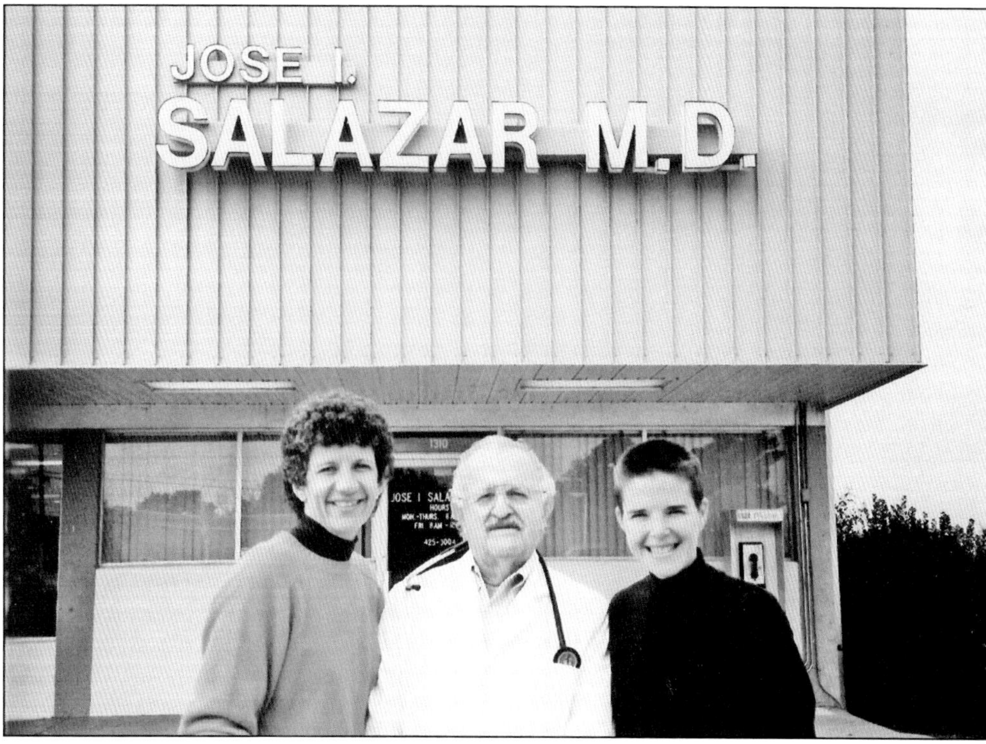

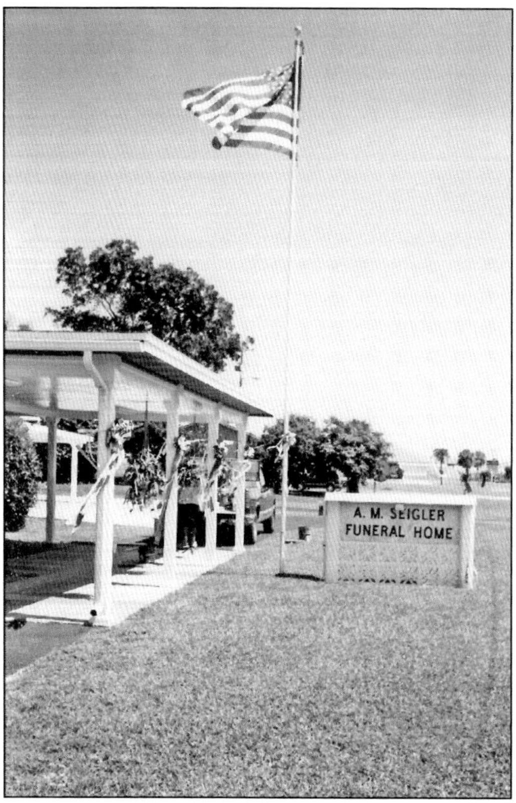

Mulberry went years without a practicing doctor within its city limits. The city's search committee encouraged Jose I. Salazar, M.D. to join the Mulberry families. Dr. Salazar is skilled and knowledgeable about the citizens' needs such as the proper care of patients with sickle-cell anemia, lupus, and treatments for the immune disorder fibromyalgia. Dr. Salazar's office is currently located on Highway 37 at 1007 Church Avenue North. (MCC.)

The A. M. Seigler Funeral Home was started by Arthur M. Seigler Sr. (1891–1956) in 1926. In 1921, Seigler Sr. became the 17th licensed mortician in the state of Florida. This was during the time when furniture stores sold caskets and bodies were returned home after embalming until burial. The business, a three-generational company owned and operated by Arthur M. Seigler Jr. and his son Mark Seigler, was passed on to Mark and his sister Sherry. Now Mark, who is the current (2005–2008) mayor of Mulberry, is the owner and operator. (MCC.)

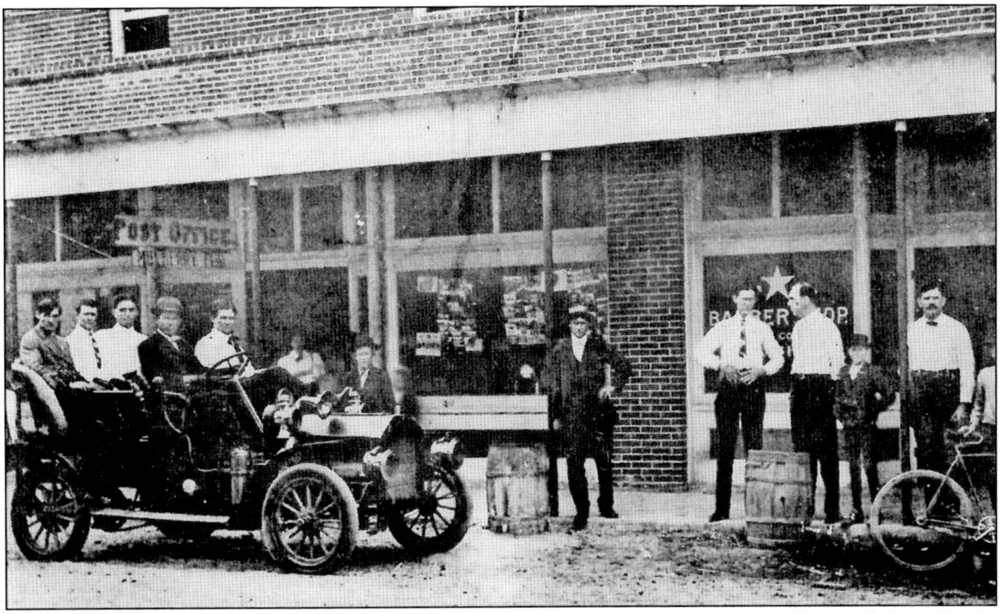

The men are waiting on the mail courier to arrive. In these early years, the mail was simply addressed with the recipients name and the city and state. Residents would ask go to the post office and ask for their mail by name. Later the post office offered boxes and finally home delivery. In 1951, Wilson C. Fugate went to work in the Mulberry Post Office and worked there until he retired in 1975. (Mulberry Historical Society.)

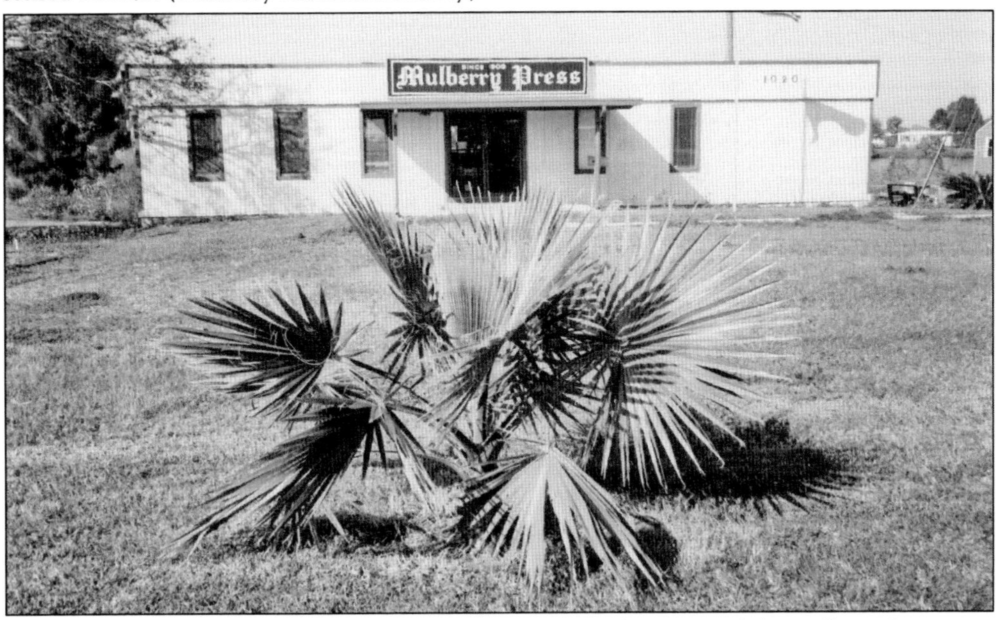

The *Mulberry Press* was started in 1909. Only three families have owned the *Mulberry Press* since 1940: the Bradley family (35 years), the Virgil Davis family (1975–1985), and the Histed family (1985–present). The paper covers news for Mulberry, Willow Oak, Pierce, Bradley, Nichols, Fuller Heights, Medulla, Pine Lake, and Christina. Geneva Richardson was one of its star photographers. The paper still publishes every Thursday, and copies can be purchased at the company's Highway 37 North (North Church Avenue) location. (*The Mulberry Press.*)

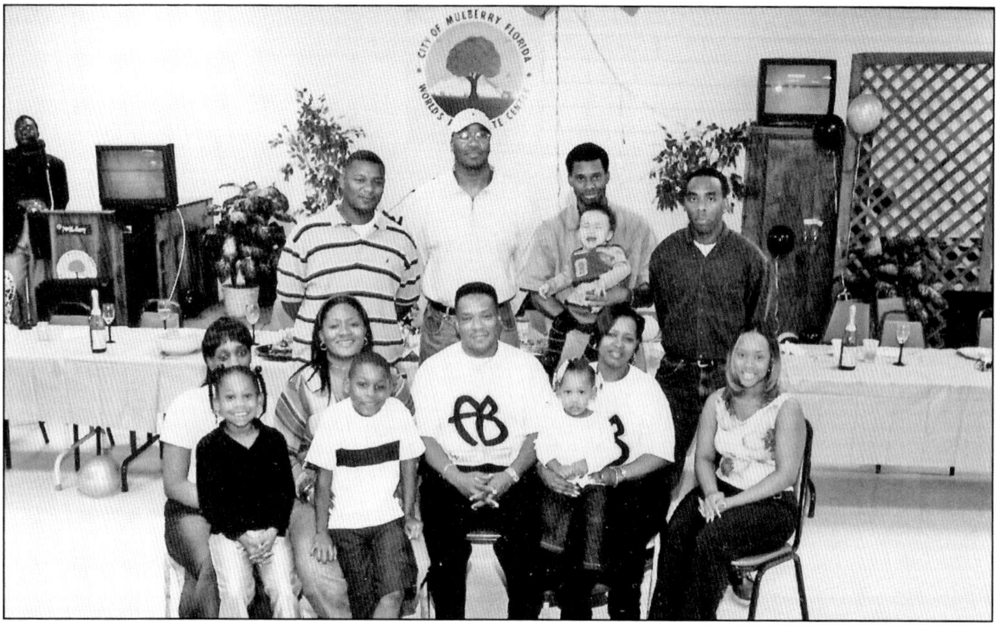

Ronald "Rico" Reed, Mulberry Police Department's first African American officer (1975–1985) and first African American lieutenant, is now the owner of Rico Reed Bail Bonds Agency and Secure Tek, Inc. In this photograph, his family is shown from left to right: (first row) Gabrielle Dukes; KT Jones; Kelsei Dukes; (seated) Alison Reed; Meki Reed; Rico Reed; Rico's wife, Gail Reed; Charrico Reed; (standing) Kerry Jones; Lester Hunt; Christian Boston, holding Ken Boston; and Bernard Stevenson. (John F. Dukes.)

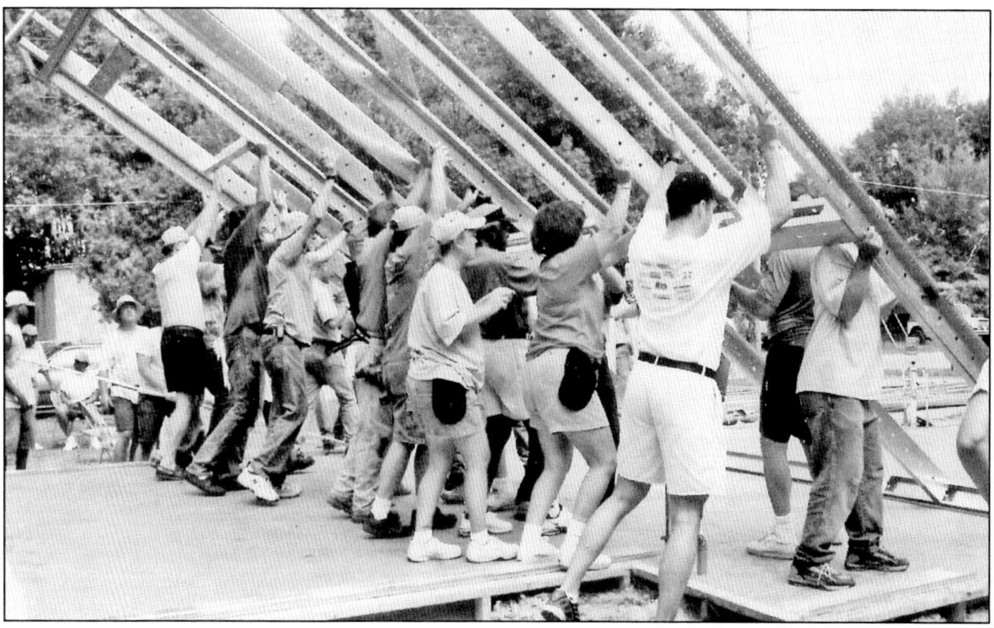

The Mulberry Chamber of Commerce sponsored a Habit for Humanity project to build a home for a needy citizen. The house was constructed in the city limits. Members of the chamber and community joined together to build the foundation. The volunteers showed compassion, respect, and friendship for everyone involved in the project. (MCC.)

Five

Church and Family

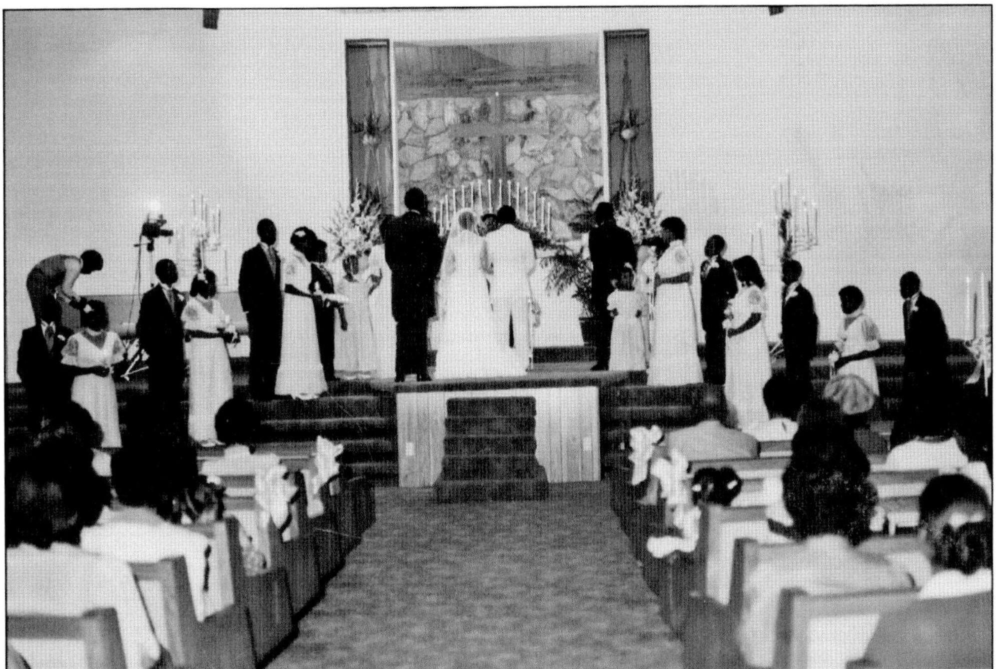

The First Assembly of God located on South Highway 60 has become the gathering place for large weddings, high school baccalaureate services, community services, and large funerals. This edifice is simply serene, and minimal decoration is required. The bridal party shown here, from left to right, includes James Sledge, Celestine Hunt, John F. Dukes, Stancilla Bell, Joseph "Cedric" Jones Jr., Gail Williams, Sherwood Daymond, Chloe Kendrick, Dina Cunningham, Joseph L. Jones Sr., bride Stephanie L. Dukes, presiding bishop Leroy Kennon, groom Jimmy R. Roland, Todd Morgan, Janail Glover, Joe Daymond Jr. (hidden from view), Monica Helper, Christopher Carson, Quintas Curry, Isom Helper IV, LaDessa Dukes, and Richie Sledge. In 2007, the chamber of commerce listed 23 churches in Mulberry.

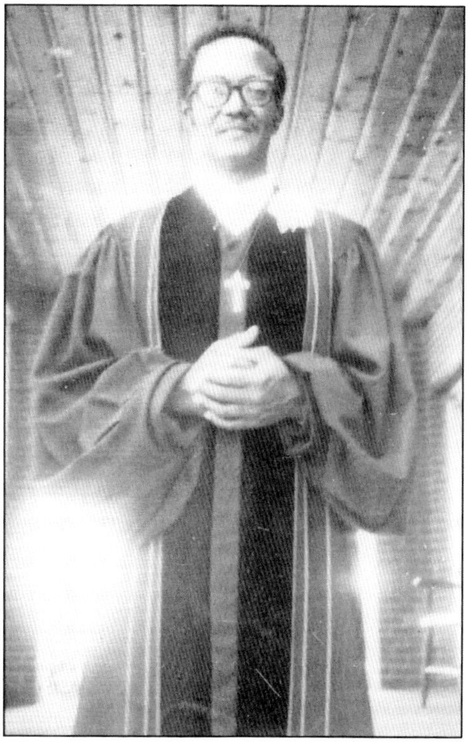

Rev. E. L. Partner, has been a pastor since 1976. He and Vera L. Partner married in 1976, and so they have celebrated 25 years of marriage. Revered Partner was the pastor for Mt. Zion AME Church in Mulberry and was very involved with the ministerial association and other community needs. (Burdell Kendrick/MBS.)

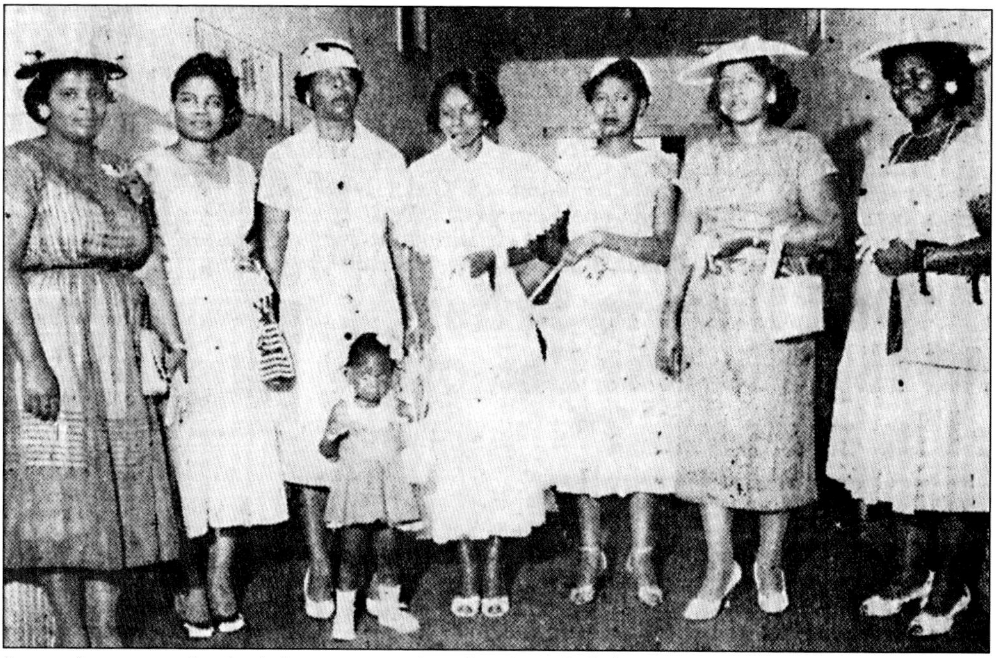

It was the custom for the ladies to cover their heads with fashionable hats or a lace covering, and to wear or carry their gloves and a hang bag with a lace handkerchief inside. Pictured here in about 1958 attending a father's day tea are, from left to right, Ola Mae Smith, Lillie Ruth Baker, Nila B. Brown, Birdell Kendrick and daughter Linda, Mae Satchel, Edith Brown, and Rosa Wade. (Essie N. Helper Morgan.)

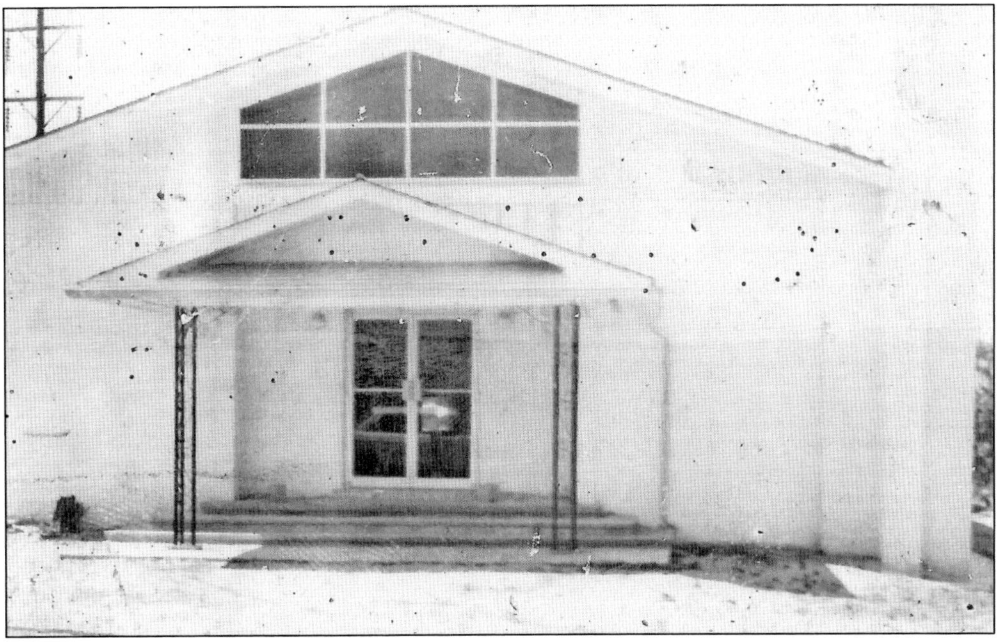

Bethel Missionary Baptist Church organized in 1908. The church caught on fire when sparks hit the wooded building from a wood-burning train engine, and its bell fell into the lake. Services were then held in the Old J. R. E. Lee School building. Essick Nelson, Walter Mapp, and others provided major financial and physical contributions to rebuild in 1969. March 2008 marks Bethel's 100th anniversary. (Ruenea Boyd Bigham.)

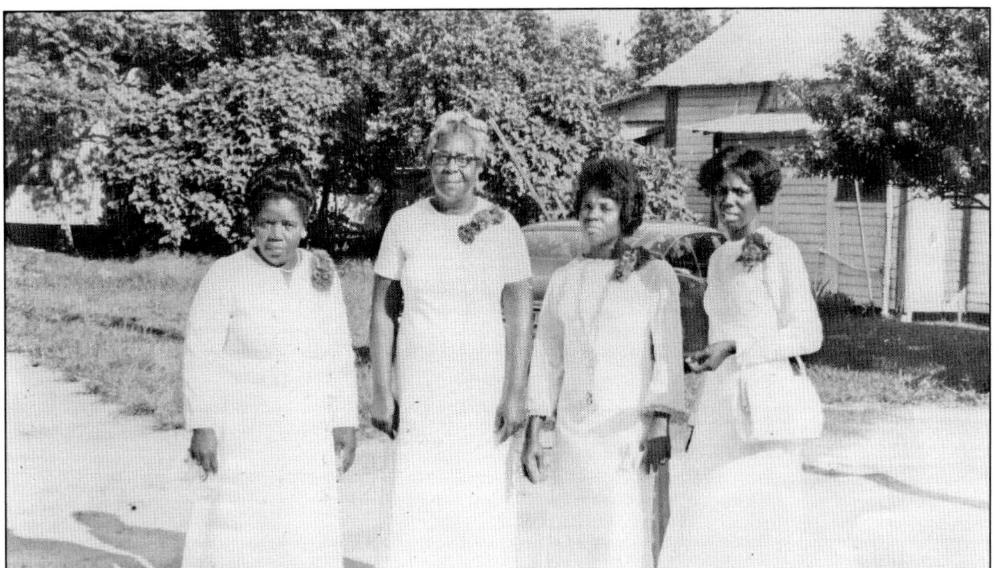

Gathered here, from left to right, are Bethel members Sr. Catherine Pope, deaconesses Nila B. Brown and Hazel Napier, and Sr. Julie Williams Taylor. The community actions of Hazel Napier, Oscar Baker, Roosevelt Baker, Walter Mapp, Pricilla Ford, Paul Napier, and others have resulted in better sewer systems, a new road allowing an alternative route to east Mulberry, playgrounds, and other improvements in the African American communities.

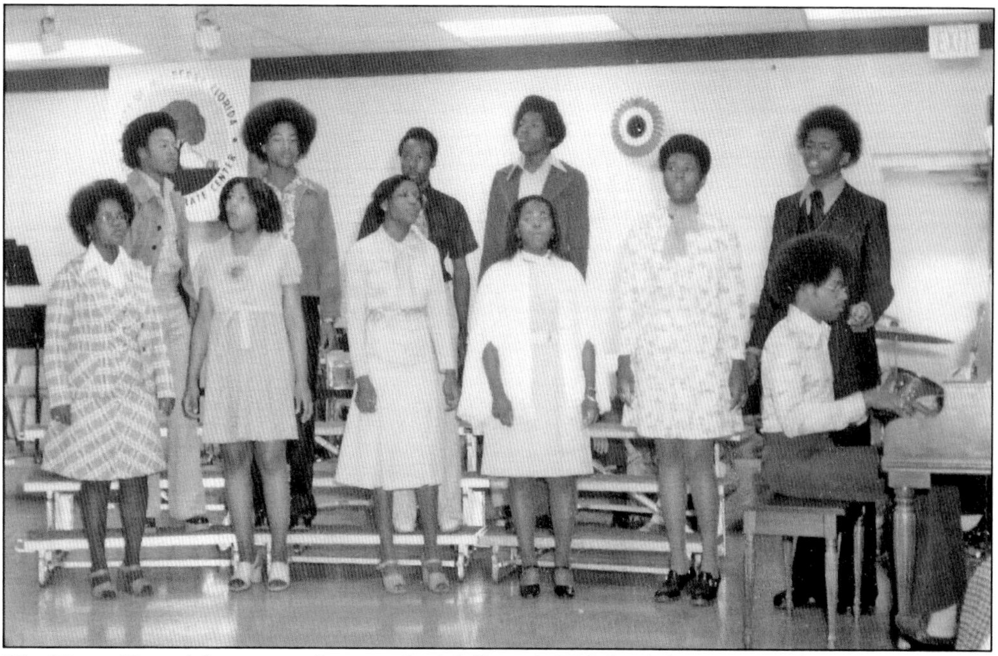

The Unity Gospel Singers perform at the Mulberry's 75th birthday party at the Mulberry Civic Center on February 12, 1976. From left to right are (first row) Linda Clayton, Wanda Kendrick, Negria Jackson, Linda Warner, Janice Smith, minister Nigel Williams, and Rev. Eugene Kendrick, who is playing the piano; (second row) Samuel Jones, Milton Morris, Rev. L. Hamilton, and minister Terry Childs.

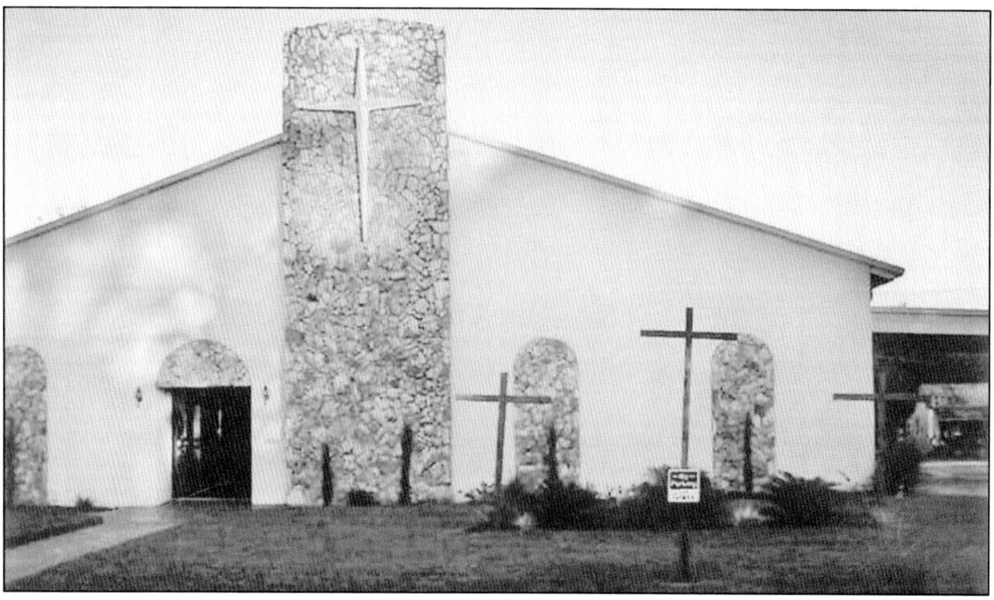

Jerusalem Missionary Baptist Church was founded in 1929. It has played an active part in community involvement. Several of its members have served as principals, city commissioners, service organizations' offices, and committee chairs. This keeps the church connected to what is going on in the community and helps to meet the people's needs. Jerusalem firmly believes that "one can be in the world and not be of the world." (Stephanie L. Dukes.)

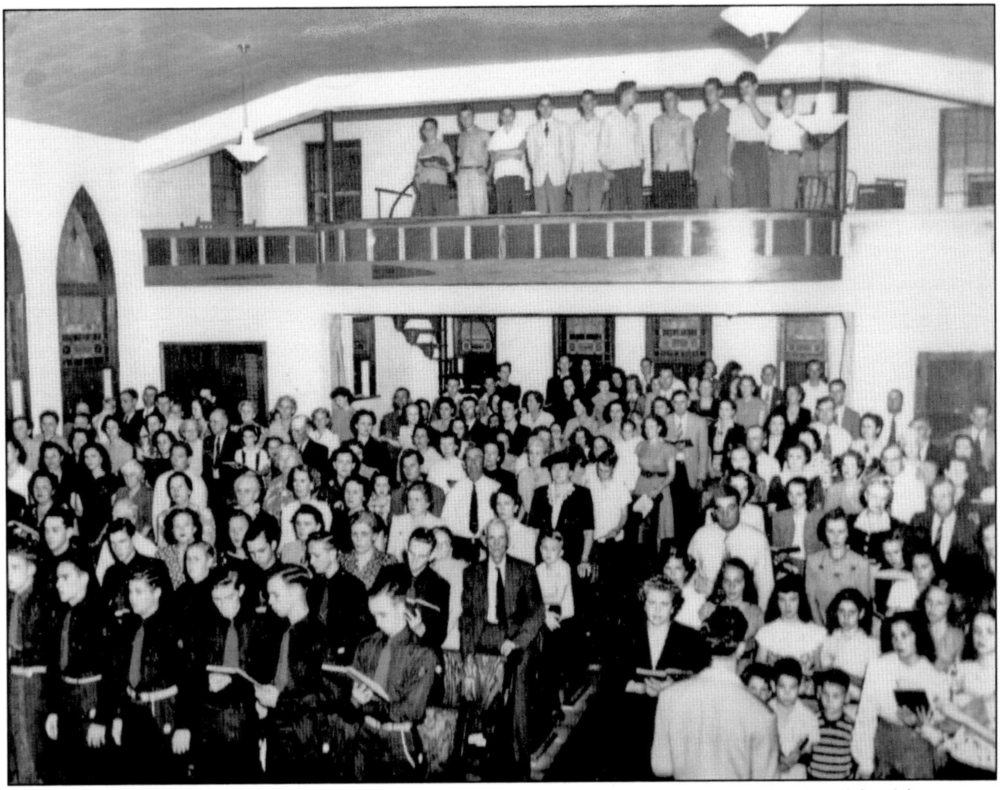

The First Baptist Church in Mulberry is located across from the second school building now known as William H. Purcell Elementary School. This 1940s picture shows the congregation honoring the Explorer Scouts. (Henrie Harned Sparkman/MBS.)

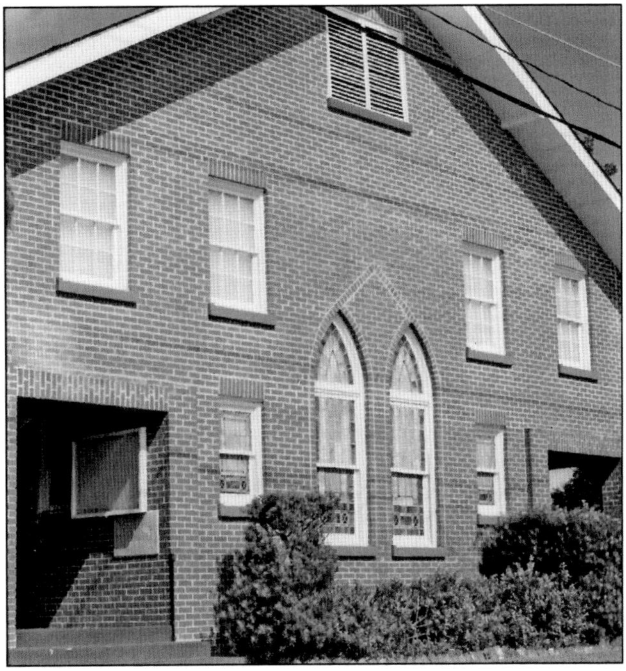

First Baptist Church is one of the churches, if not the only church, in Mulberry with stained-glass windows of this quality. The stained-glass windows start with two large windows in the front and continue around the sides and back of the church. The church's cornerstone reads "First Baptist Church A.D. 1935." Mulberry High School held the graduating class baccalaureate service here until the graduating classes outgrew the edifice. (The *Mulberry Press*.)

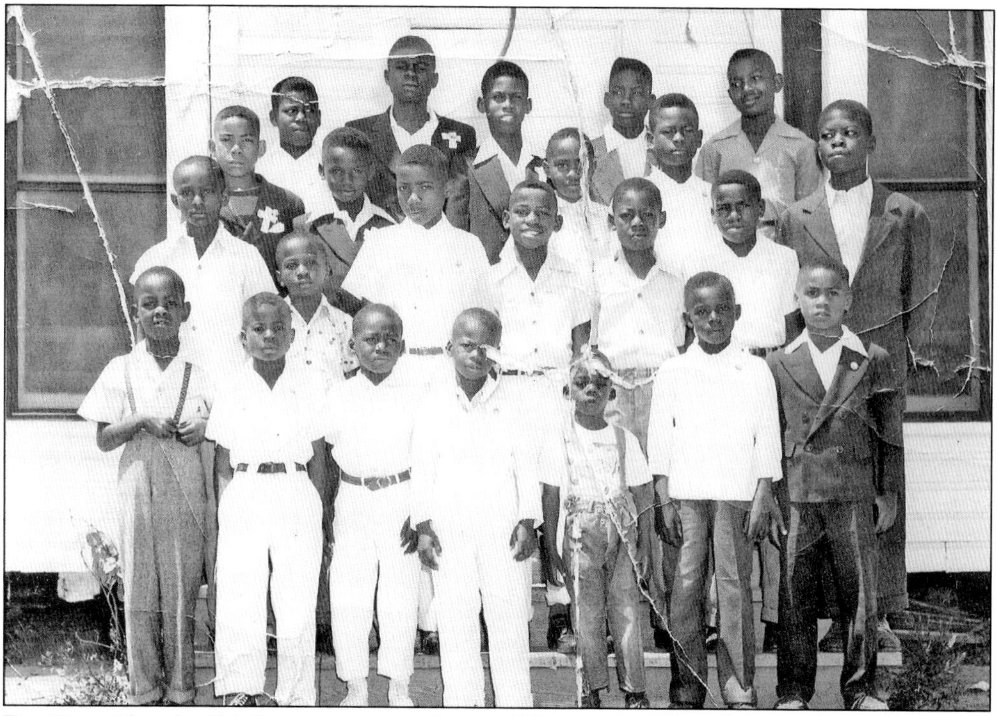

First Born Church of Mulberry group members at Old Prairie are, from left to right, the following: (first row) unidentified, Clarence Jackson, four unidentified people, and Herbert Woodard; (second row) Bernard Jackson, Graddy Jackson, unidentified, Edward "Tom Boy" Robinson, and two unidentified people; (third row) ? Wallace, Chesley Woodard, unidentified, Johnny Lee Overstreet, and Tommy Jenkins; (fourth row) Jerry Overstreet, Wogan Woodard, Lawrence Woodard, and two unidentified young men. (Herbert Woodard.)

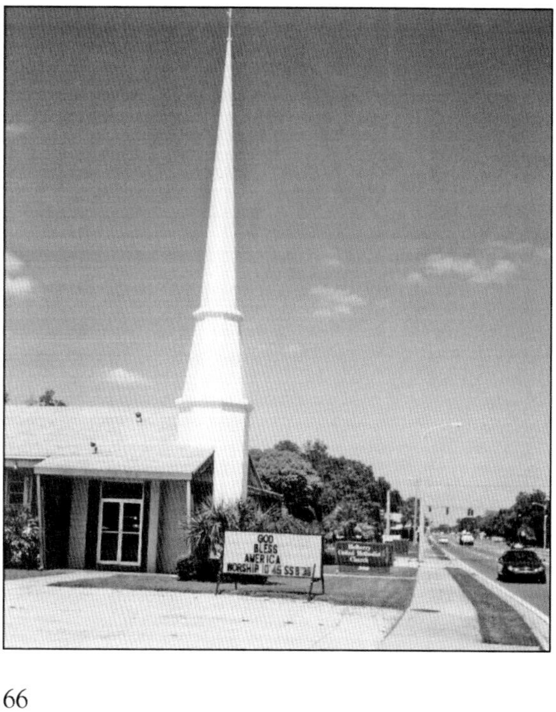

The United Methodist Church on Highway 37 began under the direction of Reverend Sumner in 1896. The Mulberry Historical Society, Inc. has partnered with the church to use its facility to host its annual Celebration Day program. The program honors Mulberry citizens who have made outstanding achievements and excelled in community involvement. This event is held in October of each year. The society meets the second Thursday of each month at the phosphate museum. All are welcome to attend. (The *Mulberry Press*.)

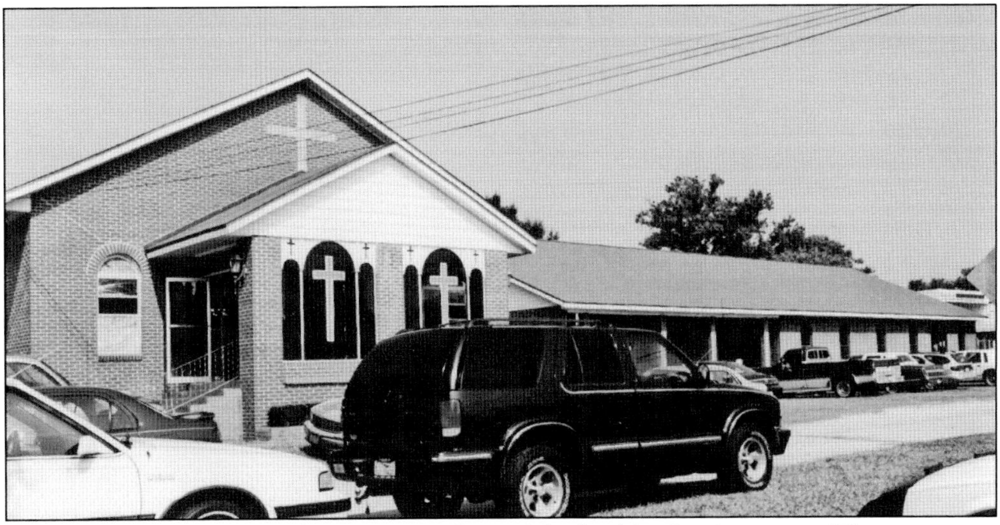

In 1909, William Clement and Annie Sprutt donated this land for church purposes. The cornerstone reads, "Mt. Zion A.M.E. Church Mulberry, Florida." Stewards include Lloyd Gibson, Theodore Williams, Noah Brown, Evon Aiken, Bernice Cromartie, Luella Bentley Sec. Trustees: Marguerite E. Holland, Will L. Bentley, John R. Thomas, Ed Clark, Frank McGill, Tom Smith, S.S. Supt. Bessie Kennon, Pastor Rev. W. E. Spell, Arch. & Builder: Rev. G. A. Rutledge, Presiding Bishop Rev. L. G. Hatcher." (The *Mulberry Press*.)

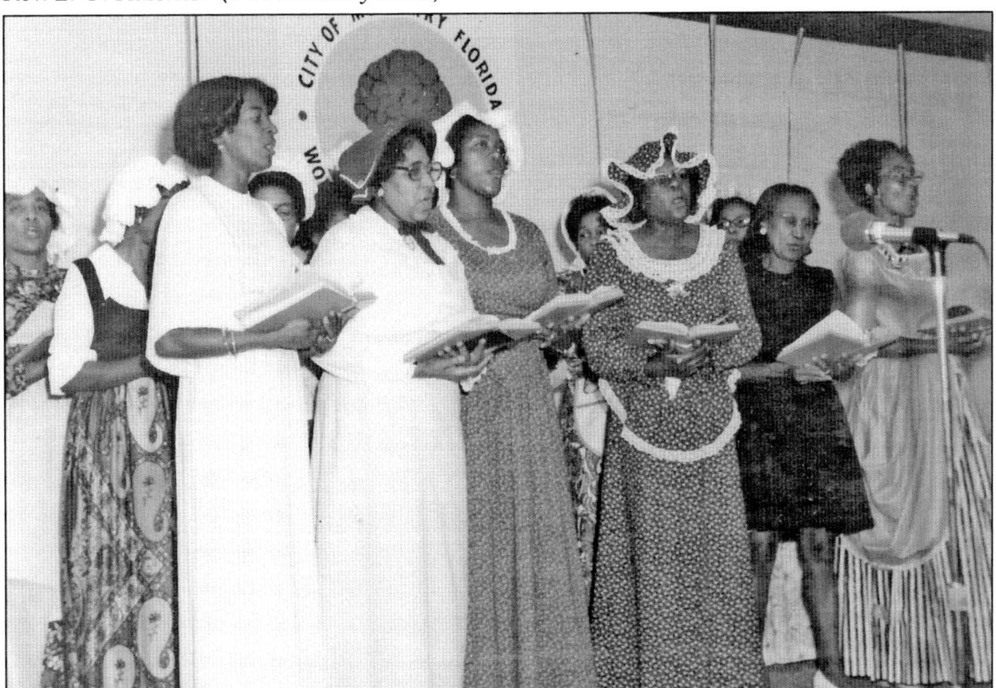

Pictured here is the Mt. Zion AME Church choir singing at the bicentennial celebrations held at Mulberry's Civic Center in 1976. From left to right are the following: (first row) Emily Bell, Gertrude Niece, Helen Francis, Virginia White, Betsy Kennon Cooper, and Ruth Stewart; (second row) unidentified, Lillie Ruth Baker, unidentified, Barbara Jean White, and Margie Mapp; (third row) Dorothy Morris. (MBS.)

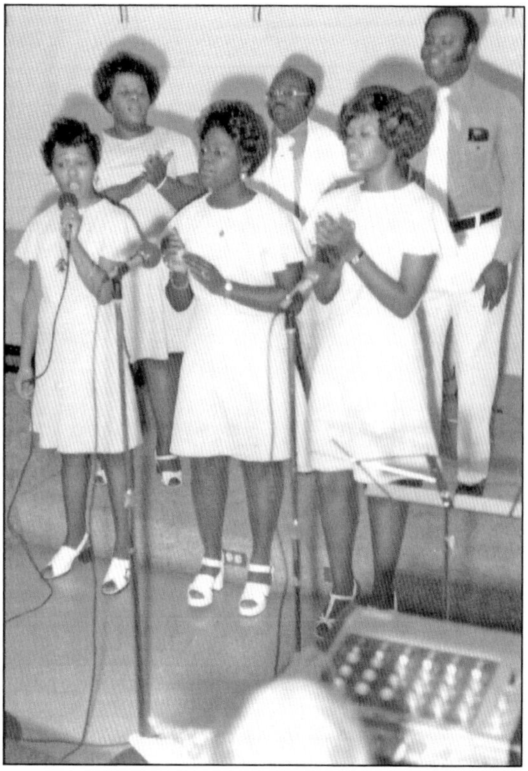

Here the choir of St. James Primitive Baptist Church of East Mulberry sings at the 1976 bicentennial celebration. From left to right are as follows: (first row) Evelyn White, Robin Brooks and unidentified; (second row) Carrie Walker, deacon Willie Brooks, and deacon Otis Bell. The Brooks are part of Mulberry's legendary Brooks Singers.

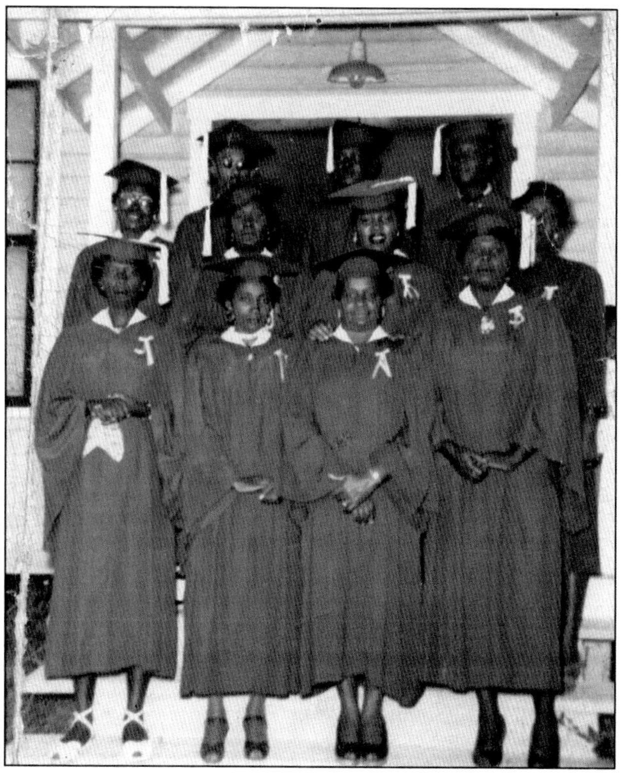

Mount Carmel Primitive Baptist Church was organized in 1955 to serve the growing needs of the community of Nichols, Florida, along with the members of the Amie Chapel Missionary Baptist Church. This 1950s photograph shows members of Mount Carmel's choir in their uniforms, which looked much like graduation attire. The choir was known to move their tassels from side to side during certain songs. From left to right are (first row) Martha Smith, Salley Mae Robinson, Rebecca Swilley, Annes Smith; (second row) Trudie Grant, Ruby Grant, Azore Grant, Georgia Lee Sirmons, unidentified; (third row) Earl Smith Jr., Leroy Swilley, and Alfrazier Murray.

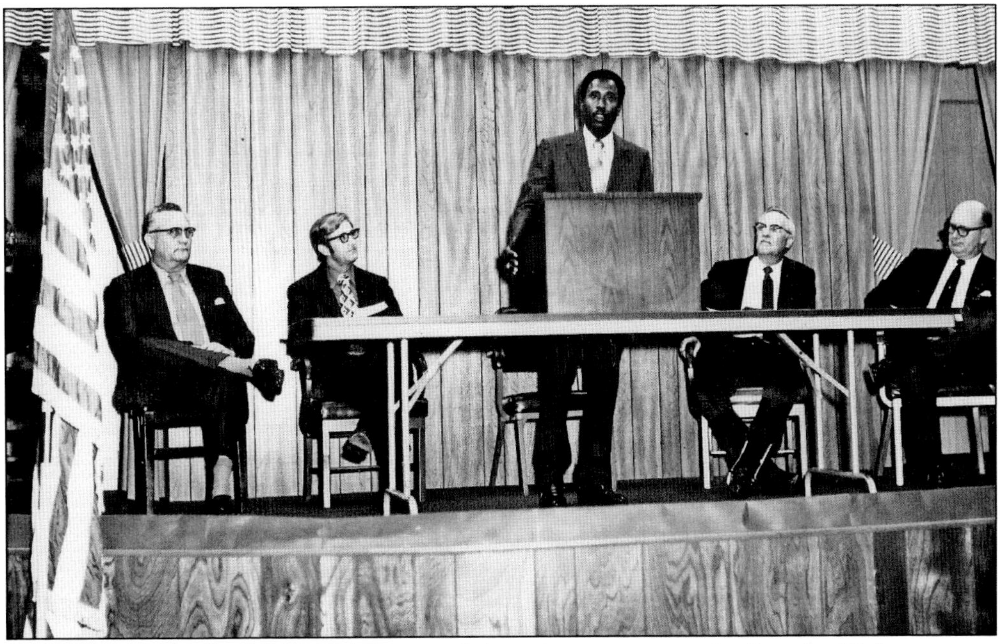

In the late 1960s, the Mulberry Ministerial Association sponsored a Fourth of July program. Seated from left to right are Rev. Leon Boswell, Rev. Travis Hudson, Rev. Leroy Kennon, Rev. W. E. Kircher, and Rev. Max Holleyman. The association also sponsors canned food drives during the Thanksgiving and Christmas seasons. (Geneva Richardson/Mulberry Historical Scrapbook collection.)

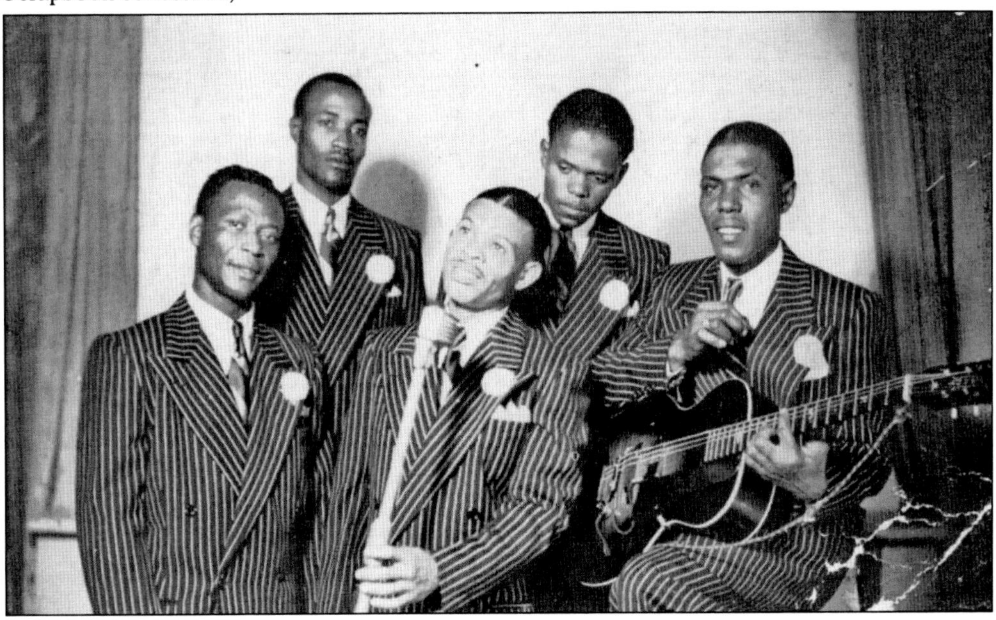

The Swanee Jubileers of Lakeland were a gospel singing group that traveled and performed throughout the South. The members pictured above, from left to right, are L. J. Ackers, T. Thomas, Jake B. Miller (at microphone), Roosevelt Baker, and Fish Willie. A female gospel group was also formed, with members Nila B. Brown, Emily Bryant Bell, and Bernice Culpepper. (Roosevelt and Lillian Baker.)

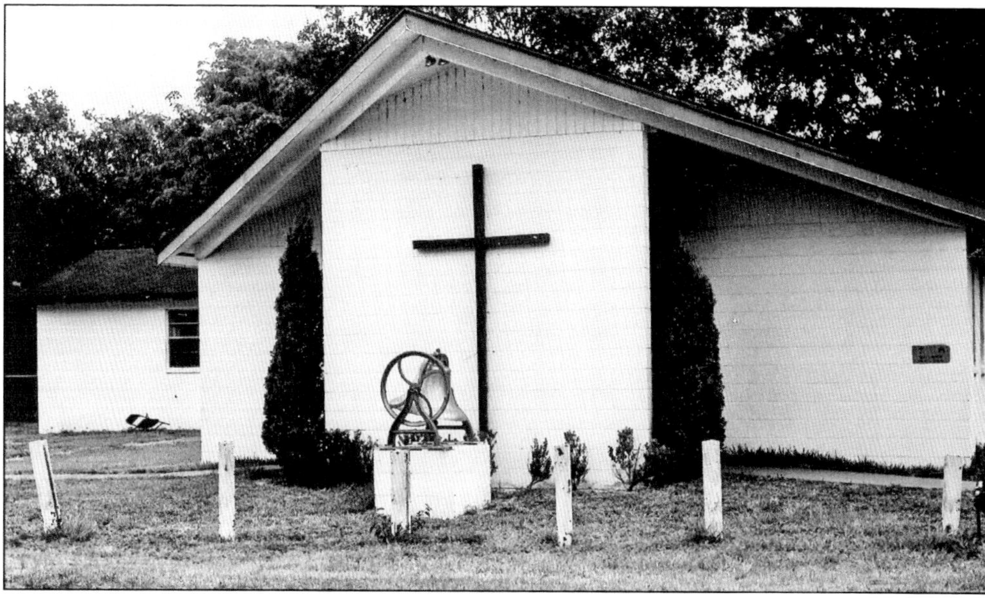

This church was organized by Rev. Sye J. Johnson in April 1949. He served as pastor until June 1993. The bell out front was once a part of the old church. It was known throughout the community that the toll of the bell signaled the calling of the community together for worship and other occasion,s such as the death of a community member. As of 2008, Rev. Wesley Mitchell is the pastor and Penny Morris Mitchell is the first lady. (Essie N. Helper Morgan.)

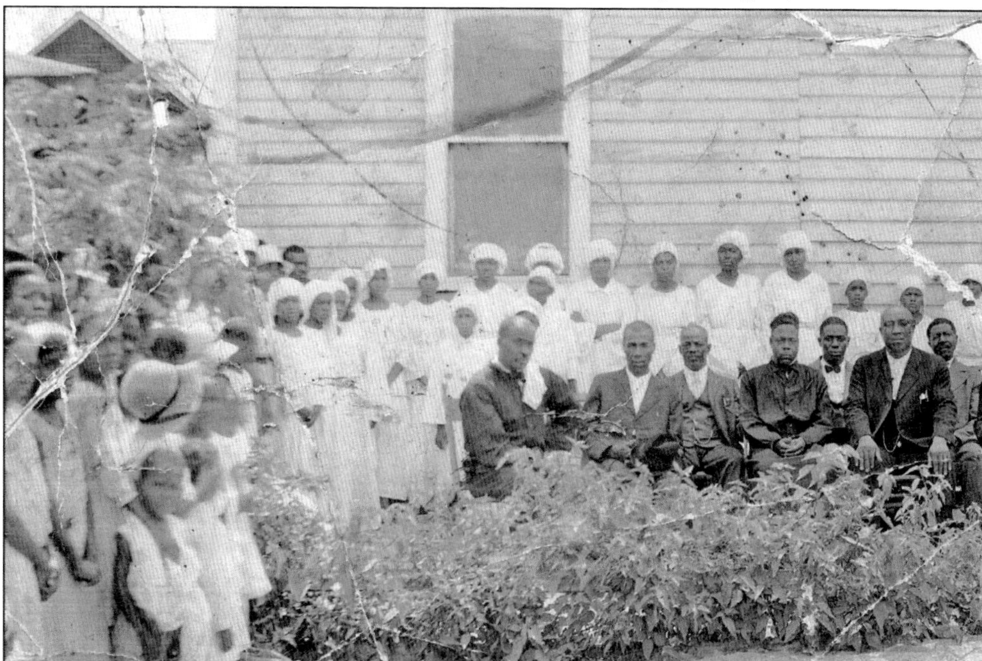

This late 1950s photograph shows the gathering of the First South Florida Baptist Association Congress Number 5 meeting at Bethel Missionary Baptist Church. The candidates dressed in white are moments from being baptised in the pool in front of the church by the bishop, pastor, and deacons. (Ruenea Boyd Bigham.)

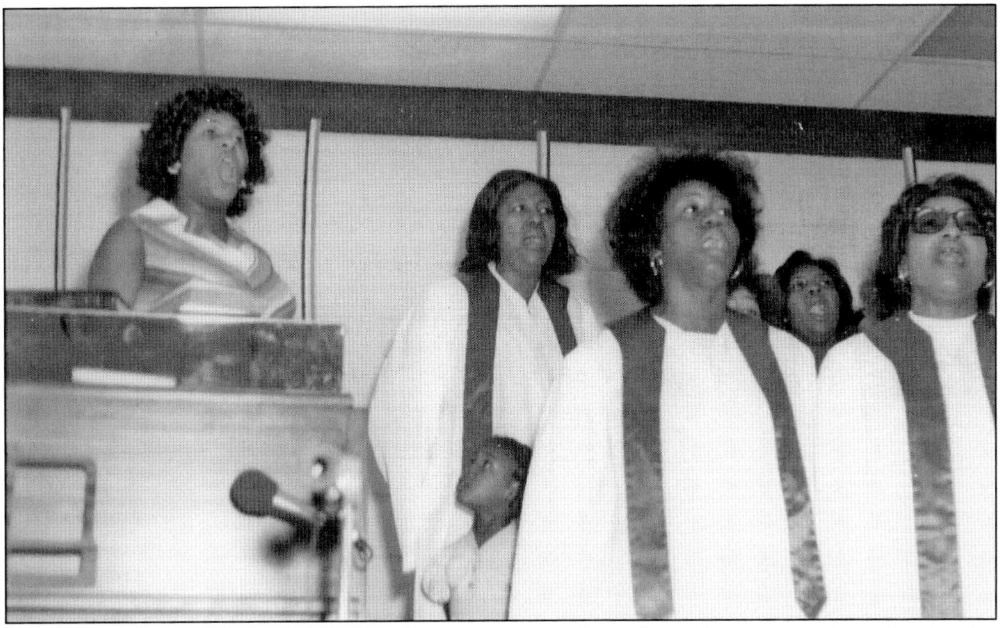

St. Paul Missionary Baptist Church in Pierce is known throughout the community as having the most talented vocalists including the Kendrick family, which now belongs to Mt. Olive of Bradley where Rev. Eugene Kendrick is pastor. The McPlatt family is gifted with musical talent along with the Stephens, Jacksons, and other families. Pictured here from left to right are as follows: (first row) Louise McPlatt and Miriam Wallace; (second row) Wanda Jackson Kendrick, Mary Pete, two unidentified people, and Rosa Gundy. (MBS.)

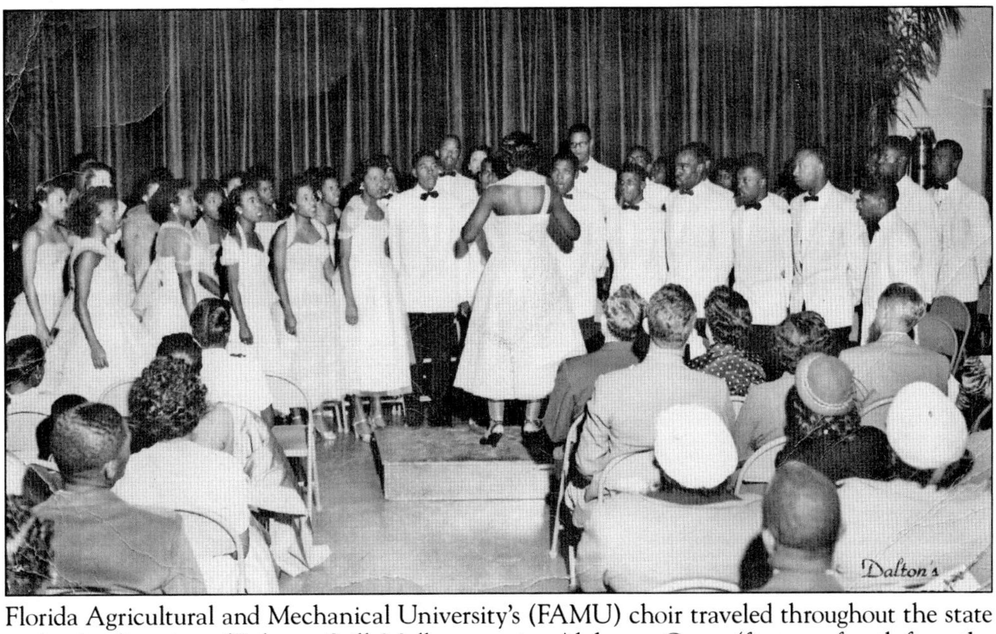

Florida Agricultural and Mechanical University's (FAMU) choir traveled throughout the state under the direction of Rebecca Still. Mulberry native Alphonso Green (first row, fourth from the right) graduated from FAMU, taught school in Polk County, and recorded a 45 single, "I Want to Be Home for Christmas" along with David Helper, Will Stevenson, Ben Smith, and Otis Webster. The B-side was "The Joke on Santa." (Ruenea Boyd Bigham.)

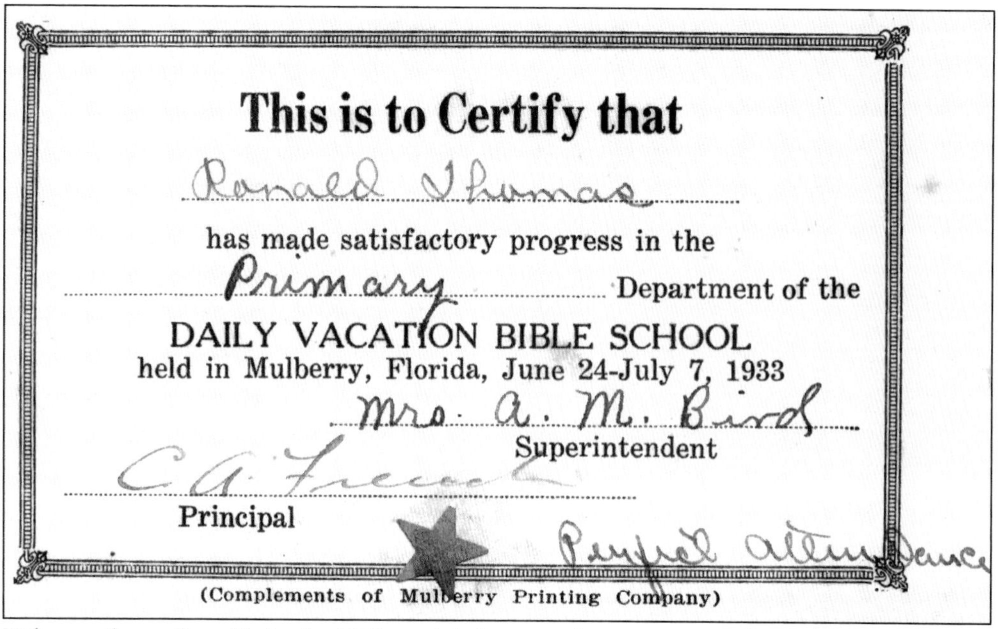

This is to Certify that

Ronald Thomas

has made satisfactory progress in the

Primary Department of the

DAILY VACATION BIBLE SCHOOL

held in Mulberry, Florida, June 24-July 7, 1933

Mrs. A. M. Bird

Superintendent

C. A. French

Principal

Perfect attendance

(Complements of Mulberry Printing Company)

Kids stayed out of trouble in the 1900s mainly because the community planned activities for the children. They could count on having snacks, learning scripture verses, and seeing their special friends everyday. This certificate shows that Ronald Thomas had perfect attendance. Notice the Mulberry Printing Company's support. (Ronald Thomas.)

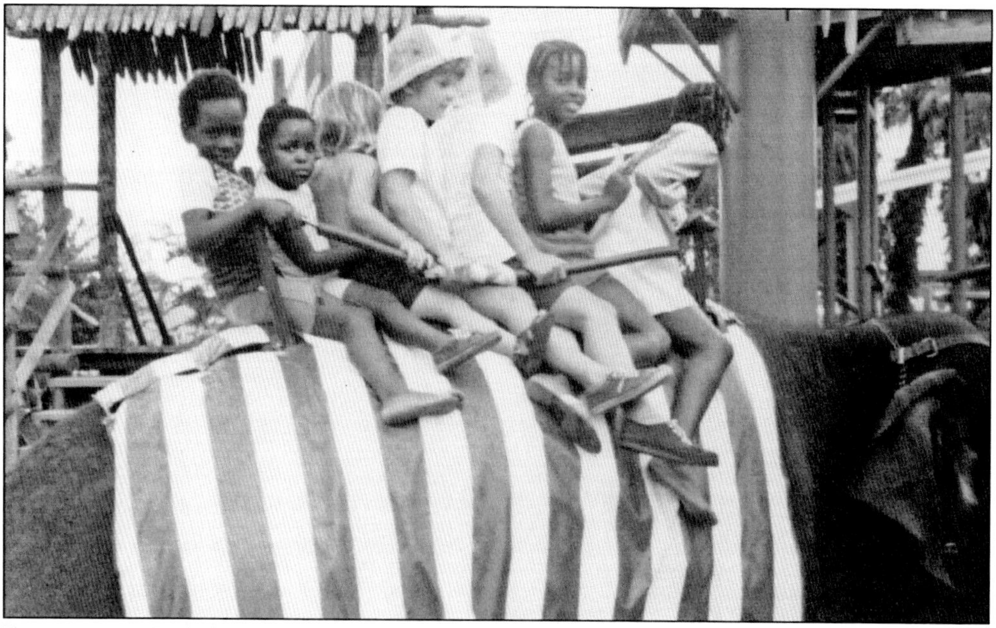

Every summer, Bethel Missionary Baptist Church would reward its Sunday school and Summer Bible School students with "Fun in the Sun." The summer of 1974, under Sunday school superintendent deacon Emanuel Doleman, students were taken to Busch Gardens in Tampa, Florida. Shown here are students Cedric Jones, Sharon Thomas, unidentified, unidentified, Vanessa Smith, and Sharon ? riding a tamed African elephant. Other school superintendents include Deacon Ollie Anderson and Rev. John Smith Jr. (Nila Helper Jones.)

Six

EDUCATION

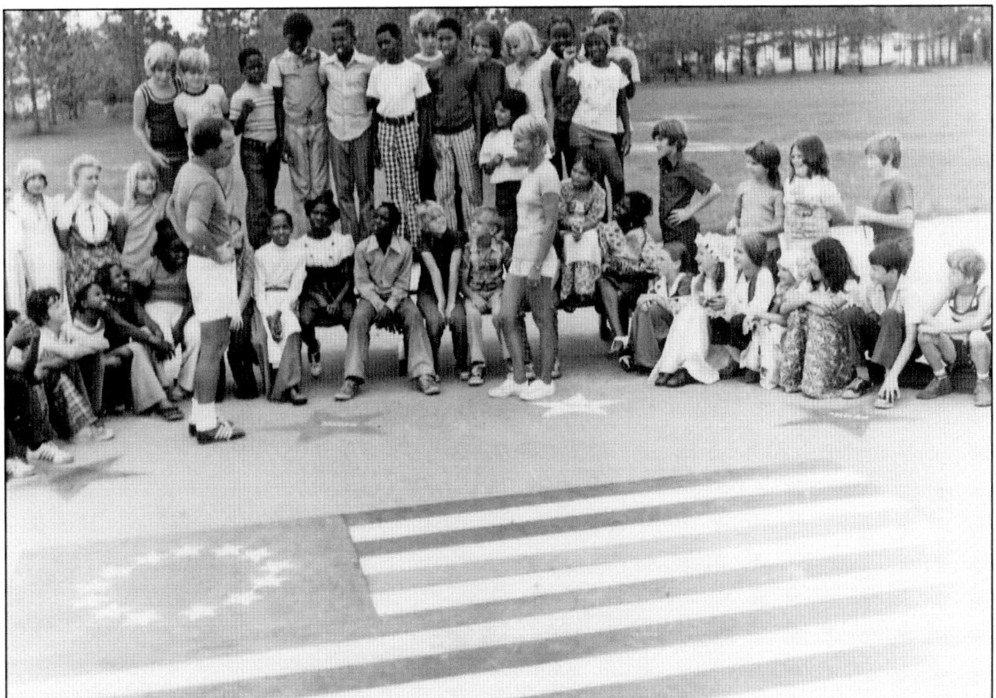

All Mulberry schools joined in Mulberry's 75th anniversary celebration and the nation's bicentennial celebration. Coach George Hatch, Mulberry High School's principal from 1996 to 2008, is pictured here with Mulberry Elementary School's bicentennial display. Mulberry Middle School contributed a banner entitled "Flying to Freedom." George Hatch is the father of two, husband of Nancy, brother of Geraldine, son of Gerald Sherwood and Marie Black Hatch, and stepson of Isla Paxton Hatch.(Geneva Richardson/Mulberry Historical Scrapbook Collection.)

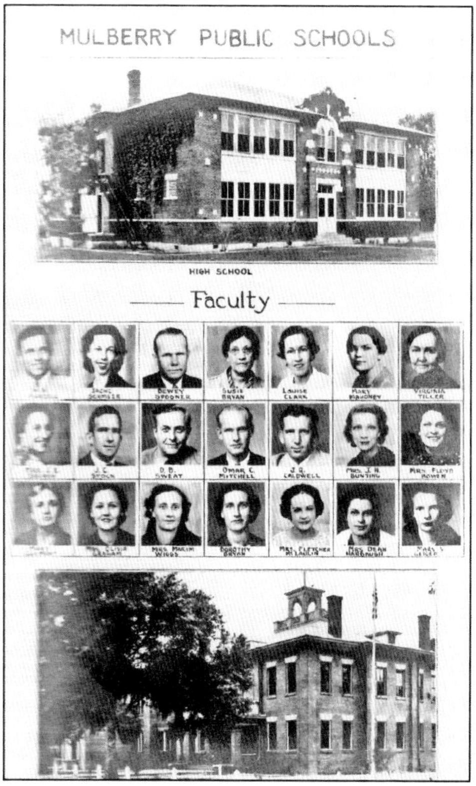

The land for the high school, featured in the image above, was donated in 1924 by Levi N. Pipkin. This campus became Mulberry Elementary School and later was named William Purcell Elementary School. In the middle of this image are the 1937 faculty members of Mulberry High School. The first Mulberry elementary school, constructed in 1898–1899, located at the corner of Canal and Church Streets, was originally located where the tree is in the image below. The building pictured here in 1909 is the elementary and junior high school.(Raymond L. Driver.)

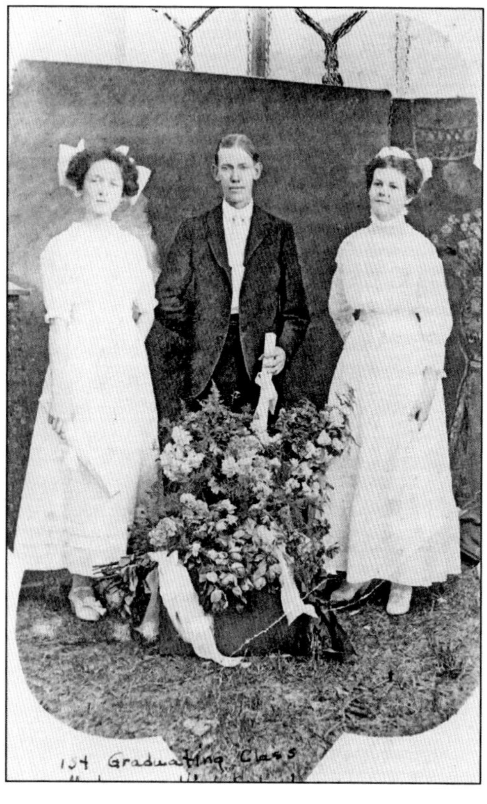

The three-member class of 1911 was Mulberry High School's first graduating class: from left to right are Maude Davis, James Bond Gibson, and Selma Allene Smith. O. J. Moore was the principal. The approval to organize a high school came in 1908, making Mulberry the third organized high school. The other high schools were in Bartow and Lakeland. The building for the high school classes would come later, in 1924. (MBS.)

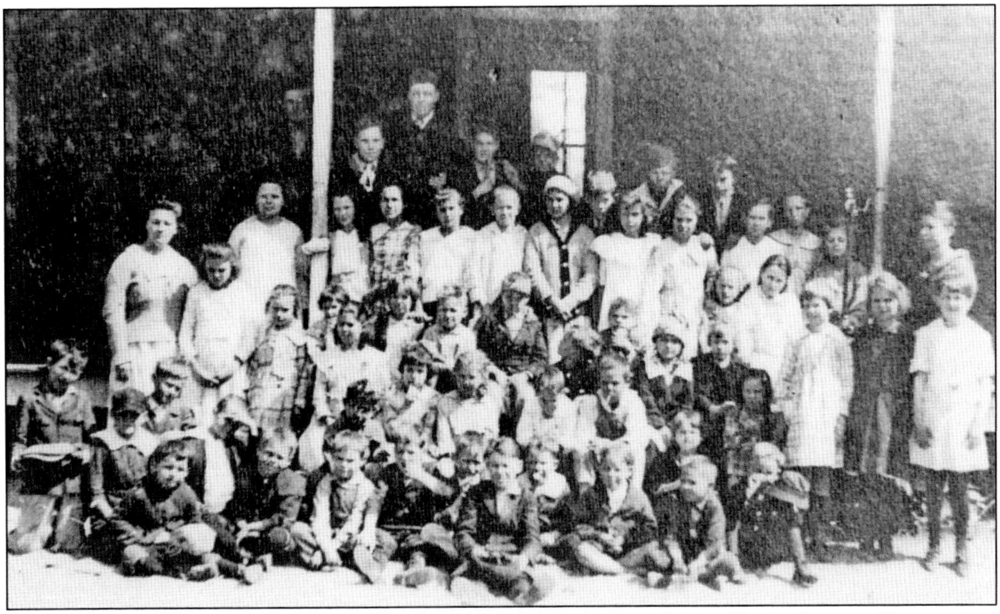

The Phosphate Mining Company was formed on April 12, 1906, by E. C. Stuart, Christopher Gustavus Memminger (1865–1930), and H. E. Memminger. The general manager, Paul Hamilton Fuller, ensured that a school and church were part of the Nichols mining town when it was completed in 1921. It is said that the community of Fuller Heights is named for him. This photograph depicts the Nichols' School students and teachers around 1921. (SLAF.)

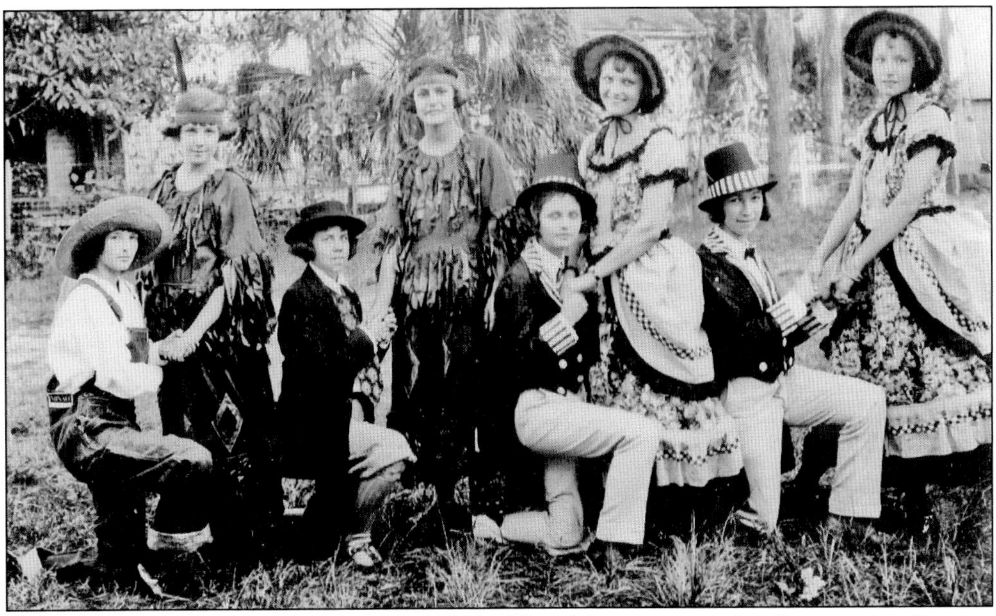

The class of 1924 presented a play entitled *Ten Years Hence*, written by class member Bernice Haynsworth. Cast members, from left to right, are (kneeling) Edwina Bruton, Abbie Vassie, Eva Whidden, and Inez Clark; (standing) Naomi McLalin, valedictorian Myrtle Carter, Bernice Haynsworth, and Mildred Overstreet. Class members not pictured include Paul Anderson, Helen Byrd, Harold Weaver, Henry Clements, Lula Mae Fletcher, Lillian Fulghune, Maggie Carter, salutatorian Ruth Collins, and Harold Brokaw. (Bernice Haynsworth Allen/MBS.)

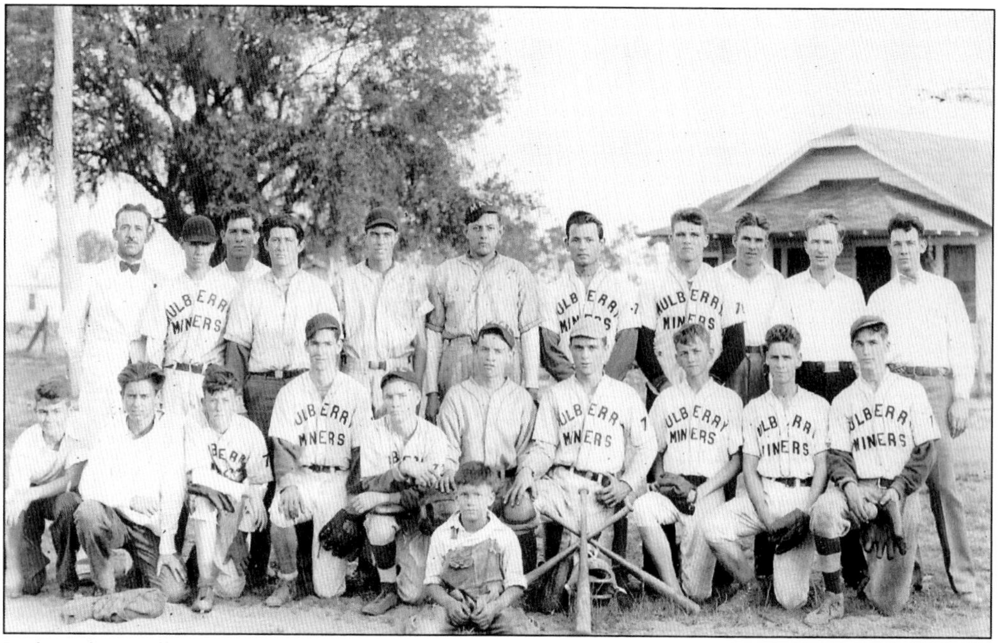

Before the Mulberry sport teams were known as the Panthers, they were dubbed the Miners. Shown here from left to right are as follows: (first row) mascot Nic Gandy; (second row) Norton Wilson, Osline McDonald, James Spyrcem, Carter McLaulin, Harry Driver, Roddie Bryan, Alva Burris. J. D. Hicks, Dick McLaulin, and Carl Evers; (third row) professor Harry B. Mullon, Fredie Denmark, Wilbur Jones, Clifton Hall, Gray Martin, Woody Woodall, J. E. Brown Jr., Billy Turner, Carl Ellis, and Coach Huskey. (Raymond L. Driver.)

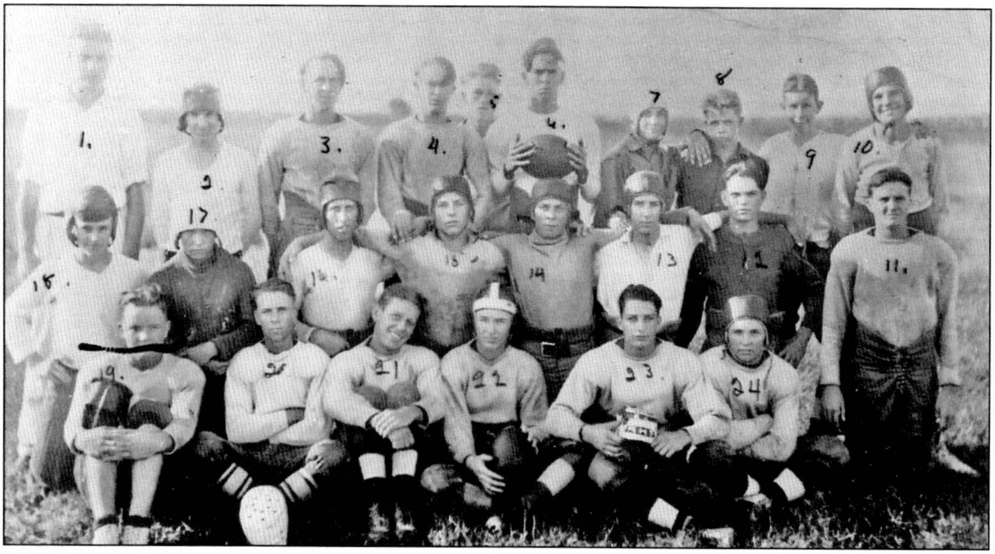

The first Mulberry High School football team was organized in 1924. Here the members are pictured from left to right: (first row) Clark Pixton, Roy Turner, Curtis Clark, Joel Eves, Austin Graham, and Irwin Haynsworth; (second row) Hugh Sutton, Bernie Green, team captain Marion Wiggs, Justin Lovell, Jim Sutton, Wimpus Simpon, Cecil Sweat, and Harold Hooker; (third row) coach Loraine Saunders, Robert Mitchell, Charles Lovell, Lamar Evers, Teaford Holland, Bennie Jones, Emory Fitts, Hubert Collins, B. J. Sapp, and Parker Hall. (Raymond L. Driver.)

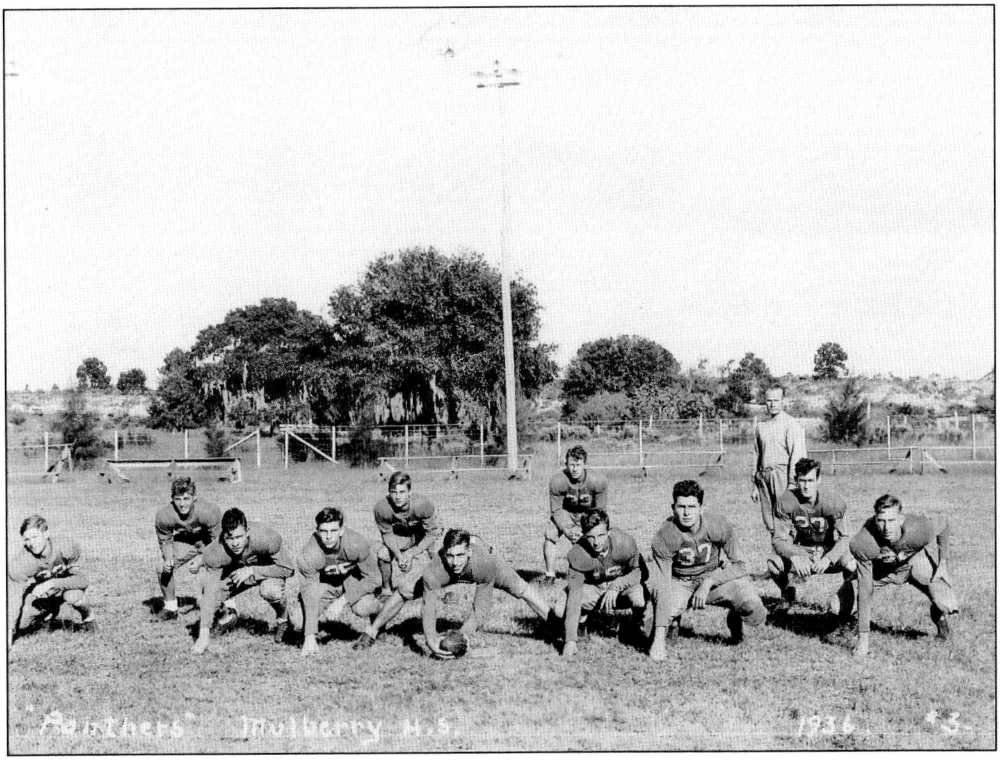

Extracurricular activities are said to improve the sensory perception. Shown here from left to right are the members of the football offense line for the 1936 Mulberry High School Panthers: Raymond L. Driver, right end; Lester Carter, right tackle; Sims Cozart, right guard; Jerry Duke, center; Vernon Jordon, left guard; Jack Jones, left tackle; and Murphy Lewis, left end. The backfield players included Frederick McCook, quarterback; Duke McDonald, halfback, Julian Mullis, full back; and Percy Cribb, halfback. (Raymond L. Driver.)

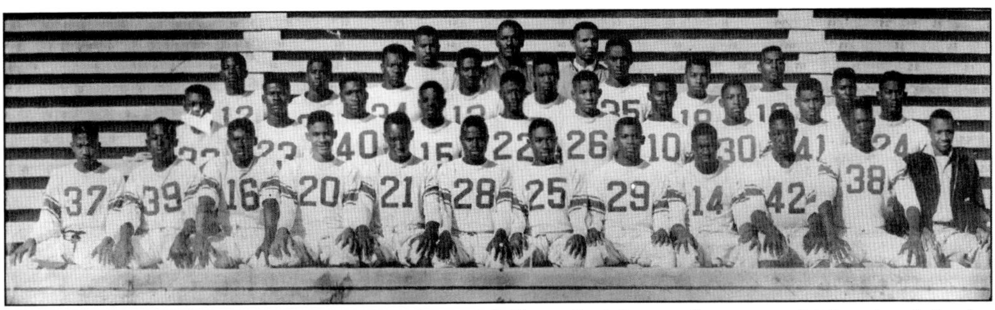

The 1954 football team at Union Academy, Mulberry's African American high school, had a 10-0 season, scoring 526 points and holding the opponents to 43; three members of the team were drafted to professional football. The identified Mulberry players include Bernard White, second row, eighth from the left; Alphonso Newkirk and Roosevelt Smith, third row, second and third from the left, respectively; and Coach Jordan Corbett, fourth row, third from the left. Floyd Robinson is not pictured. (Bernard White.)

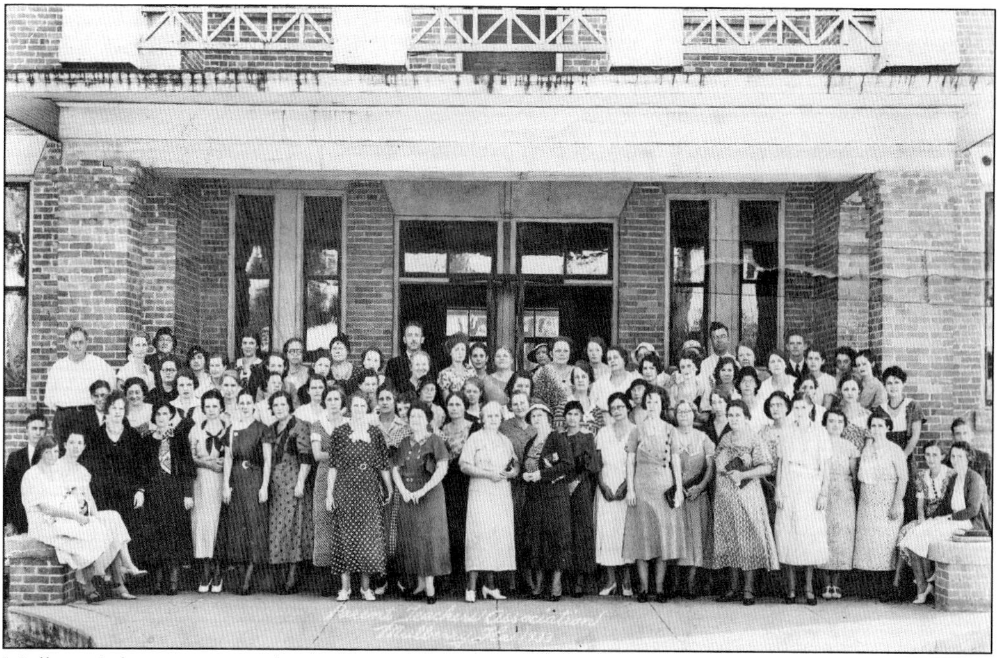

Mulberry's first parent-teacher association (PTA) was organized in 1933. This photograph features the faculty and staff, including almost every mother of children attending the school. The principal was Harry B. Mullon. The first president of the organization was Maude Clements Driver, who served three consecutive years. (Raymond L. Driver.)

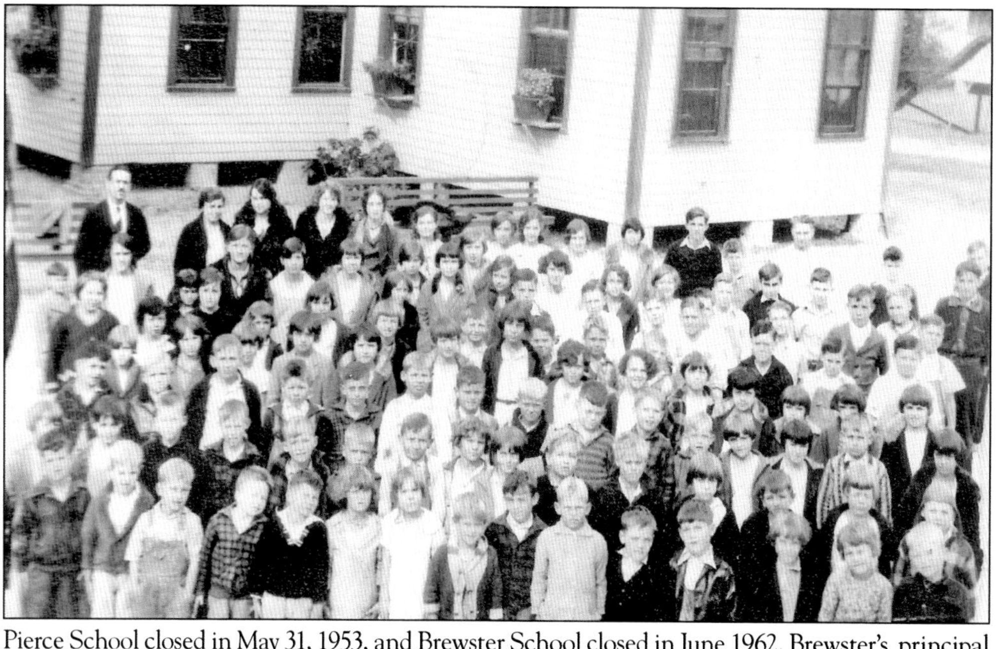

Pierce School closed in May 31, 1953, and Brewster School closed in June 1962. Brewster's principal from 1952 to 1959, Anton Dudek, became principal of Mulberry Elementary School (1959–1970). In August 1962, all students from the areas south of Mulberry started attending the newly opened Kingsford Elementary School. Construction of this new school cost $200,000 and produced 12 classrooms to house grades one through six. (MBS.)

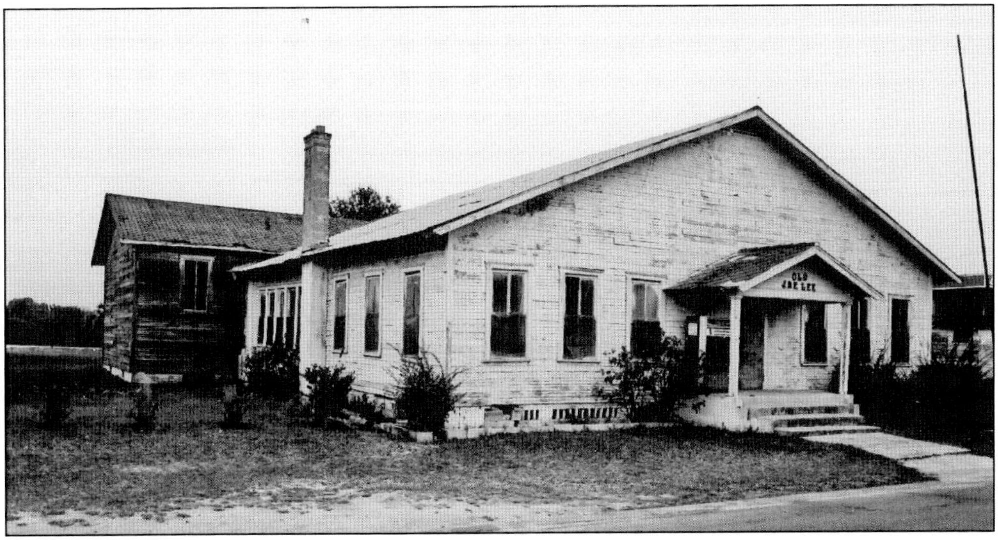

The J. R. E. Lee School opened in August 1910 to educate African Americans during segregation. The first teachers were W. T. Young and Sadie Young. Other former teachers living in Mulberry are Gertrude Bentley Niece, Essie N. Helper Morgan, Malvis B. Simmons, and John Glover. Students from J. R. E. Lee Junior High attended Union Academy in Bartow, Florida, for completion of high school. The multipurpose auditorium and classroom was pictured in the background was added in the 1938–1939 school year. (Sandra Brown.)

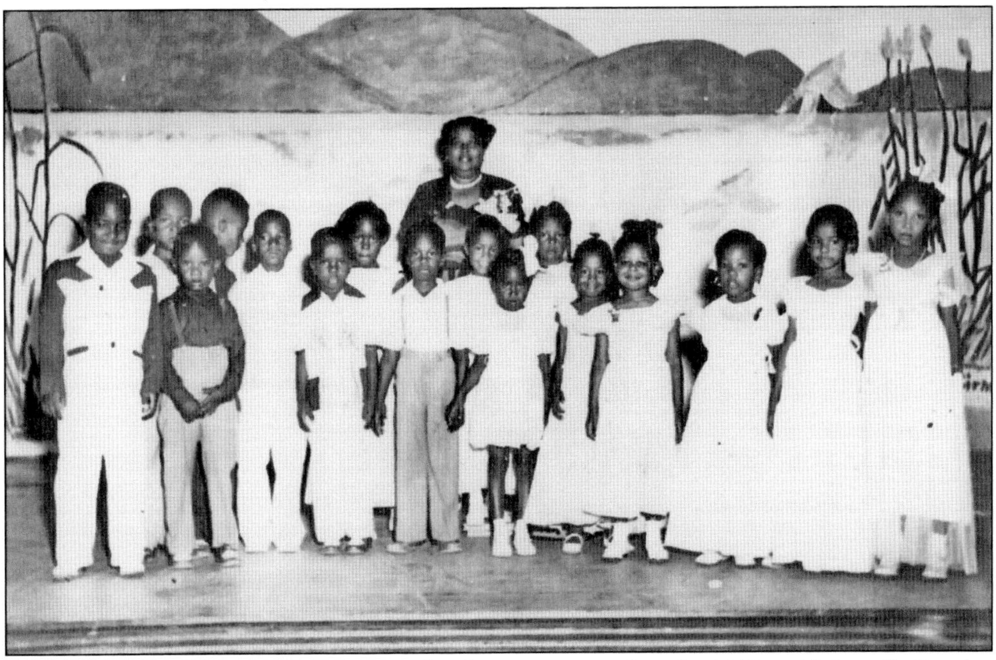

The first African American community kindergarten started in the 1940s, with Louella Bentley as the teacher. Students are standing on the stage of the old J. R. E. School. From left to right are the following: (first row) Albert Johnson, Willie Herbert Stancil, Robert Stevenson, Bruce Stewart, Voncille Stewart, Estelle McGill, Brenda Brown, Sharon Helper, Virginia Walker, Vera McGill; (second row) Willie Frank Brown, Eugene Frances, Maxine Smith, Ethel Bell, Gwendolyn Simmons, and Mrs. Louella Bentley. (Gertrude Bentley Niece/MBS.)

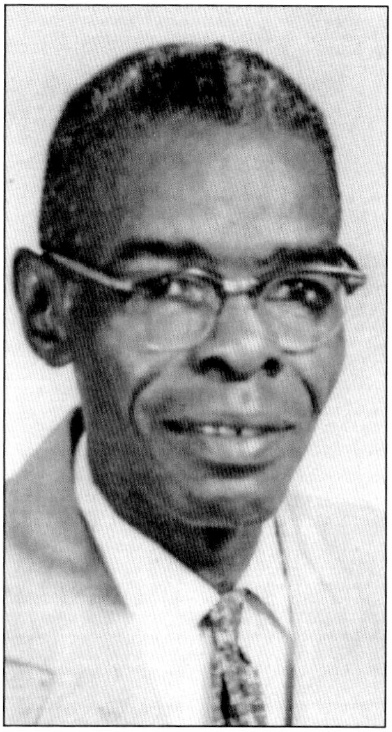

Leroy Johnson stressed the importance of education to his son Woodrow (pictured) and his two siblings. Before walking to Union Academy High School in Bartow, 10 miles east of Mulberry, Woodrow would go to work at the Juanita Hotel. He continued his educational pursuit until he became a teacher; he taught for more than 30 years. (John and Ruth Glover.)

In the early 1900s, many students had to perform their chores before going to school. Children were encouraged to come to school wearing whatever made them feel comfortable. The individuals in the first row are listed here from left to right: teacher Lucille Davis, William Brown, Alphonso Jenkins, ? Coleman, Benjamin Franklin, ? Tillman, Edward Sanders, David Smith, Palmer Francis, James Raymond Dawson, Nathaniel Hall, and one unidentified boy. Those students in the second row are listed here from left to right: unidentified, Elizabeth Williams, unidentified, Dorothy Smith, Marg Parrish, Idella Parrish, Hattie Howell, Willie Mae Harmon, Lillie Ruth Cromotie, Pearlie Lee, ? Jones, Edith Cromotie, and Vanilla Edwards. (Palmer Francis.)

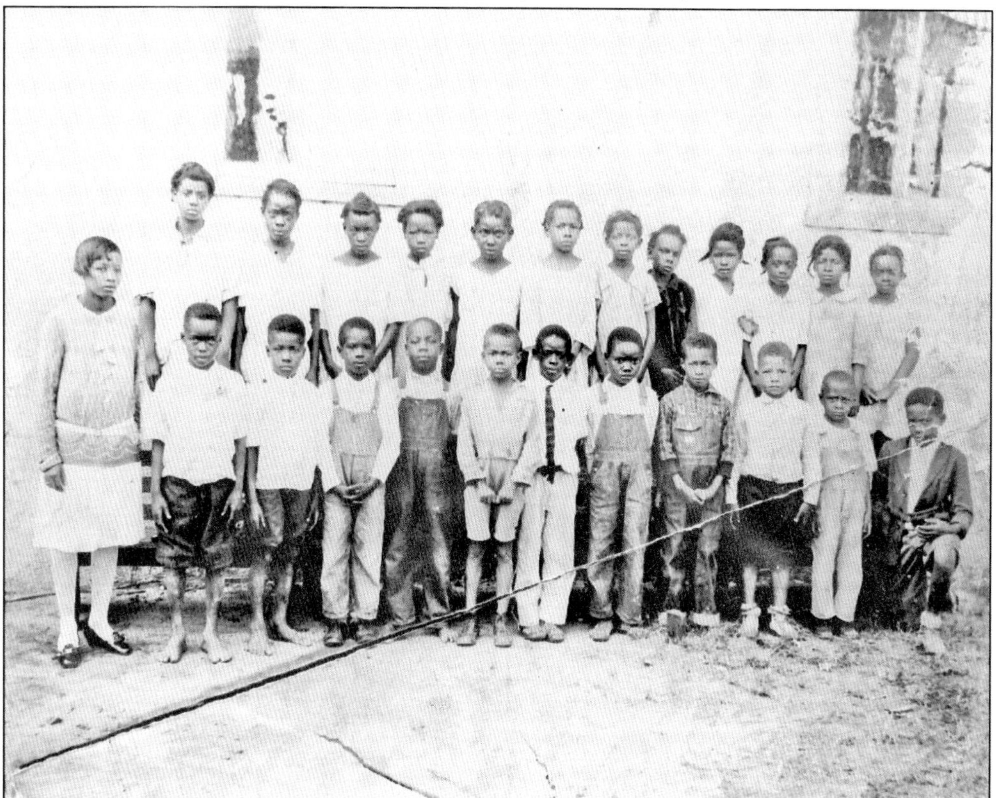

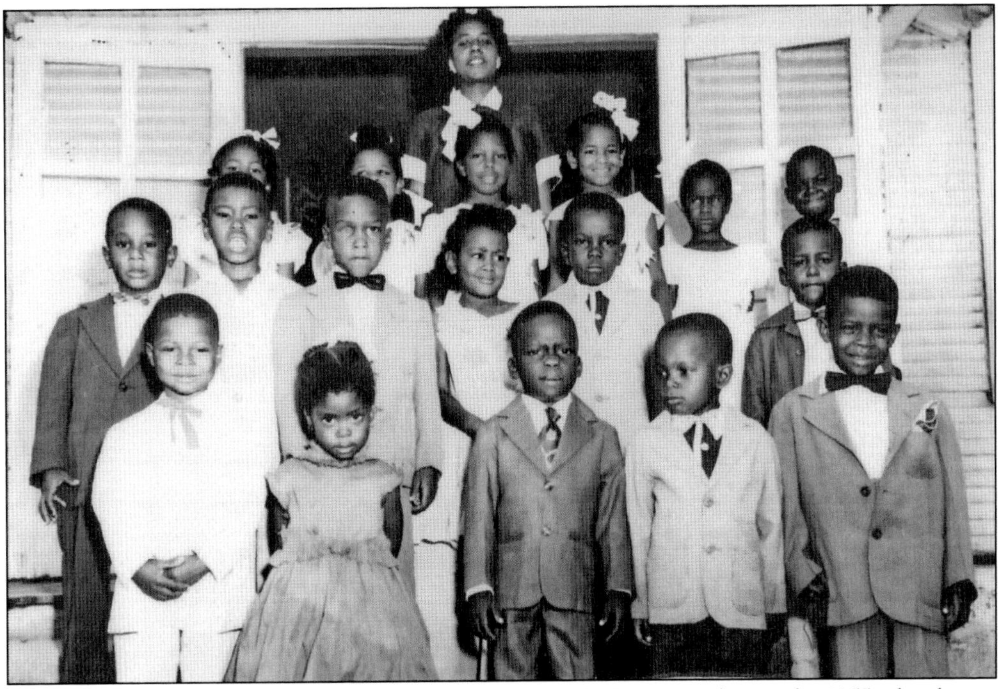

From left to right are members of the combined grades of J. R. E. Lee during the 1955 school year: (first row) Emanuel Doleman, Esther Williams, York Dukes Jr., Eugene Kendrick, and Leo Dempsey; (second row) Willie Hurbert Stancil, Frank Satchel Jr., Ernest Branch, Estella McGill, Wiley Kendrick, and Howard Glover; (third row) Ethel Bell, Brenda Brown, Gwen Simmons, Virginia Walker, Voncille Stewart, Harry Ford, and teacher Inez Brown. (Berdelle Kendrick/MBS.)

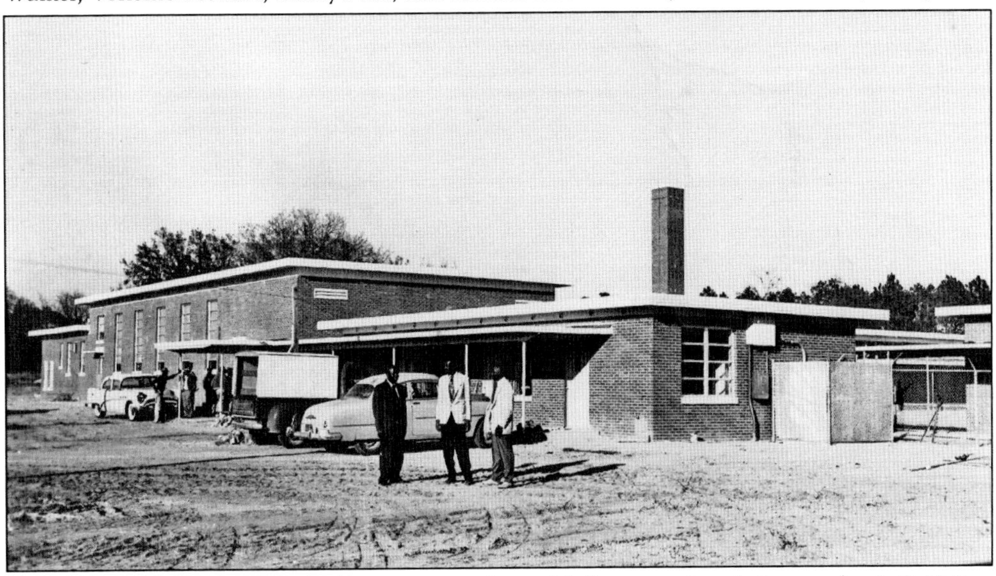

This site located at 500 Ninth Avenue in southeast Mulberry replaced the wooden J. R. E. Lee School located at Southwest Fourth Avenue. The school housed grades one through eight for African American students of Mulberry and its surrounding communities. Pictured from left to right are Isom Helper II, Frank Conoly (principal from 1954 to 1968), and Samuel Montgomery. Construction workers are in the background. (Essie N. Helper Morgan.)

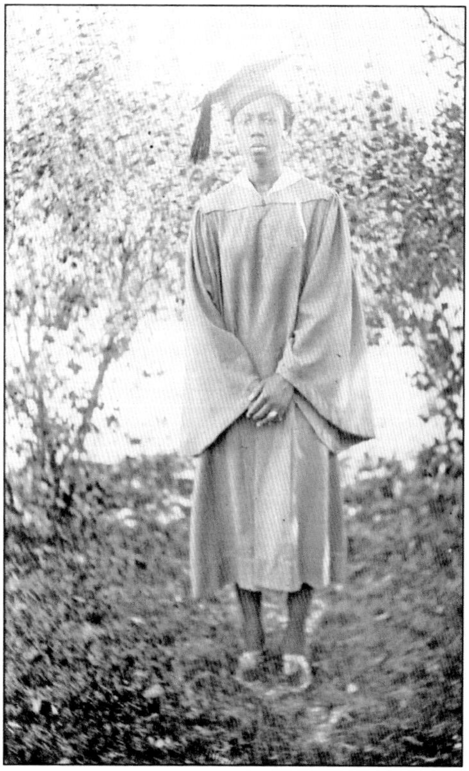

Essie Marie Nelson graduated as valedictorian of the Union Academy's class of 1938. Classmates included Dorothy Allen, Annie Belle Brown, Estella Jackson, Erkie Lee Bouie, Lola Ford, Mamie Ford, Frederick Geathers, Adele Taylor, Lillie Taylor, Lelia Robinson, Asonia Waldon, Naomi Webster, Willie Lee Bentley, James Gardner, ? Cobb, Kenneth ?, Marble Lee Seabrooks, Albert Young, and ? Green. (Essie N. Helper Morgan.)

In 1959, the 16th graduating class of the Sunlight School of Beauty Culture held its graduating exercises at New Salem Primitive Baptist Church, Tampa, Florida. The identified graduates of Mulberry are Viola Law (Kennon), fourth row, fourth from left; Christine Overstreet (Curry), fourth row, fifth from left; and Nila Helper (Jones), sixth row, first from right. (Nila Helper Jones.)

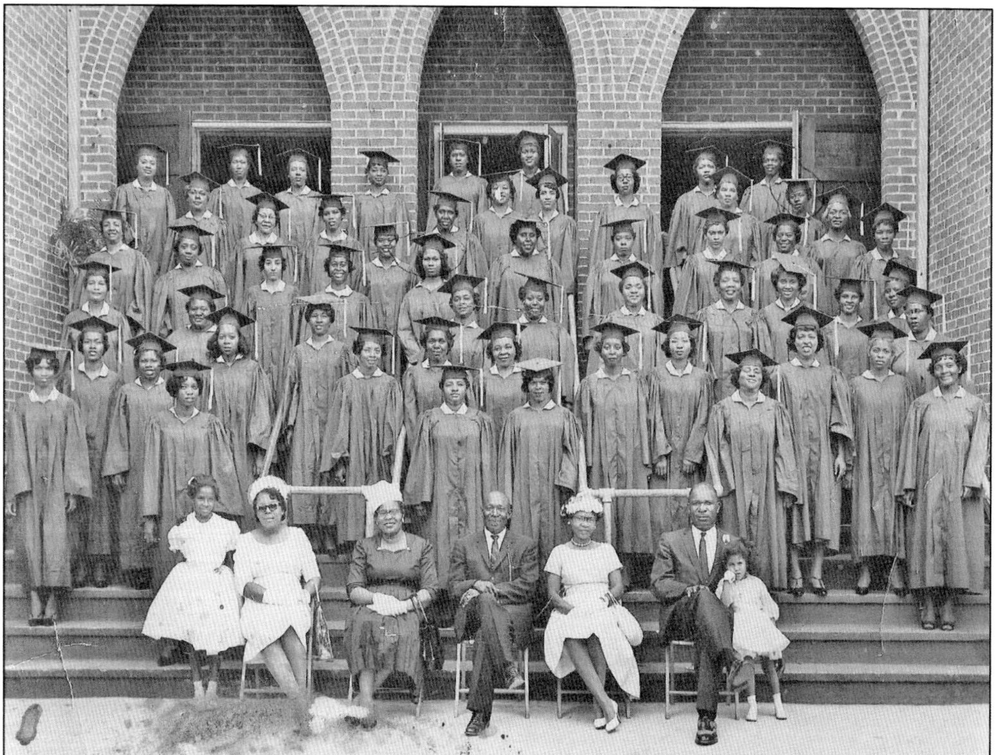

Commissioner Collins Smith (2002–present), known as Coach Smith, graduated from Union Academy and Bethune Cookman College. Coach Smith was an assistant football coach and head basketball coach at Mulberry High School, working as an educator for 36 years. He is the proud father of four; husband of Ellistine; son of Kay and Marie Smith; and brother of Margaret, Evelyn, Roosevelt, Azzie, Altamease, Robert, Emma, Maxine, Katie, Kay, Blondene, and Charles. (The *Mulberry Press*.)

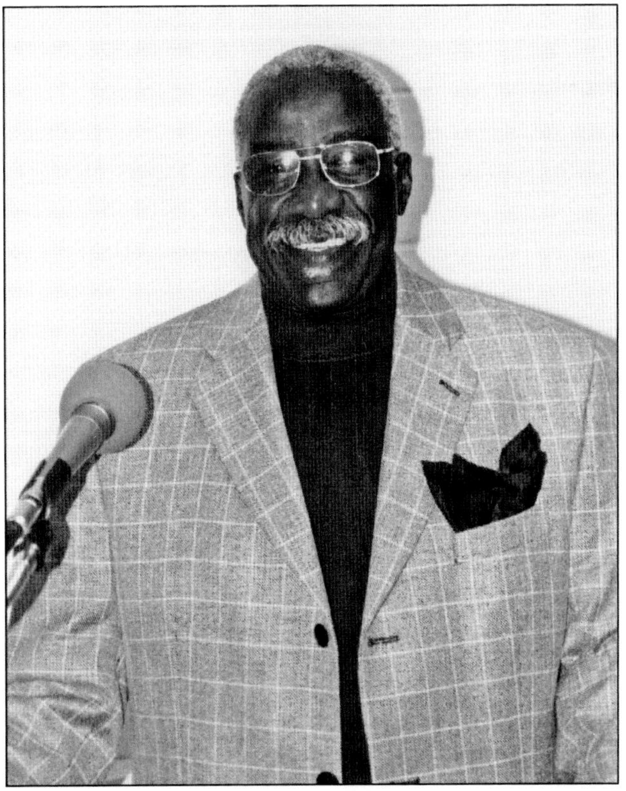

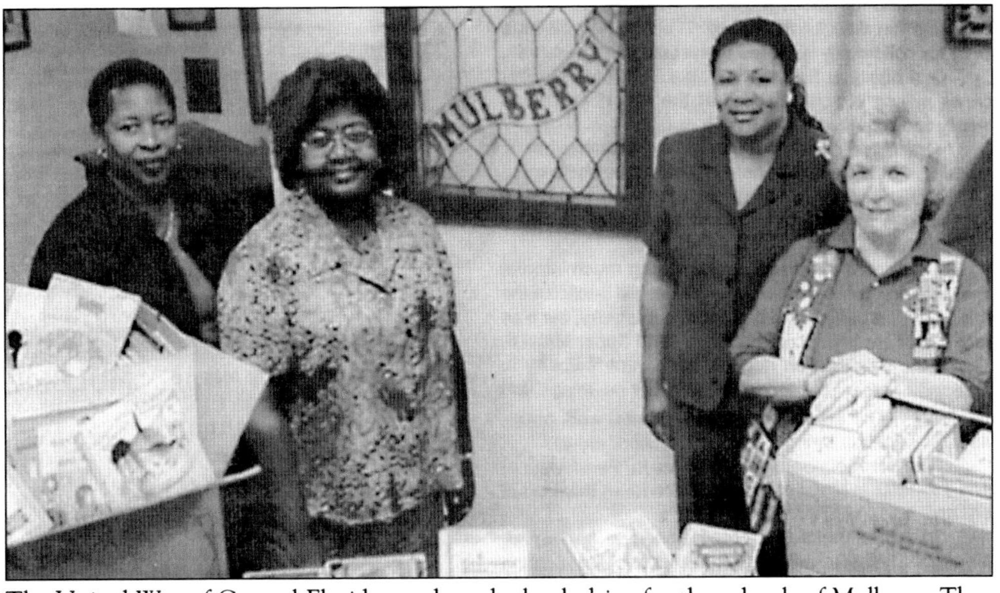

The United Way of Central Florida conducted a book drive for the schools of Mulberry. They collected more than 400 books for students to read from employees of local businesses. This photograph taken by Michael Gordon shows, from left to right, United Way volunteer and Florida Southern College employee Brenda Lewis; Wilbur Hallam Purcell Elementary School principal Ellistine Smith; Mulberry Middle School principal Patricia Barnes; and Kingsford Elementary School principal Sharron Jones. (The *Mulberry Press*.)

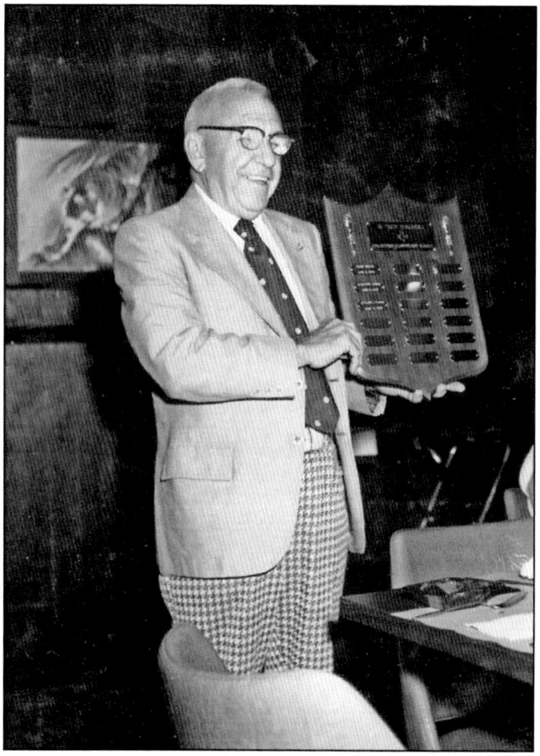

Gerald Sherwood Hatch served as principal of Kingsford Elementary School from 1962 until his retirement in 1976, 14 years of his 37 years in education. Gerald was born in Silver Springs, New York. He received his bachelor of science and master of arts degrees from Florida Southern College. Gerald served his community as chairman of Mulberry Housing Authority and in other civic organizations. Gerald married Marie Black and, after her passing, Isla Paxton. He is the father of Geraldine and George. (Geneva Richardson/MBS.)

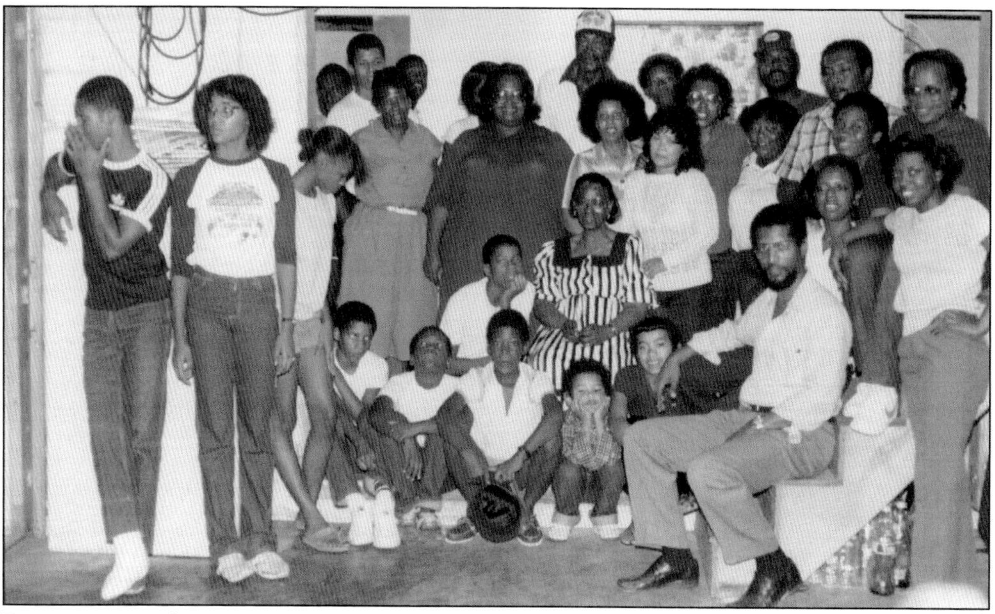

Essie Marie was born on October 16, 1918, to Essick and Theola Nelson. After graduating from Union Academy in 1938 and obtaining her associate of arts degree from Florida Agriculture and Mechanical University (FAMU), she started teaching in 1941 and earned a bachelor's degree of education in 1956. Throughout her 41 years of teaching , she taught at Union Academy, in the mining community schools of Nichols and Swift/Agricola, J. R. E. Lee, Mulberry Elementary School, and Kingsford Elementary School. (Essie N. Helper Morgan.)

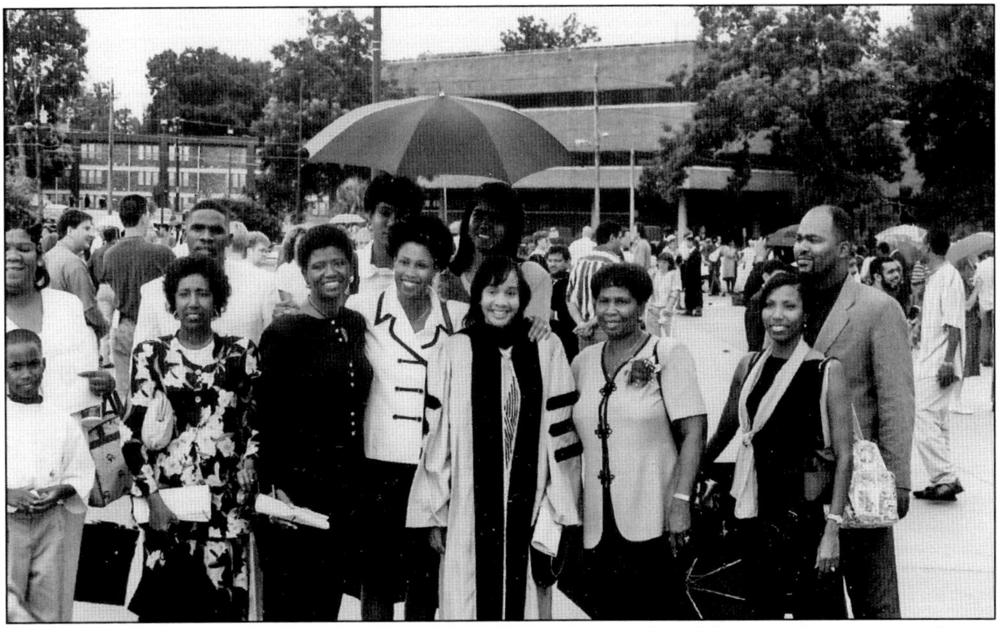

Dr. Maxine LaVon Montgomery, associate professor, is the first African American to obtain tenure in the department of English at Florida State University. She authored many great works, including *Conversations with Gloria Naylor* and *The Apocalypse in African American Fiction*. The fourth daughter of Samuel and Mollie Montgomery, Maxine married Nathaniel Crawford, and they have one daughter, Samantha, named in honor of Maxine's father. (Stephanie L. Dukes.)

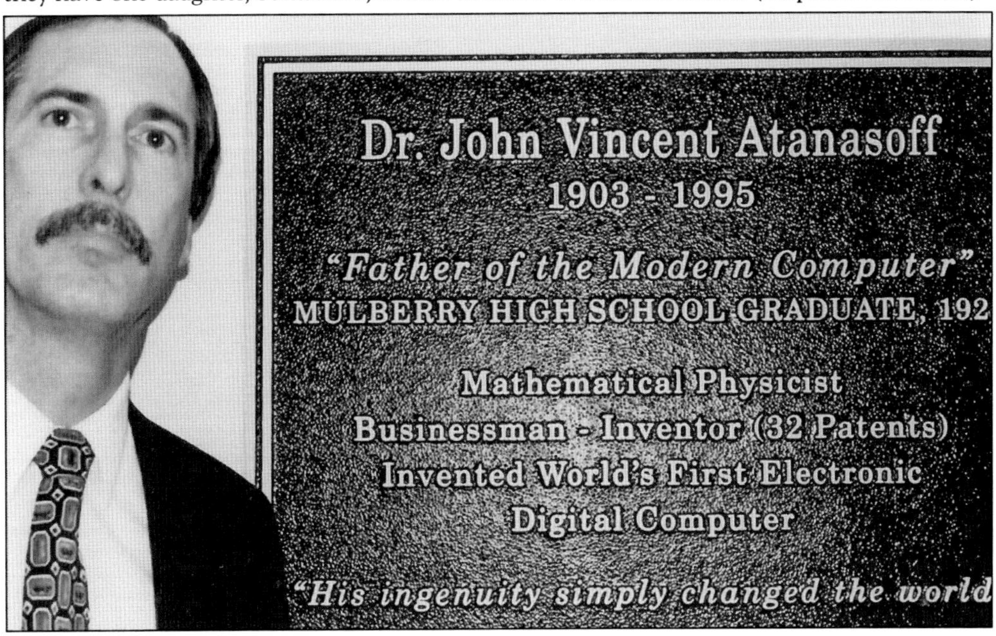

Here Dr. Steven Petrie, principal of Mulberry High School from 1988 to 1996, stands next to the plaque noting the outstanding accomplishments of Mulberry High School class of 1924 graduate Dr. John Vincent Atanasoff. The computer lab at Mulberry High School was named in his honor. John married Laura Meeks and is the father of three children: Elsie, John, and Joann. (The *Mulberry Press*.)

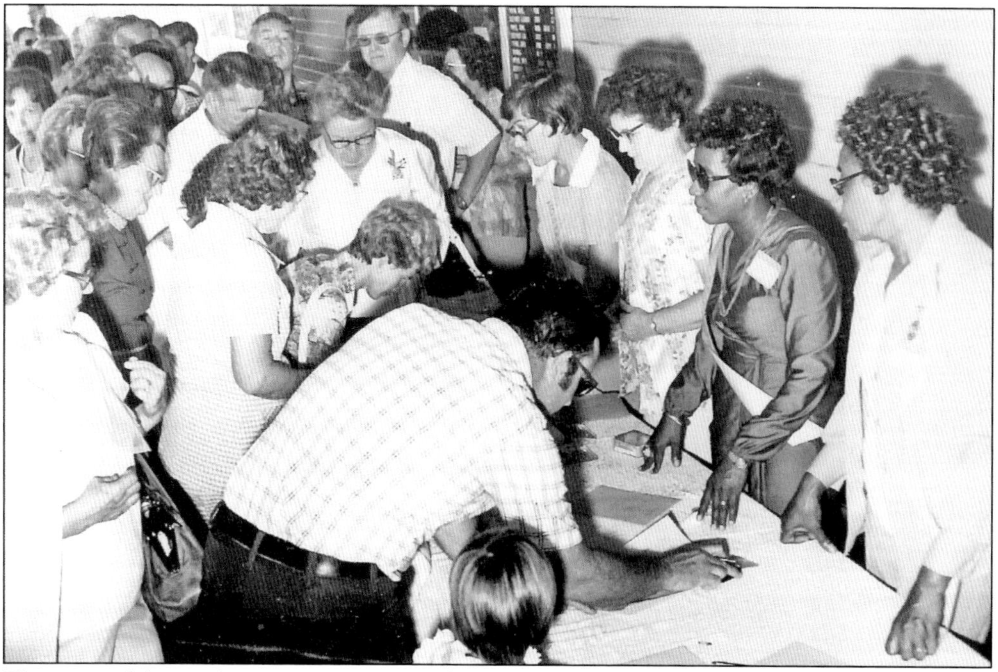

These two African American women, Barbara Jean White (left) and Inez Brown, are lifelong residents of Mulberry. Even though they graduated from Union Academy instead of Mulberry High School (MHS) due to segregation, they joyfully assisted with the MHS bicentennial reunion registration because their children benefited from the Supreme Court's decision in the case of *Oliver L. Brown et. al. v. Board of Education of Topeka, Shawnee County, Kansas.* (MBS.)

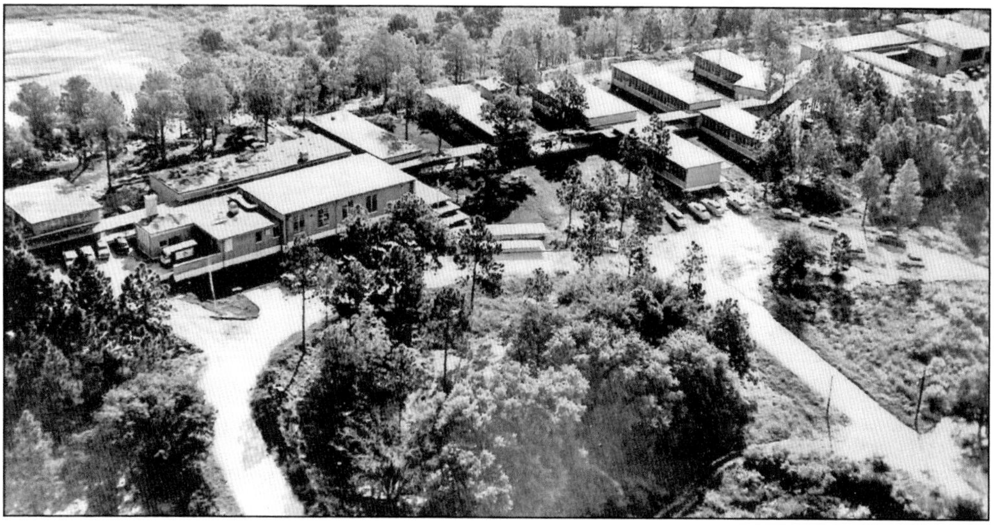

In 1965 and 1966, Mulberry became the pilot for integration of Polk County schools starting with 11th and 12th grades; the other grades followed in 1966 and 1967. J. R. E. Lee School's name was changed to Mulberry Middle School, consisting of grades six through eight. All of Mulberry's elementary school students were divided between Mulberry Elementary School and Kingsford Elementary School, based on the location of their residence. All middle school and high school students attended Mulberry Middle School and Mulberry High School. (Mulberry High School/MBS.)

Seven

EVERYONE IS SOMEONE SPECIAL

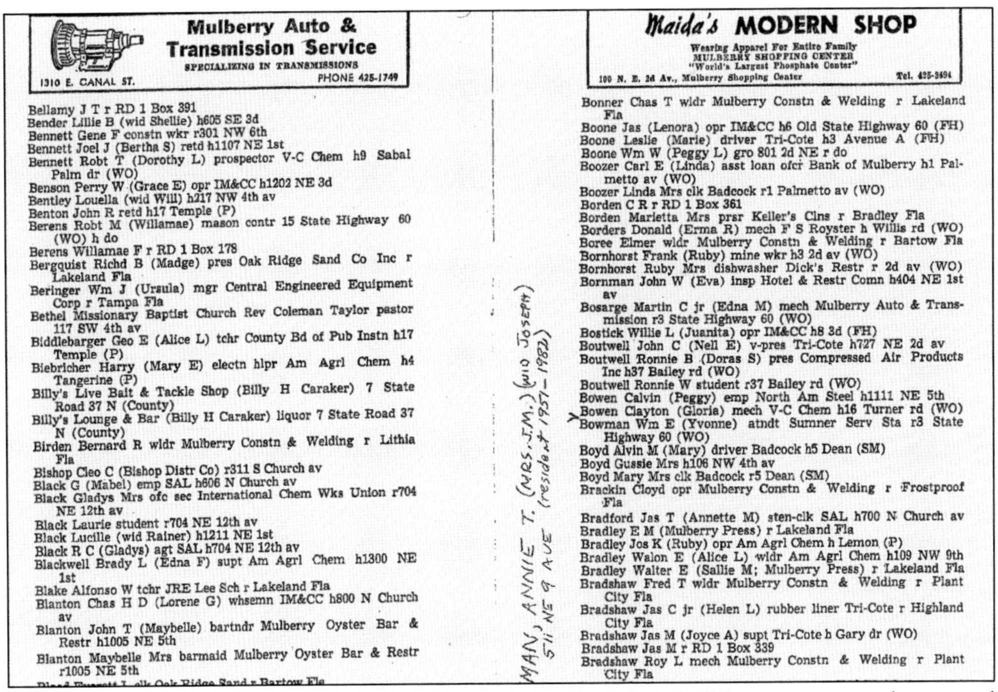

Mulberry Auto & Transmission Service
SPECIALIZING IN TRANSMISSIONS
1310 E. CANAL ST. PHONE 425-1749

Bellamy J T r RD 1 Box 391
Bender Lillie B (wid Shellie) h605 SE 3d
Bennett Gene F constn wkr r301 NW 6th
Bennett Joel J (Bertha S) retd h1107 NE 1st
Bennett Robt T (Dorothy L) prospector V-C Chem h9 Sabal Palm dr (WO)
Benson Perry W (Grace E) opr IM&CC h1202 NE 3d
Bentley Louella (wid Will) h217 NW 4th av
Benton John R retd h17 Temple (P)
Berens Robt M (Willamae) mason contr 15 State Highway 60 (WO) h do
Berens Willamae F r RD 1 Box 178
Bergquist Richd B (Madge) pres Oak Ridge Sand Co Inc r Lakeland Fla
Beringer Wm J (Ursula) mgr Central Engineered Equipment Corp r Tampa Fla
Bethel Missionary Baptist Church Rev Coleman Taylor pastor 117 SW 4th av
Biddlebarger Geo E (Alice L) tchr County Bd of Pub Instn h17 Temple (P)
Biebricher Harry (Mary E) electn hlpr Am Agrl Chem h4 Tangerine (P)
Billy's Live Bait & Tackle Shop (Billy H Caraker) 7 State Road 37 N (County)
Billy's Lounge & Bar (Billy H Caraker) liquor 7 State Road 37 N (County)
Birden Bernard R wldr Mulberry Constn & Welding r Lithia Fla
Bishop Cleo C (Bishop Distr Co) r311 S Church av
Black G (Mabel) emp SAL h606 N Church av
Black Gladys Mrs ofc sec International Chem Wks Union r704 NE 12th av
Black Laurie student r704 NE 12th av
Black Lucille (wid Rainer) h1211 NE 1st
Black R C (Gladys) agt SAL h704 NE 12th av
Blackwell Brady L (Edna F) supt Am Agrl Chem h1300 NE 1st
Blake Alfonso W tchr JRE Lee Sch r Lakeland Fla
Blanton Chas H D (Lorene G) whsemn IM&CC h800 N Church av
Blanton John T (Maybelle) bartndr Mulberry Oyster Bar & Restr h1005 NE 5th
Blanton Maybelle Mrs barmaid Mulberry Oyster Bar & Restr r1005 NE 5th

MAN, ANNIE T. (MRS. J.M.) (wid JOSEPH)
511 NE 9 AVE (resident 1951–1982)

Maida's MODERN SHOP
Wearing Apparel For Entire Family
MULBERRY SHOPPING CENTER
"World's Largest Phosphate Center"
100 N. E. 2d Av., Mulberry Shopping Center Tel. 425-3494

Bonner Chas T wldr Mulberry Constn & Welding r Lakeland Fla
Boone Jas (Lenora) opr IM&CC h6 Old State Highway 60 (FH)
Boone Leslie (Marie) driver Tri-Cote h3 Avenue A (FH)
Boone Wm W (Peggy L) gro 801 2d NE r do
Boozer Carl E (Linda) asst loan ofcr Bank of Mulberry h1 Palmetto av (WO)
Boozer Linda Mrs clk Badcock r1 Palmetto av (WO)
Borden C R r RD 1 Box 361
Borden Marietta Mrs prsr Keller's Clns r Bradley Fla
Borders Donald (Erma R) mech F S Royster h Willis rd (WO)
Boree Elmer wldr Mulberry Constn & Welding r Bartow Fla
Bornhorst Frank (Ruby) mine wkr h3 2d av (WO)
Bornhorst Ruby Mrs dishwasher Dick's Restr r 2d av (WO)
Bornman John W (Eva) insp Hotel & Restr Comn h404 NE 1st av
Bosarge Martin C jr (Edna M) mech Mulberry Auto & Transmission r3 State Highway 60 (WO)
Bostick Willie L (Juanita) opr IM&CC h8 3d (FH)
Boutwell John C (Nell E) v-pres Tri-Cote h727 NE 2d av
Boutwell Ronnie B (Doras S) pres Compressed Air Products Inc h37 Bailey rd (WO)
Boutwell Ronnie W student r37 Bailey rd (WO)
Bowen Calvin (Peggy) emp North Am Steel h1111 NE 5th
Bowen Clayton (Gloria) mech V-C Chem h16 Turner rd (WO)
Bowman Wm E (Yvonne) atndt Sumner Serv Sta r3 State Highway 60 (WO)
Boyd Alvin M (Mary) driver Badcock h5 Dean (SM)
Boyd Gussie Mrs h106 NW 4th av
Boyd Mary Mrs clk Badcock r5 Dean (SM)
Brackin Cloyd opr Mulberry Constn & Welding r Frostproof Fla
Bradford Jas T (Annette M) sten-clk SAL h700 N Church av
Bradley E M (Mulberry Press) r Lakeland Fla
Bradley Jos K (Ruby) opr Am Agrl Chem h Lemon (P)
Bradley Walon E (Alice L) wldr Am Agrl Chem h109 NW 9th
Bradley Walter E (Sallie M; Mulberry Press) r Lakeland Fla
Bradshaw Fred T wldr Mulberry Constn & Welding r Plant City Fla
Bradshaw Jas C jr (Helen L) rubber liner Tri-Cote r Highland City Fla
Bradshaw Jas M (Joyce A) supt Tri-Cote h Gary dr (WO)
Bradshaw Jas M r RD 1 Box 339
Bradshaw Roy L mech Mulberry Constn & Welding r Plant City Fla

This is a page of the 1965 Mulberry City Directory, which listed all known persons living and working in Mulberry alphabetically by last name. The directory also listed heads of household, spouse, occupation, employer, and residence. Businesses are listed by name, owner(s), type of business, and location. In the 1921 city directory, street addresses were divided into quarters, named for the most populous families in the area. The Sprott Quarter was said to consist of more than 40 houses owned by W. C. and Annie L. Sprott. The McKillops Quarter is another listed in the 1921 directory. (Polk County Historical Society.)

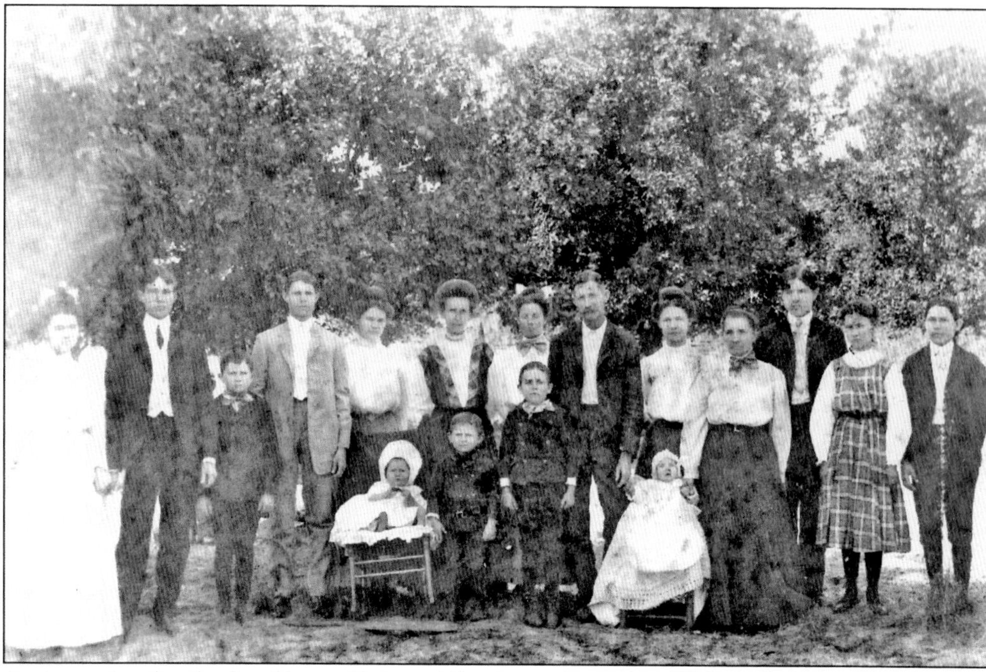

A pioneering family that Henry Nelson Allen homesteaded in Willow Oak in 1884 is shown here in 1906. Allen was involved in farming, raising cattle, and was also a citrus grower until his retirement in 1930. This family included 13 children: Ruth (Alderman), Agnes (Moore), Lillie (Sweat), Lessie (Taylor), Etta Allen, Jim Allen (whose wife is Sindrilla), Walter (whose wife is Hattie, and whose daughter is Juanita), Ethan, Owen, Oscar, Aaron, Roy, and Chester. (Bernice Haynesworth Allen/MBS.)

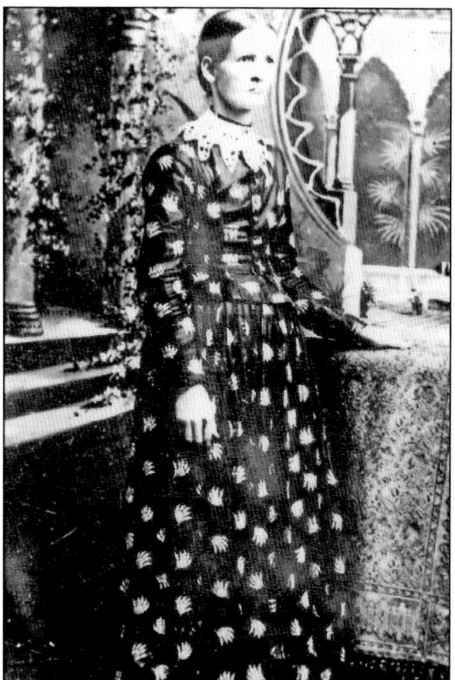

Mary Taylor (1844–1892) married James L. Whidden (1826–1906) in Ware County, Georgia. His father was J. O. Whidden, and his family settled in Brewster, Florida, in the area of Tiger Bay. Mary is buried in Elam Cemetery in Bartow, Florida. (Evalyn Kilpatrick Stephens/MBS.)

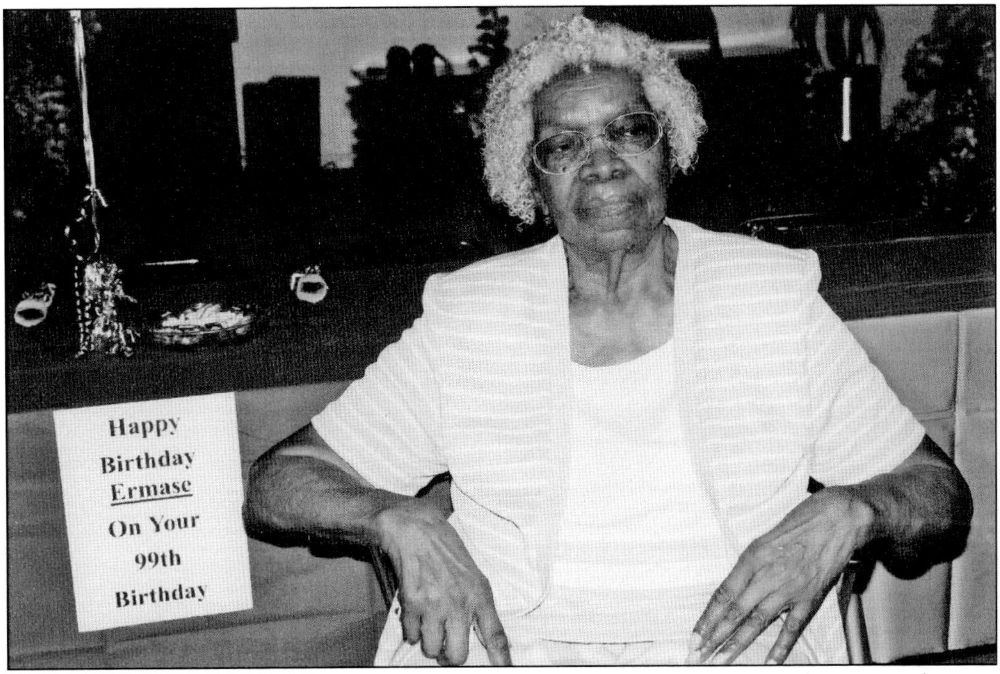

Ermase Lucas Evans, 105 years old on August 5, 2008, is the daughter of Frank Lucas and Angie E. Lucas Thomas of Ray City, Georgia. Ermase and her husband, Charlie Evans, had a daughter, Rosa Elizabeth (1930–1993). On March 4, 1933, the family moved to Mulberry for Charlie to pursue work in the sawmill as a lumber checker. Ermase and Charlie's grandsons are Earvin, Gregory, and James Wade Jr. Their granddaughters are Minnie and Lawrencena. Ermase's siblings include John Thomas, Malachi Thomas, Robert Thomas, Willie Thomas Young, and Lillie Thomas Montgomery. (The *Mulberry Press*.)

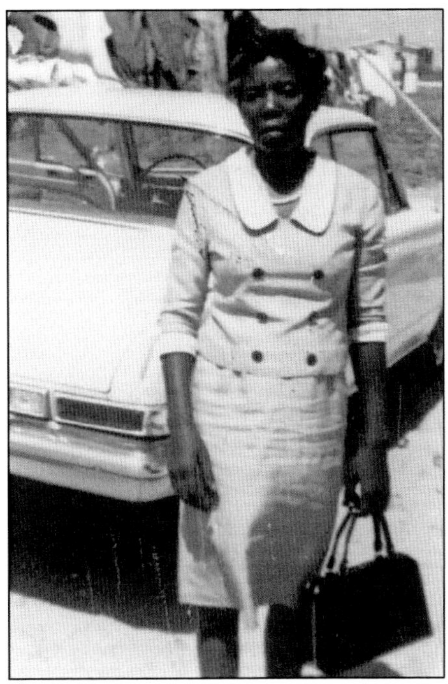

Lillie Thomas Montgomery, a lover of the English language, became an outstanding orator, faithful church servant, and founder of the Very Important Teenage Club for community youth. She was the daughter of Rev. Abraham Lincoln Thomas Sr. and Angie Elizabeth, wife of both York Dukes Sr. and Hezekiah Montgomery, and mother to David, John, York Jr., Ruth, Erma, Rose, Ophelia, and Hattie. (Gail Lula Ruth Dukes Bell.)

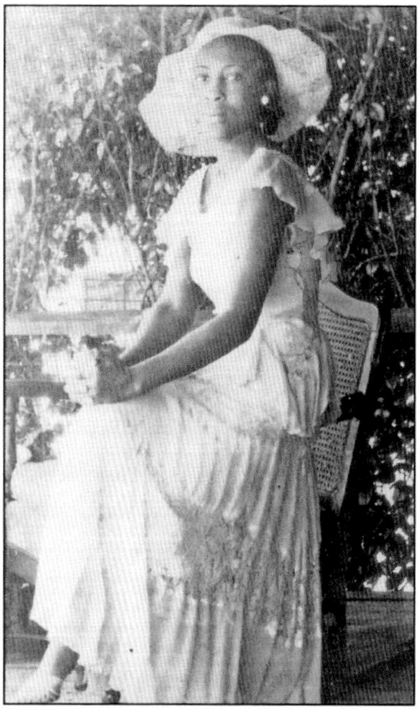

Ruth Bailey White Stewart was born to Tom and Belle Bailey in 1916, becoming sister to Geneva, Marie, Addie, and Lorenzo. Ruth celebrated her 90th birthday with her family and friends at the recreation center in Bartow, Florida, in 2006. She will celebrate her 92nd birthday on September 13, 2008. Ruth is the mother of Bernard, Marion Bruce, Patricia, Voncille, Ruth, Sheila, and Nadine. (James W. Helper.)

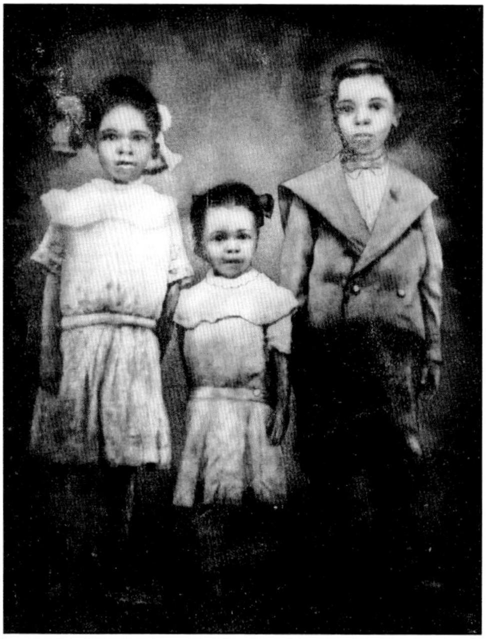

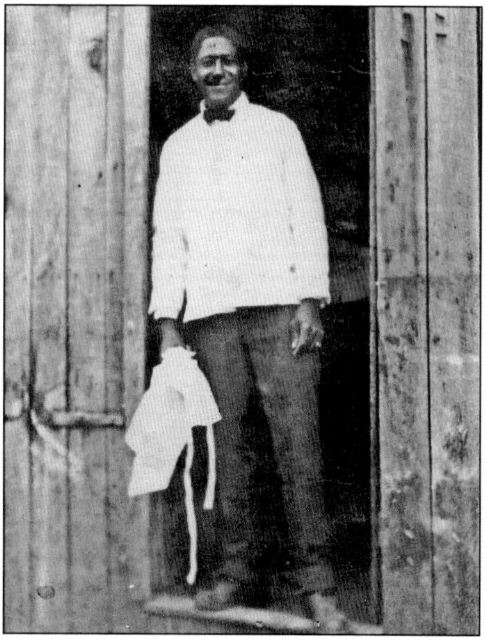

At left, shown from left to right, are Alberta, Margaret, and Leroy, three of the six children of Henry and Janie Palmer Johnson. Their other siblings are Henry Jr., Woodrow, and Albert. Alberta had a daughter named Helen. Leroy's children are Curnita and Aaron. Henry Jr.'s daughter is Jackie. Woodrow's daughter is Evelyn. No children were born to Margaret. Pictured on the right during the 1920s is Henry Pearson Jr., posing on the train where he worked as a cook. Henry worked on the Flagler East Coast Railroad to support his family. He always said he enjoyed traveling around "meeting the wealthy folks." He shared stories of these encounters with his children, nieces, and nephews, mostly to the tune of play the piano or picking the guitar. (Left, Palmer Francis.) (Right, Essie N. Helper Morgan.)

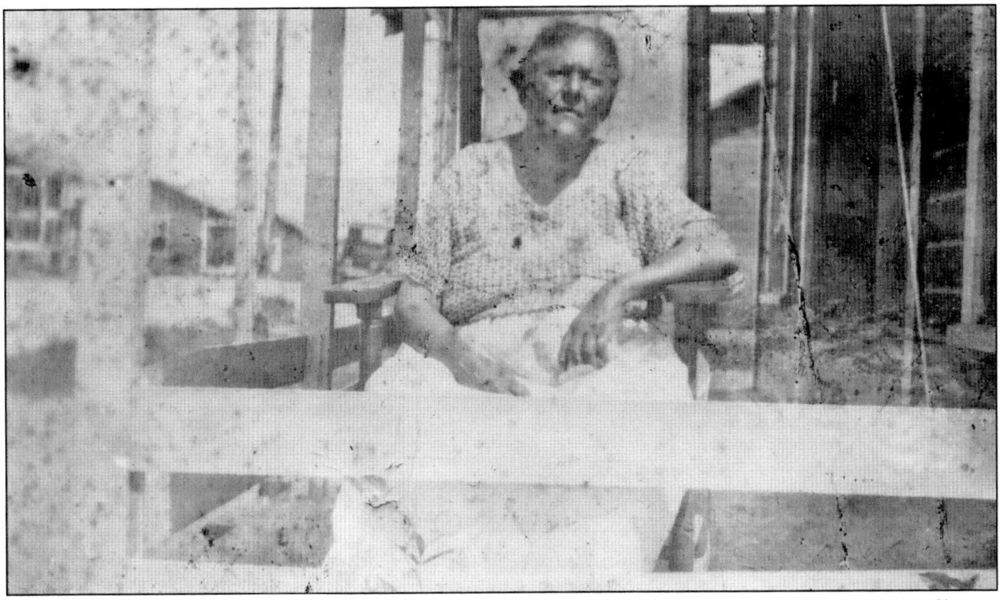

Fannie Wilcox Pearson Williams (1858–1934) was born in Coffee County, Georgia. Williams told her grandchildren that she was five years old when freedom was declared in 1863. She is the daughter of Millie Wilcox and Elijah Lott, a slave owner. Williams had 24 siblings who were sold into slavery. Williams married Pearson and of this marriage, five children were born: Carrie, Henry Jr. Mattie, Joe, and Eb. (Essie N. Helper Morgan.)

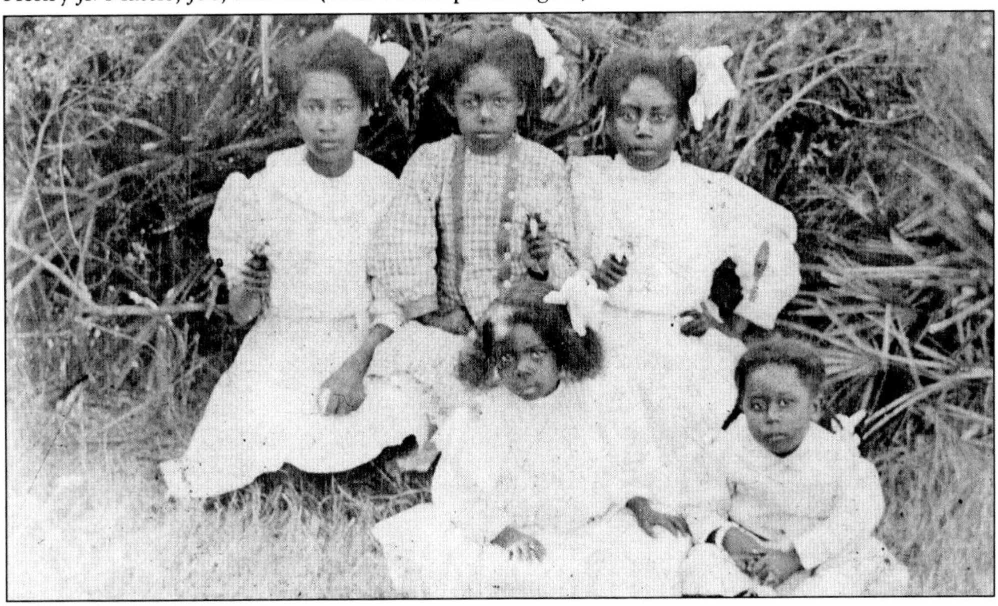

The mothers of these children died at early ages, so they were raised by their grandparents, Fannie Wilcox Pearson and Willie "Billy" Williams, who was Native American by heritage. Fannie moved to Bradley Junction after their house and store in Mulberry burned. Pictured from left to right are the following children: (first row) Marie and Thelma Pearson, whose mother was Mamie Pearson; (second row) Fannie Turner, whose mother was Carrie Turner; Theola Turner, whose mother was Mattie Turner; Willie Mae Turner, whose mother was Carrie Turner. (Essie N. Helper Morgan.)

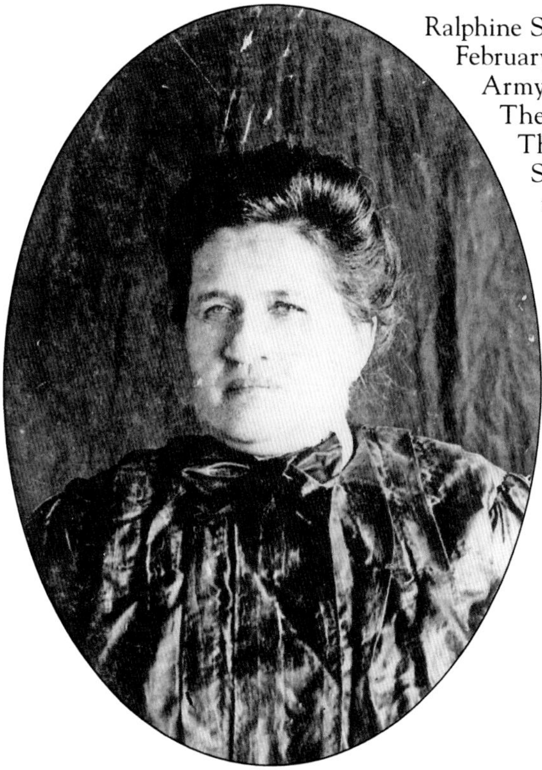

Ralphine Shuman Kelley married Samuel B. Kelly on February 1, 1877. Samuel was in the Confederate Army, Roll Company I, 1st Florida Reserves. Their children are Joseph Edward, Rogene Thomas, Grover Cleveland, James Martin, Sophia Cornelia, and Maida Virginia, who married Henry M. Clark. (Henrie Harned Sparkman/MBS.)

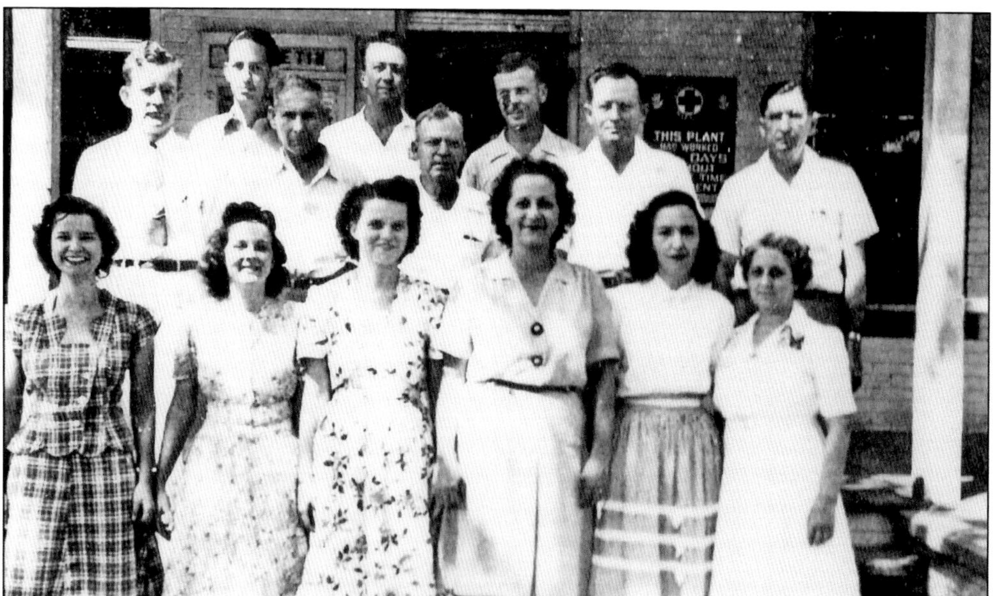

Pictured here in September 1945 from left to right are International Minerals and Chemical Corporation office personnel: (first row) Eunice Moody, Mary E. Cosey, Harriet Pearce, Eunice Martin, Myrtice Martin, and Mrs. Dugger; (second row) Earl Plurvis, D. T. Byrd, H. M. Byrd, F. R. Berquist, and Lamar Johnson; (third row) Dan Woodall, Bob Evans, and George Fifer. (Mary E. Cosey Terry/MBS.)

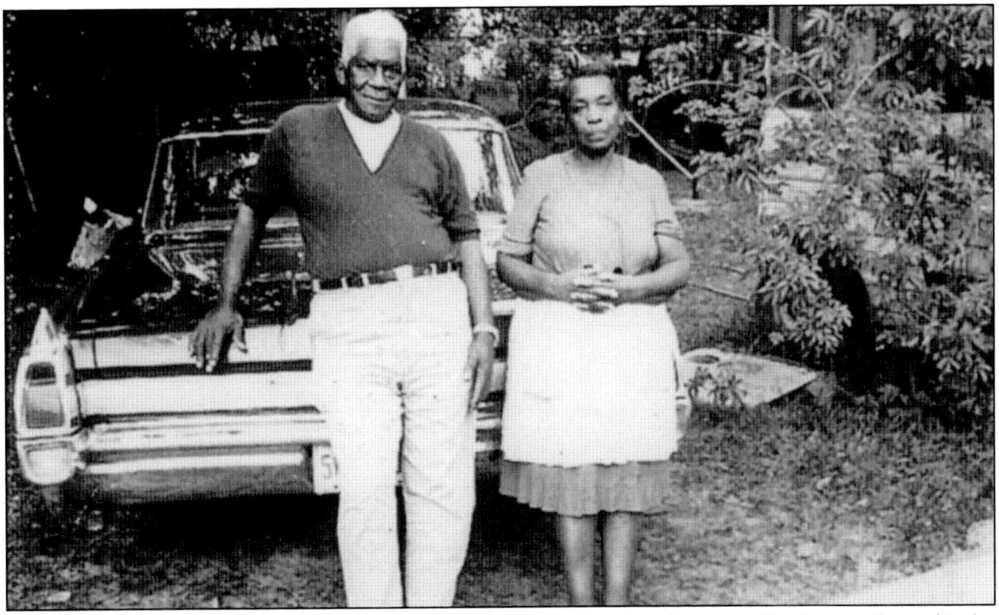

Samuel and Mary Jackson came to Bradley from South Carolina by way of Jacksonville and Lake Wales. Samuel was employed by the railroad company in Brewster and by Brewster Phosphate Company. The Jacksons owned a candy store and restaurant operated by Mary. They were one of the few families in their community with a car. The Jacksons were the parents of two sons: James and Cicero. (Chandry Jackson Cook.)

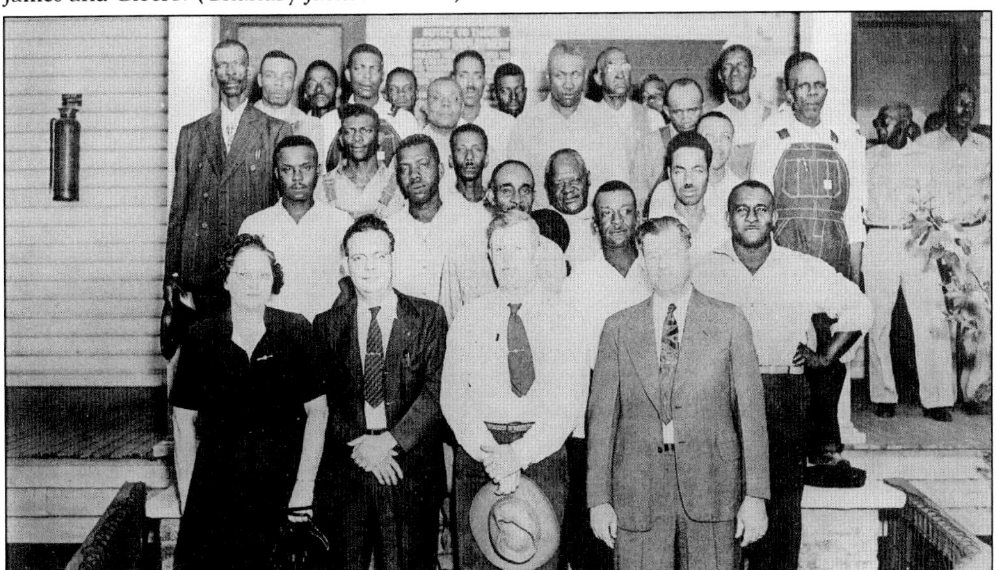

The Brewster Phosphate Company in 1940 recognized workers with 20 years of service. The following individuals are listed from left to right: (first row) Nora Bryan, Holland Miles, Otis Wilson, and Harless Bryan; (second row) Luther Hall, Leroy Henderson, Lawrence Boyd, James Simpkins, Reuben Boyd; (third row) Leo Borders, Jason Jones, Rev. Linear Luther Stuckey, George Brown Sr.; (fourth row) Dea McBride, Thomas Rollins, Walter Meadows, J. W. Borders Sr., Ivory Mims, Charlie McDuffie, Junior Gordon, Ben Smith, Ruben Randall, Jack Houston, Leslie Reid, Henry Best, Steve Williams, Rich Willis, Roy Carlton, and Nat Solomon. (SLAF.)

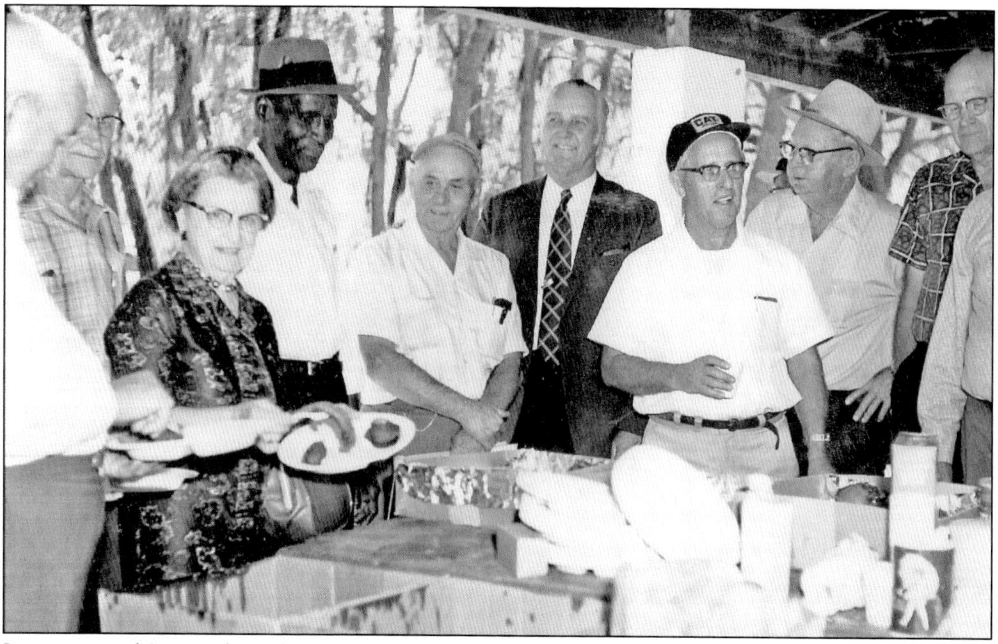

International Minerals and Chemical Corporation hosted a picnic for its retired employees in 1971 at Christina Park. From left to right are John Moore, John Simmons, Lessie Collins, Eddie Woodard, Joe Ward, Floyd Bowen, Willie Wiggs, H. J. Norman, and Fletcher McLaughlin. (Geneva Richardson/MBS.)

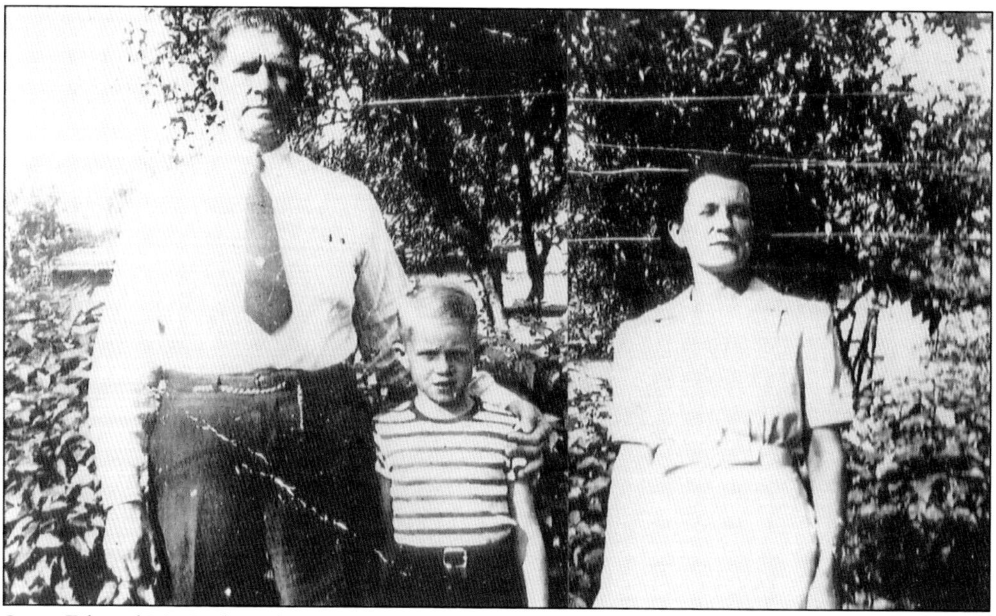

Stacy Edward McNeal was born in Pearson, Georgia, on November 22, 1902, and came to Florida in 1920. He was married in Mulberry to Annie Dell Plair in 1922. They had five children: Edward, Helen (Prevatt), Mary Adele (Neslein), Catherine (Larramore), and Laverne (Bass). Stacy owned the Texaco Station from 1928 to 1935 and the Standard Station on the corners of Highways 37 and 60 from the latter 1930s until 1945. He served as constable in 1947 and 1948. (Mary Adele McNeal Neslein/MBS.)

George T. Harned was born on July 21, 1890, in Rahway, New Jersey. George worked for Phosphate Mining Company in Nichols, Florida, as superintendent. He also served as justice of the peace and, for 20 years, judge of the small claims court for district one in Polk County. He married Inez Clark and fathered two children: Henrie and George Jr. (Inez Clark Harned/MBS.)

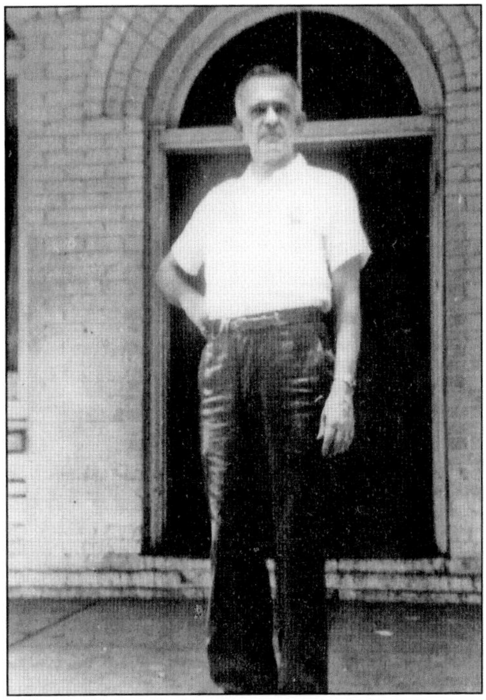

Inez Clark Harned was born in Polk County. She attended Florida State College for Women, now know as Florida State University, in Tallahassee, Florida. Inez served as executive secretary and/or bookkeeper for several organizations: Phosphate Mining Company, R. H. Clark Equipment Company, Badcock Corporation, and for the justice of the peace. Later she was elected to the office of justice of the peace. She had two children: George Jr. and Henrie (Sparkman). (Inez Clark Harned/MBS.)

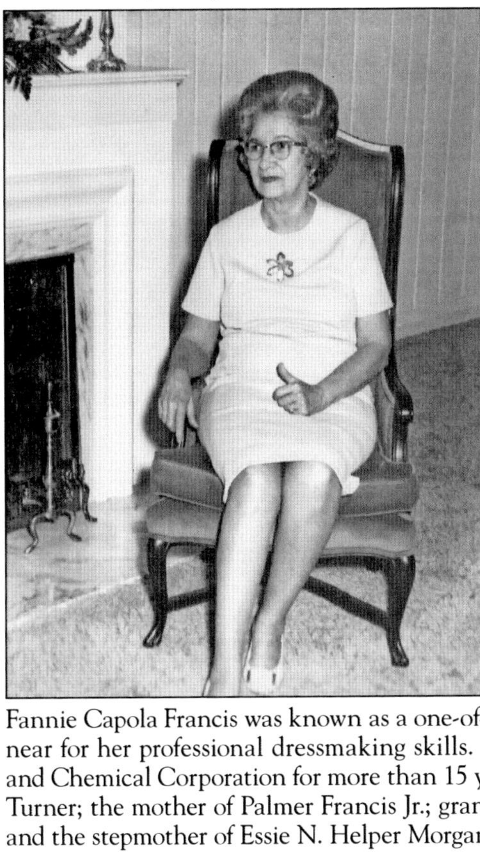

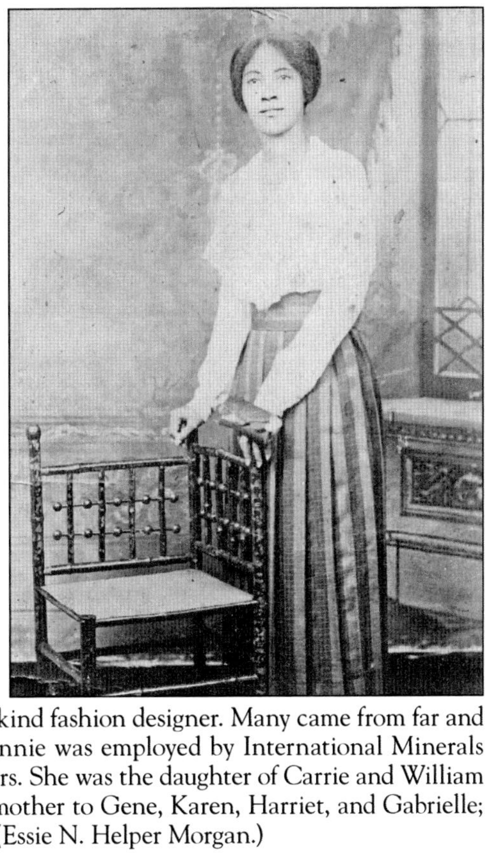

Fannie Capola Francis was known as a one-of-a-kind fashion designer. Many came from far and near for her professional dressmaking skills. Fannie was employed by International Minerals and Chemical Corporation for more than 15 years. She was the daughter of Carrie and William Turner; the mother of Palmer Francis Jr.; grandmother to Gene, Karen, Harriet, and Gabrielle; and the stepmother of Essie N. Helper Morgan. (Essie N. Helper Morgan.)

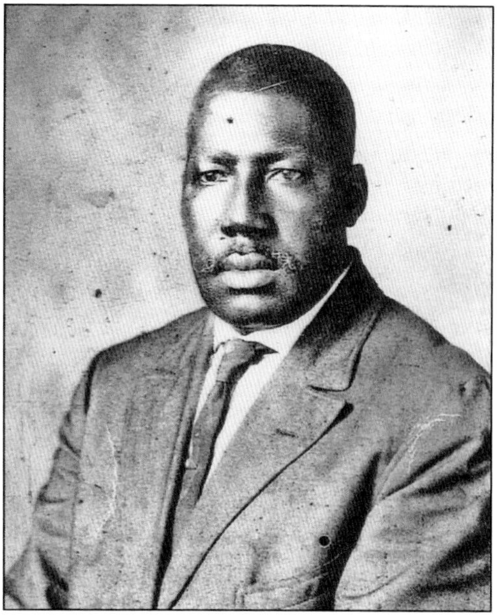

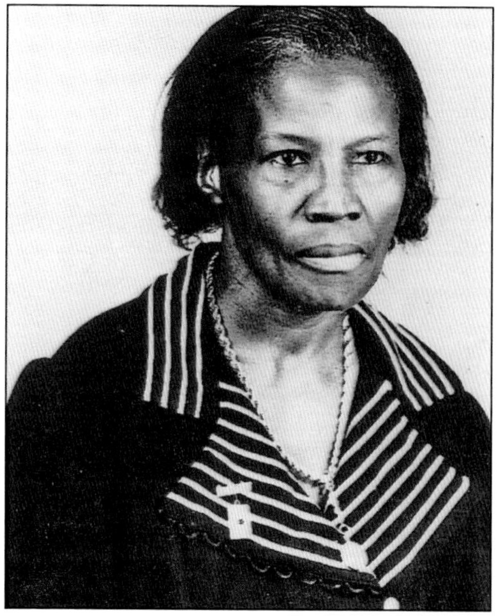

Anthony (left) and Emily Brown (right) came to Mulberry in 1909 when the town had stables, horses, buggies, and clay roads. They had one son, whose name is unknown, and two daughters, Marguerite and Anna. Anthony was the private cook for Mr. Sprott at a rooming house called the Whole and Wall, and for mine superintendent Harry Meade. He also cooked at Johnny Mitchell's Café. He died in 1938. (Maguerite Holland and Anna Williams/MBS.)

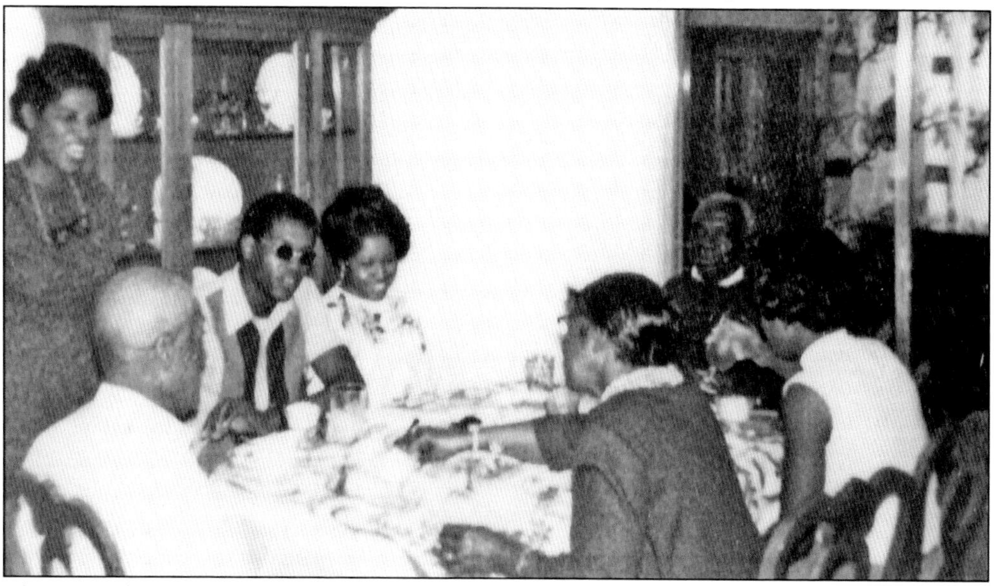

Thomas and Bernice Cromotie celebrate their 50th wedding anniversary with family and friends. Sharing these happy moments are, from left to right, the following: daughter Lillie Ruth Baker (standing), grandson Willie Frank Brown, friend Virginia Cunningham, friend Frank Sirmon, and granddaughter Sandra Brown (in white shirt with back to camera). Coming to Mulberry at the age of 16, Thomas worked for Old Prairie Mines, Seaboard Railroad Company, and served 22 years with International Minerals and Chemical Corporation. The Cromoties' three daughters are Edith, Lillie Ruth, and Mary. (Burdelle Kendricks/MBS.)

Virginia White (1905–1995) came to Mulberry in 1909 with her parents, Rev. Edward and Elizabeth Jackson. She attended Old J. R. E. Lee School, Old Union Academy High School, and Bethune Industrial Boarding School for Girls in Daytona Beach, Florida. She married Dan White, and they were blessed with nine children: Frances, Evelena, Bennie, Arthur, Emory, Edgar, J. D., Letha Mae, and Bobby. (Berdelle Kendrick/MBS.)

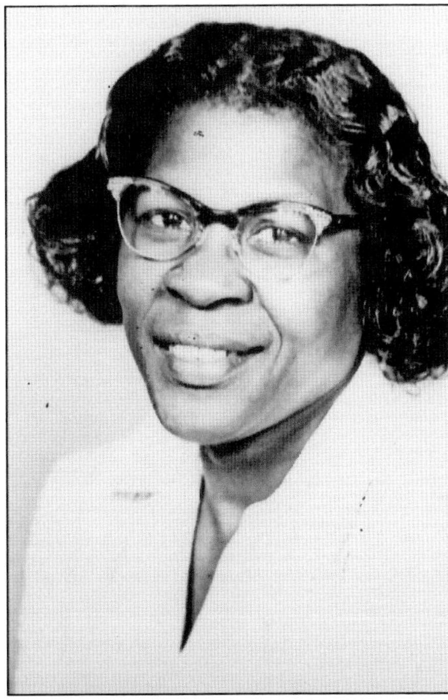

The son of Japhus Lloyd Dawson and Naomi Warren Dawson, Warren Hope Dawson (below left), a Mulberry native, graduate of Union Academy, Florida Agriculture and Mechanical University, and Howard University, has practiced law for over 40 years and earned the high honor of becoming a member of the National Bar Association Hall of Fame in 2007. Warren's mother, Naomi, was the community piano teacher and the pianist and choir director for Mount Zion African Methodist Episcopal Church of Mulberry for 51 years (1930–1981.)

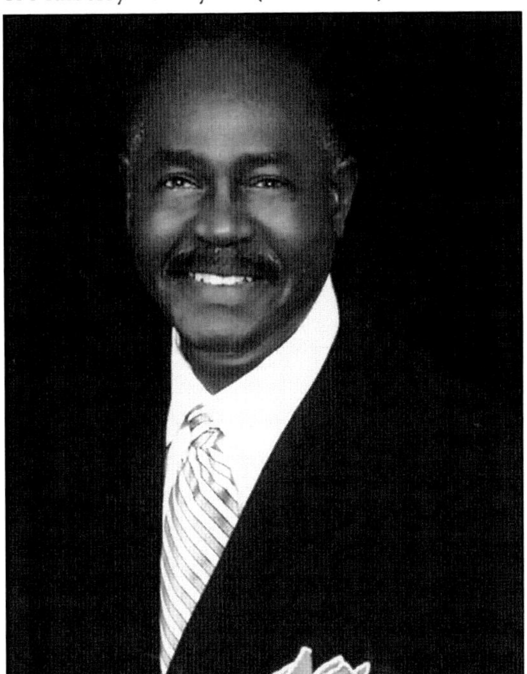

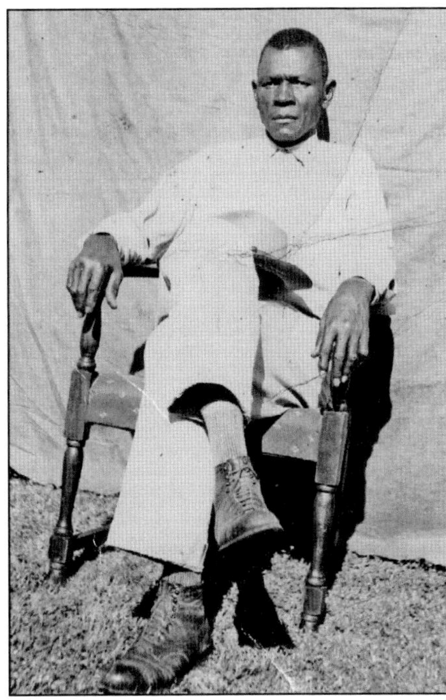

Essick Nelson (right), born in 1888 to Margaret and Tom Nelson, moved to Mulberry from Lake Park, Georgia. Essick worked for Mulberry Ice Works Company, which was owned by Edward Haskell Dudley (1877–1956), the former mayor of Mulberry. He started with the company driving a horse and wagon, and by the time he retired, he was driving an ice delivery truck. This was during the time that customers left the door unlocked for the ice man to place the ice into the icebox. Essick fathered a daughter, Essie, and was stepfather to Palmer Francis. (Essie N. Helper Morgan.)

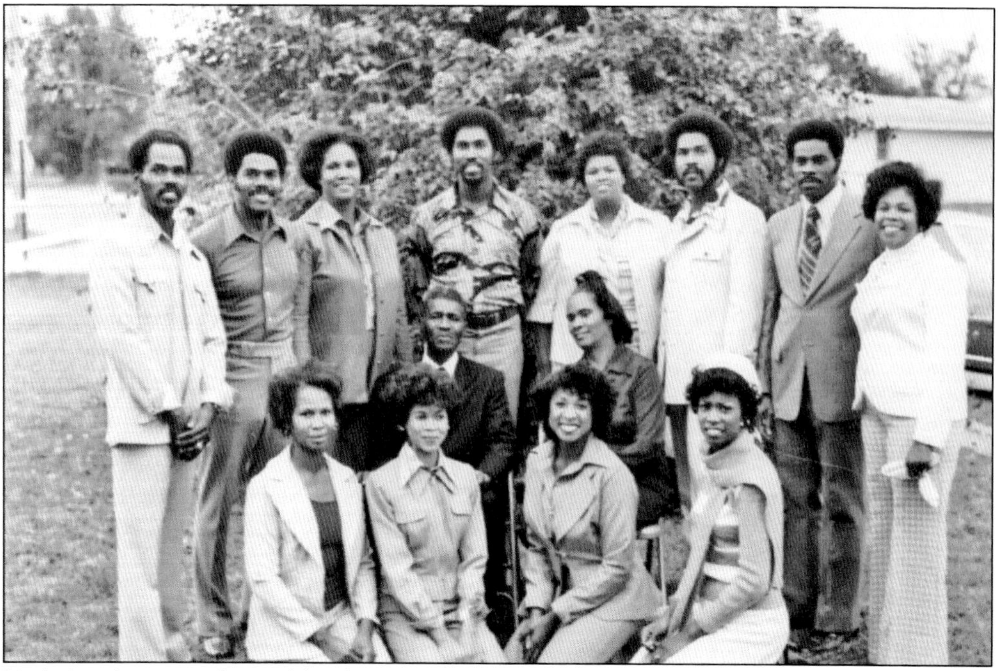

Hailed as the most educated family to graduate from Union Academy, the Woodards, Eddie and Elize, seated, educated their 12 children beyond high school. Pictured from left to right are the following: (kneeling) Annette, who pursued nursing; Julia, an educator; Gwendolyn, a counselor; and Emma, an educator; (standing) Chesley, a manager at General Motors for more than 38 years; Oziemar, who served as an administrator in the Polk County Public School system; Eddie Mae, a nurse; Lawrence, who has a Ph.D. in education; Elaine, also an educator; Herbert, a school principal; Wogan, a minister; Evelyn, who pursued business education. (Woodard family.)

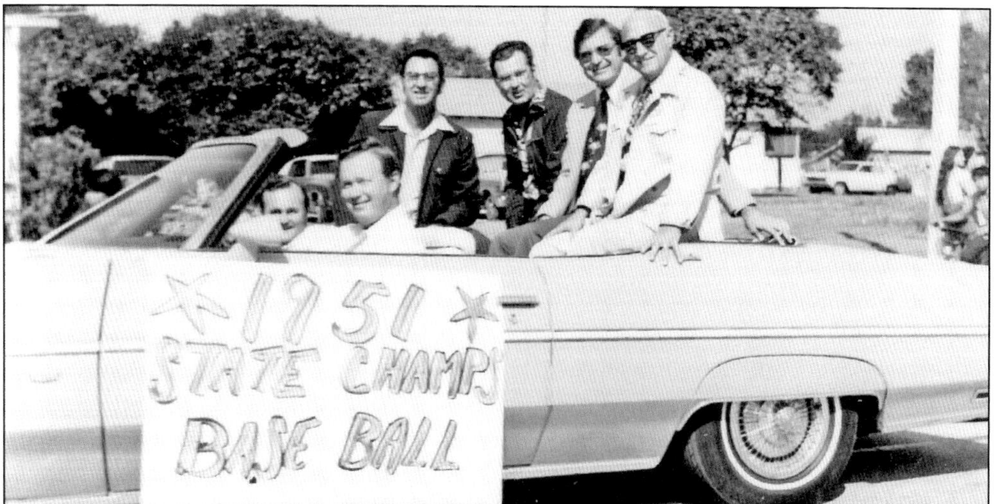

Pictured are members of the Mulberry High School baseball team of 1951, the Florida state champions. Identified team members in this image are Maxo Evans (driving) and Rooney Connell (in the passenger seat). Other state championship team members included Bob Evans, Asa Keene, Bob Ghiotto, Gene Johnson, Johnny Morrison, Jerry Williams, Dickie Hart, and Jimmy Morrison.

Eight

Service to Our Nation

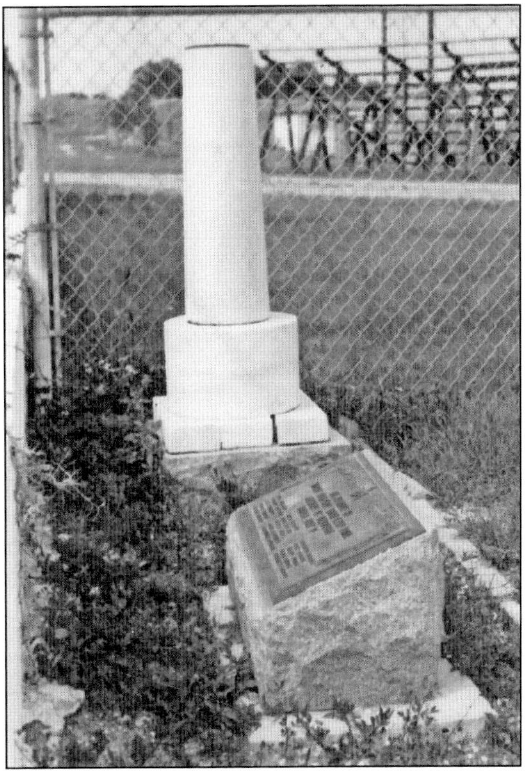

This sundial, which sits on a marble base, gives accurate time to visitors at the International Park and Bird Sanctuary in Mulberry. On Wednesday, October 3, 1951, this memorial site was dedicated to Korea War victim Cpl. Ernest Jean Cunningham. The sundial was dedicated to the Boy Scouts of America. Cunningham was a member of Scout Troop 152. The program was sponsored by the Mulberry post of the American Legion, and 150 people attended. (MBS.)

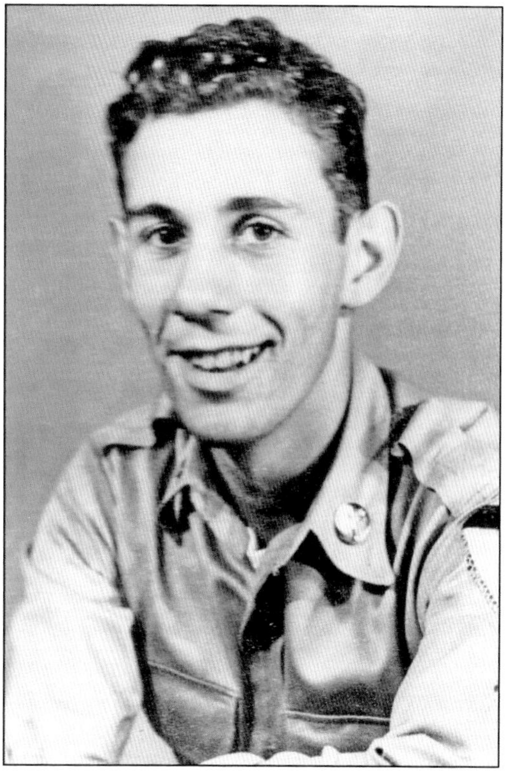

In 1936, Cpl. Ernest Jean Cunningham (1930–1950) moved to Mulberry with his family, Ernest Lee and Leila Morrison Cunningham, from Meridian, Mississippi. In November 1948, Ernest joined the U.S. Army, and on July 4, 1950, he joined the 25th Infantry in Korea. Cunningham was killed on July 16, 1950, his parents were notified on July 16, 1950, and remains were shipped home one year and two months later. Cunningham was buried on September 19, 1951, in Poplarville, Mississippi. (Leila Cunningham/MBS.)

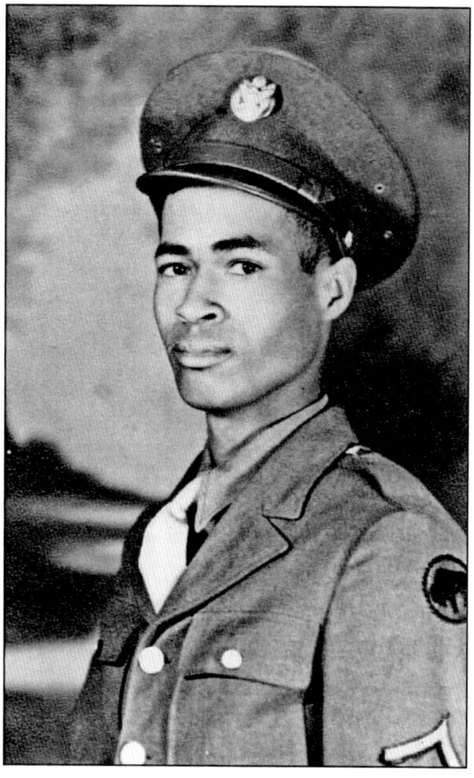

S.Sgt. Palmer Francis Jr. served in World War II as a radio chief in the Headquarters Company, 2nd Battalion, 370th Infantry and received, among his many awards, the Purple Heart. He was a buffalo soldier. He chose Helen Marie White to be his bride, and to this union, four children were born: Gene, Karen, Harriet, and Gabriella. He was employed by International Minerals and Chemical Corporation and built his own house on land he purchased in the mining town of Nichols, Florida. (Essie N. Helper Morgan.)

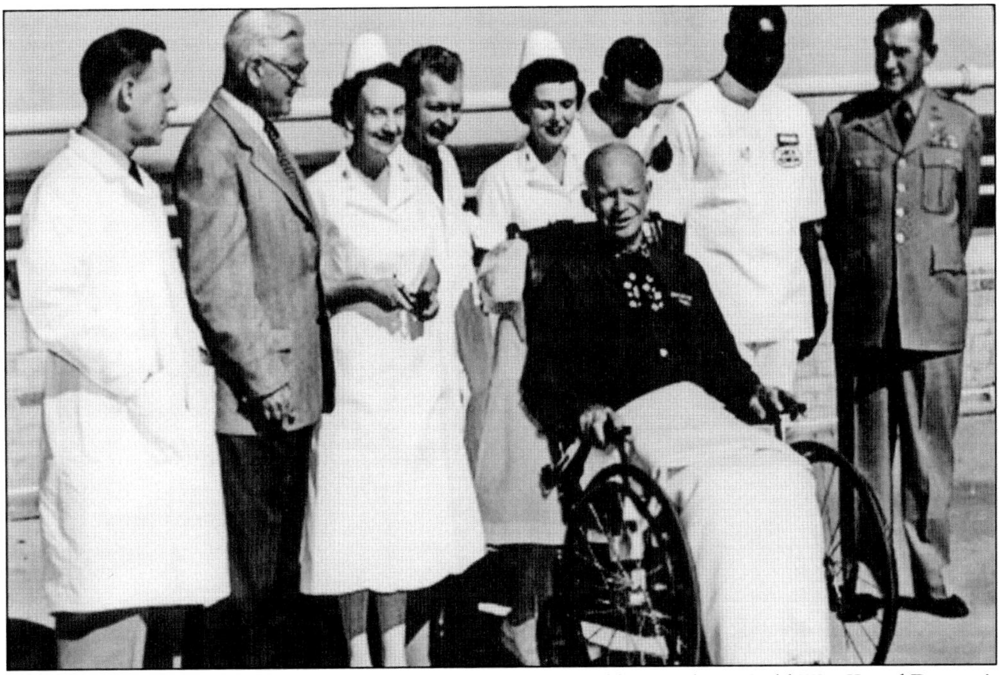

Col. Edyth Turner served as chief nurse of the 306th general hospital in World War II and Denver's Fitzsimmons Army Hospital, where she, pictured here third from the left, was honored to provide care for Pres. Dwight Eisenhower in 1955. The others pictured are Lt. Lorraine Knox, Dr. Howard Snyder, Col. Byron Pollock, Col. George Powell, M.Sgt. Donovan Walling, Sgt. Joseph Vaughn, and Maj. Gen. Martin Griffin. She is one of the first women to achieve the rank of colonel in the U.S. Army. (U.S. Army, Dwight D. Eisenhower Presidential Library and Museum.)

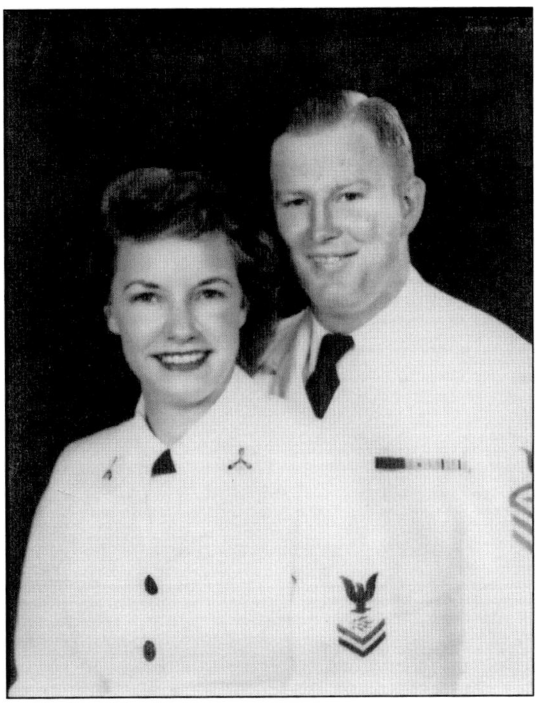

Raymond Louis and Betty Jane Driver met during their military careers. They were married for 49 years, from 1945 to 1994. Two sons were born to this union: Raymond Jr. who passed in 1954, and Daniel Joseph, who passed in 1956. The Drivers enjoyed the benefits of military life by living in China, Philippines, India, Bermuda, Brazil, and several wonderful cities of the United States. Most of all, they enjoyed being together. (Raymond L. Driver.)

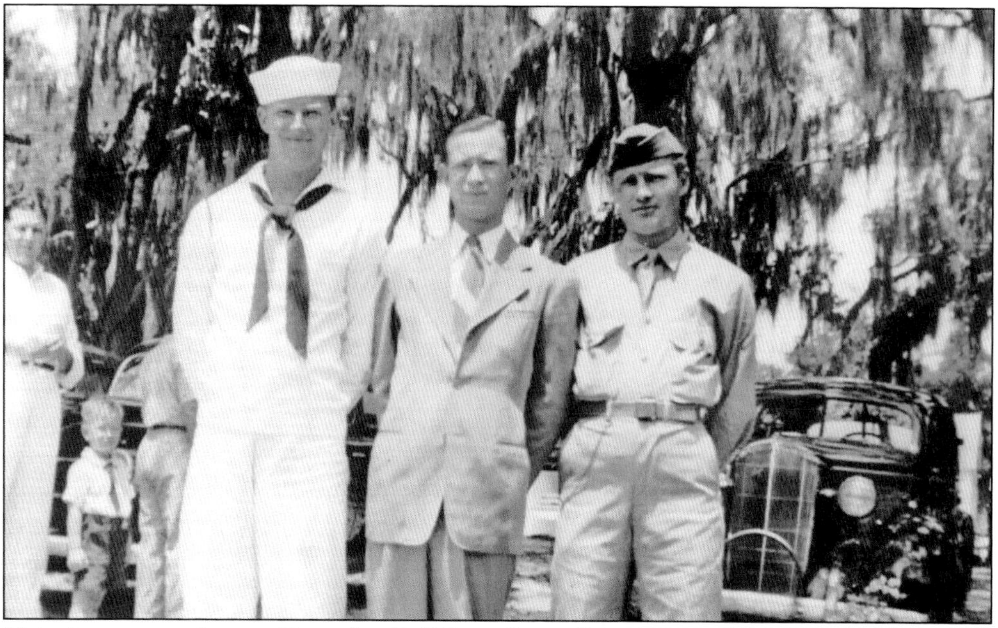

This picture was taken on December 7, 1941, at Green Cove Springs, Florida. From left to right are S1c. Raymond L. Driver, James Driver, and Pvt. Harry Driver. In the background to the left are Edgar Woodall and James Edgar Woodall. Although the brothers joined different branches of the military, they remained close. (Raymond L. Driver.)

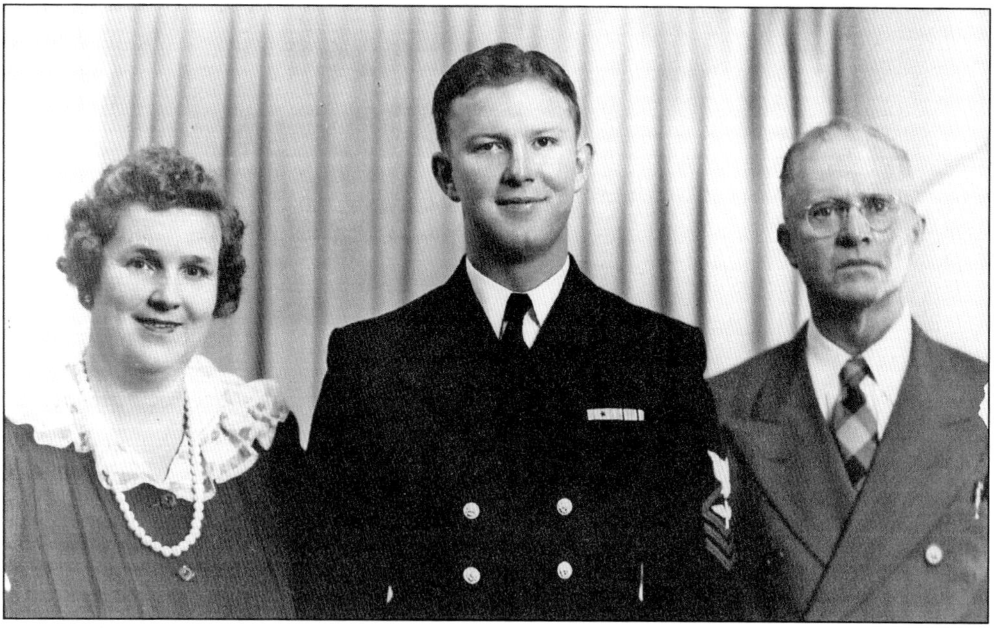

Raymond L. Driver was born in 1922 in Mulberry and serve in the U.S. Navy from 1940 to 1961, in the World War II, Korea and Vietnam conflicts. Driver earned his master's degrees from Drake University. He is one of the foremost historians on the phosphate industry and history of Mulberry. As an active 1937 alumni of Mulberry High School, Driver is a driving force behind the Gray Panther Alumni Association, the Mulberry Historical Society, the Kiwanis club, and the American Legion. (Raymond L. Driver.)

These unattributed famous words best describe the dedication of those serving in America's armed forces: "A veteran, whether active duty, retired, national guard or reserve, is someone who at one point in his life wrote a blank check made payable to 'the United States of America' for an amount of 'up to and including my life.'" Cosigned by "the family." This couple is unidentified. (The *Mulberry Press*.)

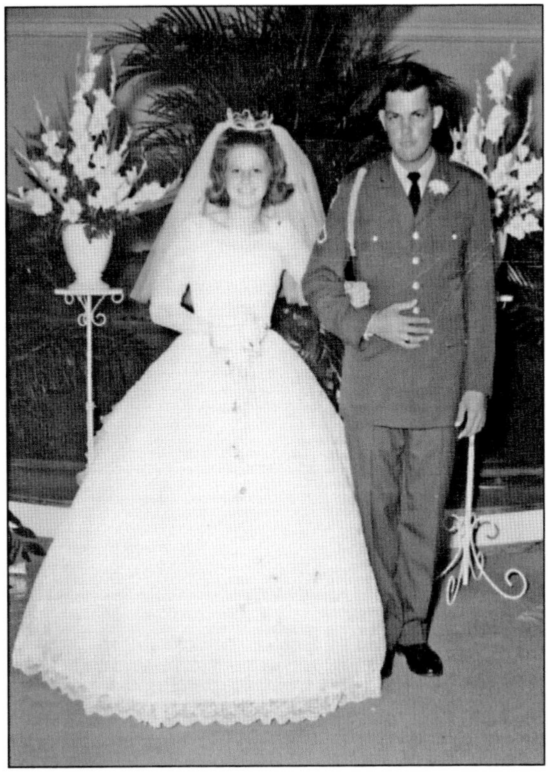

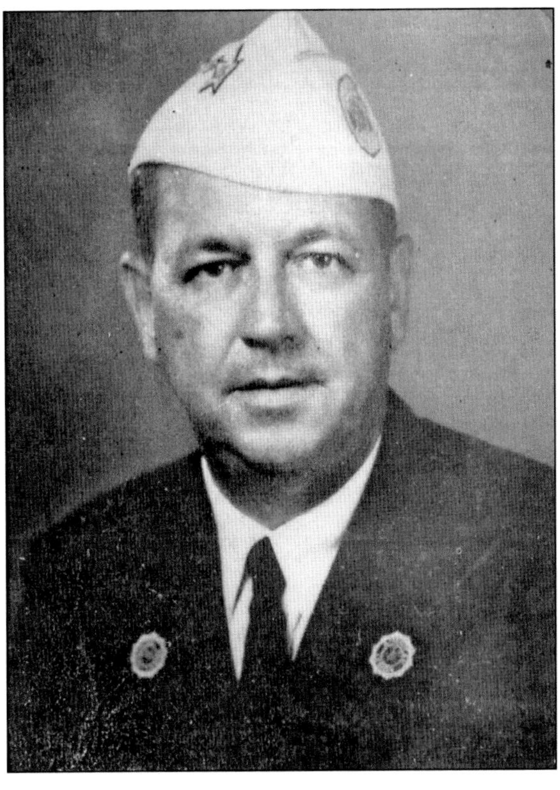

Maj. Harry Levi Mead (1800–1972), son of Henry Stephen and Amanda DuBois Mead, is a member of a family that has served in every war of the American colonies and nation from 1647 to World War II. Mead served in the army from 1917 until 1919. His sons, Harry Jr. and James, were born to his union with Helen Newman Mead. As an outstanding mining expert and engineer, Mead held many distinguished positions in the mining industry. (MBS.)

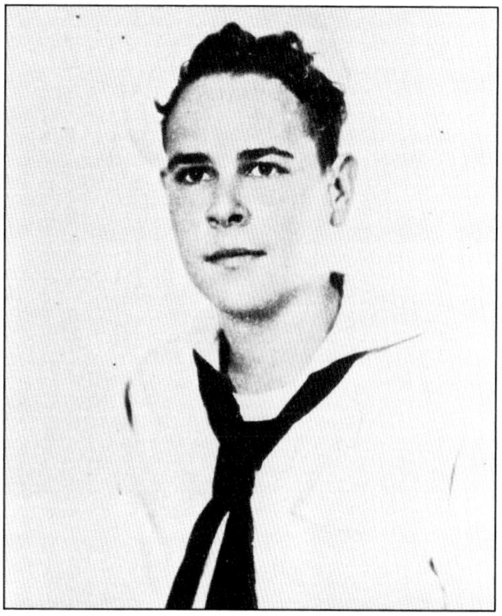

Ron Thomas is a native of Mulberry with a strong commitment to preserving the community's history. At least once a month he drives from Rockledge, Florida, to Mulberry to attend Mulberry's historical society meetings. Ron's military training provided skills necessary to work for Lockheed Martin until retirement. Ron is the proud father of one daughter. (Ron Thomas.)

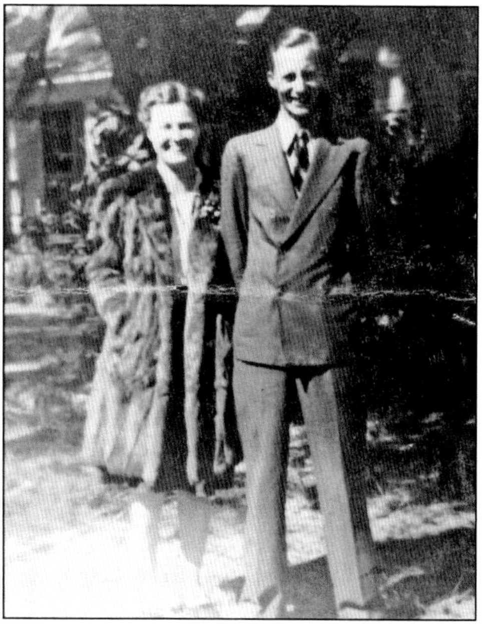

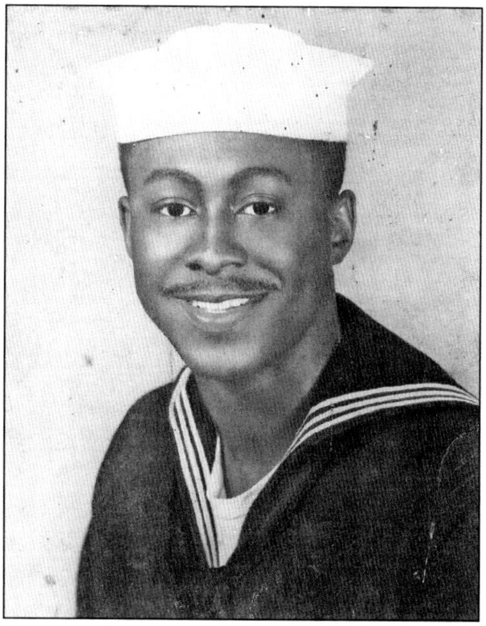

Pictured on the left, Kenneth F. Speight was called into the armed forces during World War II from his position of manager at the Mutual Store. Speight married Florence Whidden, the daughter of Eldridge Saxton and Susan Holland Whidden. The Speights had one son, Kenneth Charles, and Mrs. Speight taught in the Polk County School until retiring in 1954. Her siblings are Monte Julian, Stella, Earl, and Eve. Pictured on the right, S3c. Bernard White was born in Mulberry on August 24, 1937, to Fair and Ruth E. Bailey White. Bernard inspired 11 young men to enlist in the U.S. Navy upon graduation from Union Academy High in 1954. The group included James Battle, Curtis Carter, Simon Henry, Robert Lee Jamerson, Bull Johnson, James Jones, Ward Maning, Alfonso Newark, Floyd Robinson, and Arthur Shoulders. They had intended to join the U.S. Marines, but that recruiter was out to lunch, so the navy recruiter signed them up. (Left, Florence W. Speight/MBS; right, Bernard White.)

Ralph Collins was born on July 31, 1929, to C. R. Collins and Lessie English Collins. Lessie was a charter member of the women's club for more than 50 years and lived in Nichols, Florida. Ralph shares his birth month with his older sister, Barbara English, who was born in 1918 in Nichols, Florida. Ralph served in the U.S. Army. (Lessie Collins/MBS.)

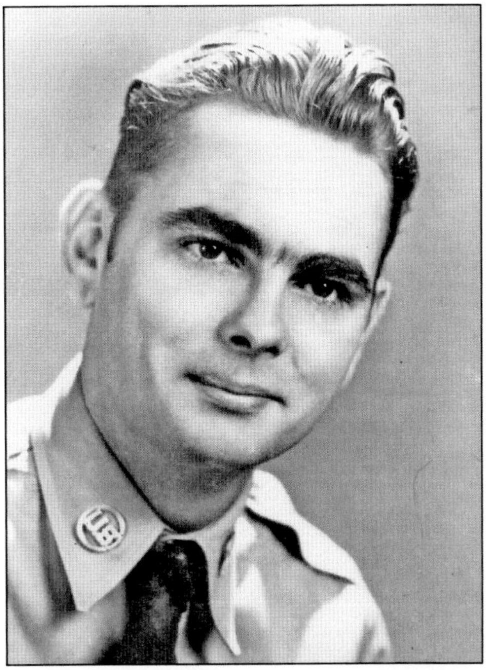

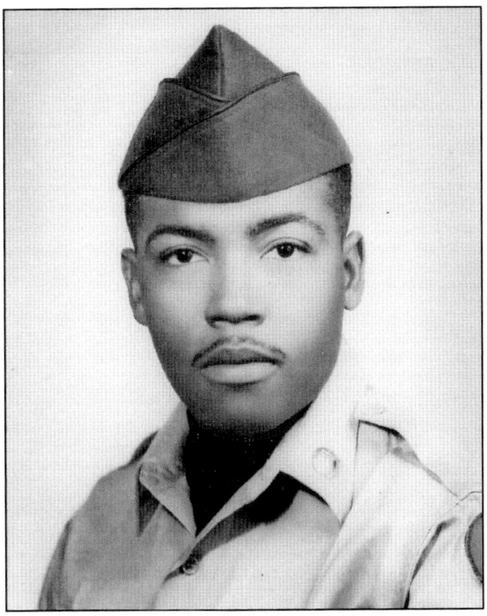

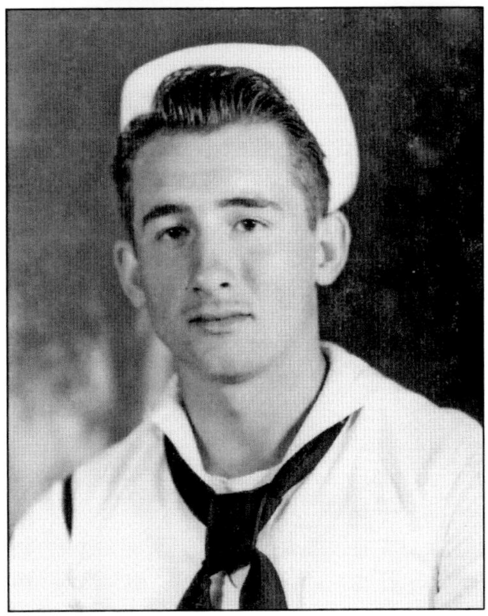

Born on March 12, 1935, in Mulberry, James Weldon Helper (left) was the son of Isom Helper and Allie Mae Aikens Helper Johnson. A graduate of Florida Agriculture and Mechanical University, Helper served in the Korean War as a member of the U.S. Army. He is the father of two daughters: Phyllis Juanita and Monica Marchei. William B. Hunt graduated from Mulberry High School while serving in the U.S. Navy. He graduated from the University of Miami. William is a member of Mulberry Methodist Church, a charter member of the Mulberry Lions Club, as well as past president of the Mulberry Chamber of Commerce. He was an agent for H. B. Hunt and Son Insurance Agency for more than 28 years. (Left, Essie N. Helper Morgan. Right, Annie Louise Lee Hunt/MBS.)

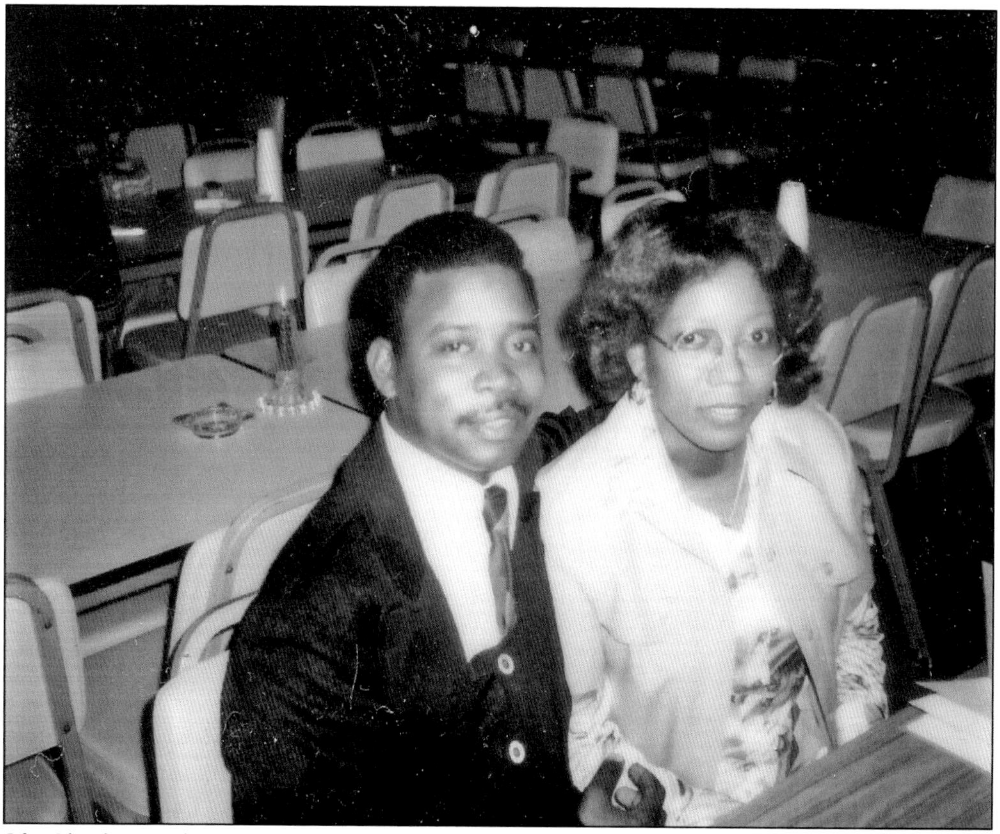

Sfc. Charles Gardner Jr. was the son of Charles and Ollie Mae Gardner. Upon graduating from Union Academy High School, he joined the U.S. Army for the career span of 21 years. Married to Carolyn Griffin of Marianna, Florida, Charles was the godfather of Tanya Leah Dukes. Charles's siblings are S.Sgt. Willie James Hayes, Esther, E. J. Williams Jr., and Gilbert Smith. Charles is pictured here with his childhood friend, Sharon Helper. Other military buddies from his childhood include M.Sgt. Ollie Bernard Smith and M.Sgt. Johnnie Lee Brown. (Nila Helper Jones.)

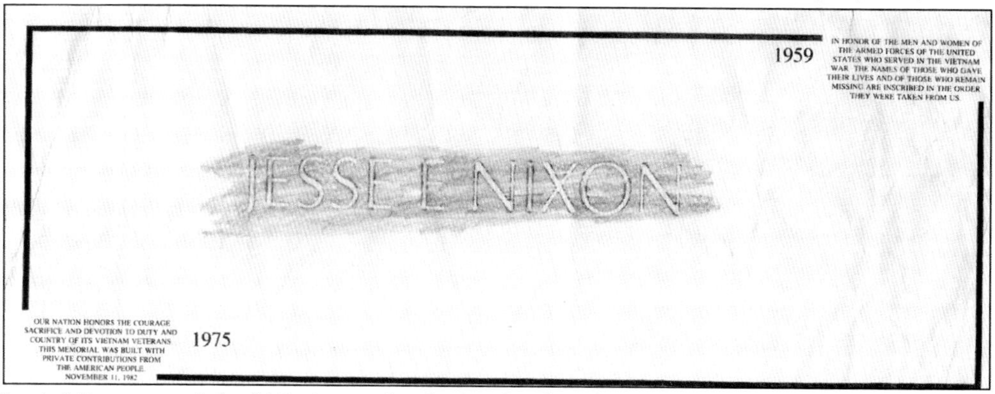

Jessie Nixon joined the U.S. Army after high school and a few months shy of his discharge in 1970. This shading is from the National Memorial Monument Wall in Washington, D.C. Jesse's name can also be found on the Florida State Veteran's Memorial in Tallahassee across the street from the capitol. Nixon's brothers who served this country and returned safely home are Samuel Chapel, Lenwood Pope, and Tyrone Pope. (Stephanie L. Dukes.)

On April 20, 1942, Thomas Leon Brown joined the family of William Matthew and Edith Cromartie Brown. Thomas attended J. R. E. Lee Junior High School and graduated from Union Academy High School. He served in the U.S. Army for more than 21 years. Brown is the father of Antonia and the stepfather of Betty, Lorotta, Diane, Paula, Alana, Dalynn, and Lessie. His siblings are Sandra, William Clifford, Willie Frank, and Roger. (Sandra Brown.)

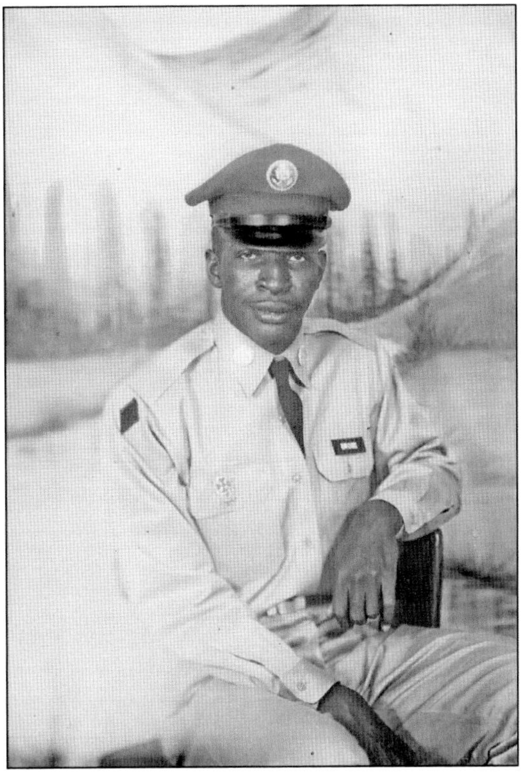

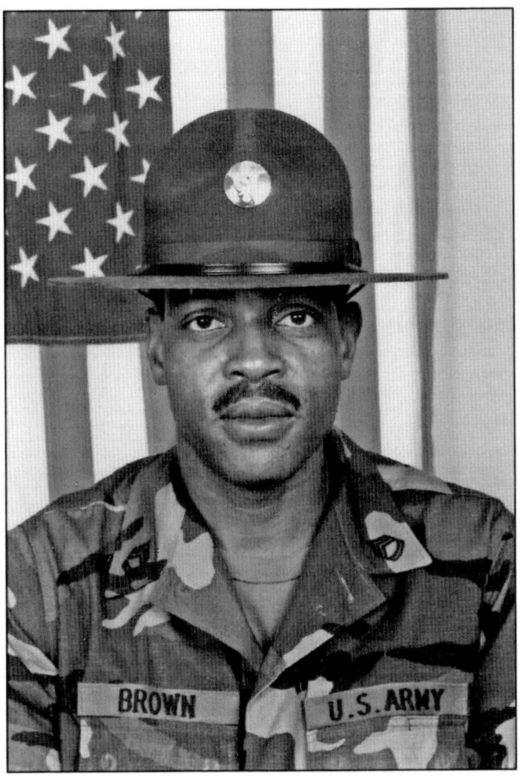

Willie Frank Brown was one of three brothers to serve in the U.S. Army. Graduating from Union Academy High School, Willie Frank thought he would join for only a few years, but all three brothers served the army until retirement. (Sandra Brown.)

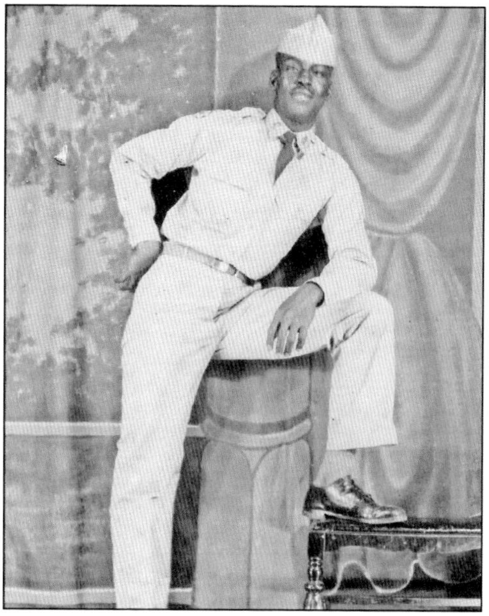

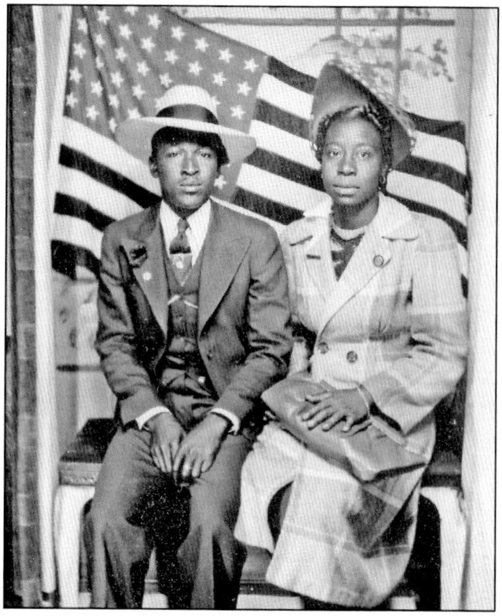

Thomas Jefferson "Zannie" Green (left) was born on January 23, 1928, to Lewis and Cora Green. Thomas, who served in the U.S. Army during World War II, is the brother of Tishia Mae, Nila, Benny, Priscilla, May Rose, Isaac, and Clyde Green. He enjoyed Sunday school and attending the Baptist Youth Training Union at Bethel Missionary Baptist Church during his younger life. Green departed this life on March 17, 1928. Fred and Nila Brown (right) are representative of the many civilians who patriotically supported the war effort by purchasing bonds and working in businesses that supplied goods and services to the military. Here are the names of just a few Mulberry servicemen: Willie Bentley, Ulysses Boone, Hubert Edwards, Isaac Green, Lister Hayes, Nathaniel Howard, Joseph Jones Sr., John Thomas, and Ivy Smith. (Left, Renuea Boyd Bigham; right, Essie N. Helper Morgan.)

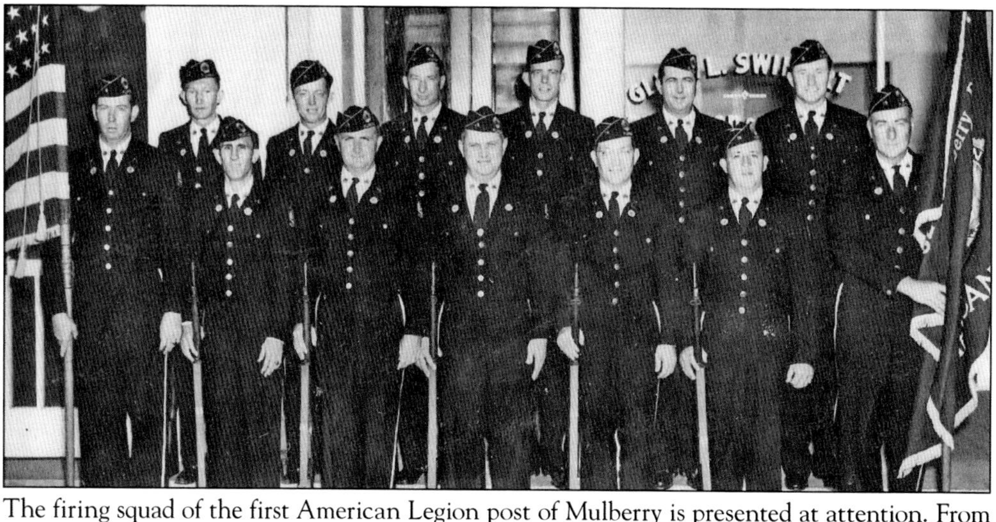

The firing squad of the first American Legion post of Mulberry is presented at attention. From left to right are the following men: (first row) Dicky Lyle, Dick Hawkins, William H. Miller, Cole Wilson, Reuben Snead, Arthur M. Seigler Jr., and Dewey Brooke; (second row) Speck Clements, George McCuthcheon, Lawrence Moore, Barney Mullis, Willie Martin, and Crook Clements. (Dick Hawkins/MBS.)

Nine

STYLE AND CULTURE

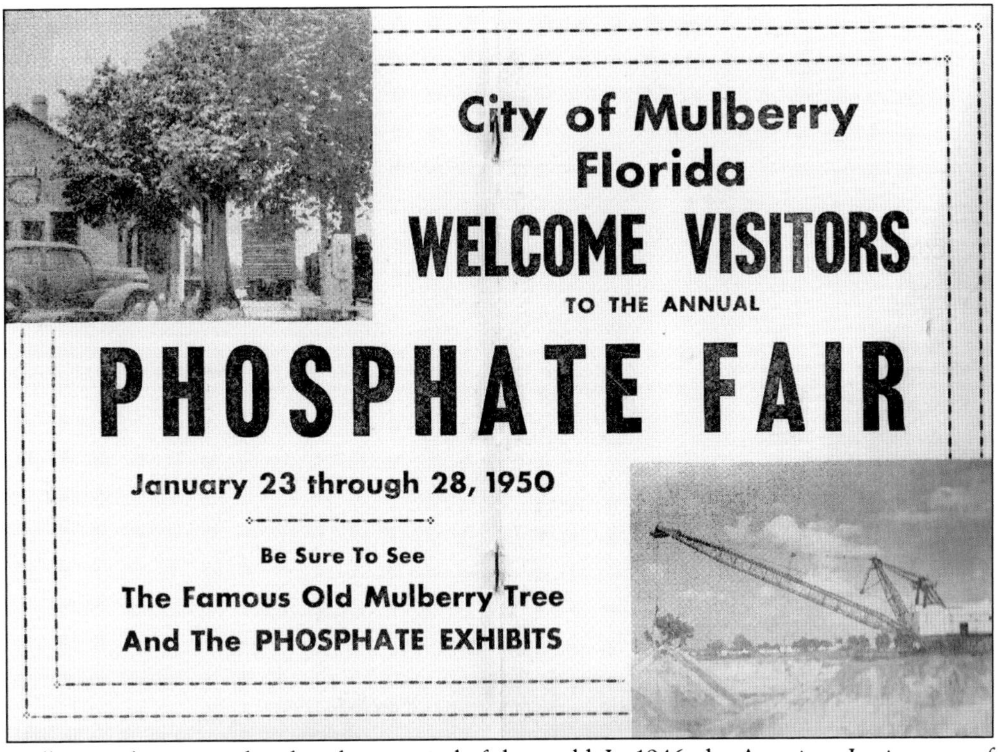

Mulberry is known as the phosphate capital of the world. In 1946, the American Legion post of Mulberry began celebrating this honor with an annual phosphate fair. This image is part of the fourth annual official fair program book. The photograph of the Mulberry tree was taken by Alva Claude Pipkin as editor for the 1949 Mulberry High School yearbook. This picture has appeared in numerous publications. Edgar H. Pipkin Sr. Alva's father, had the original photograph enlarged by a photographer in New York and had a wooden frame made. The photograph has hung in numerous places around town, including the Pipkins' residence, Johnnie Mitchell's Café, the post office, city hall, and the phosphate museum. (MPM)

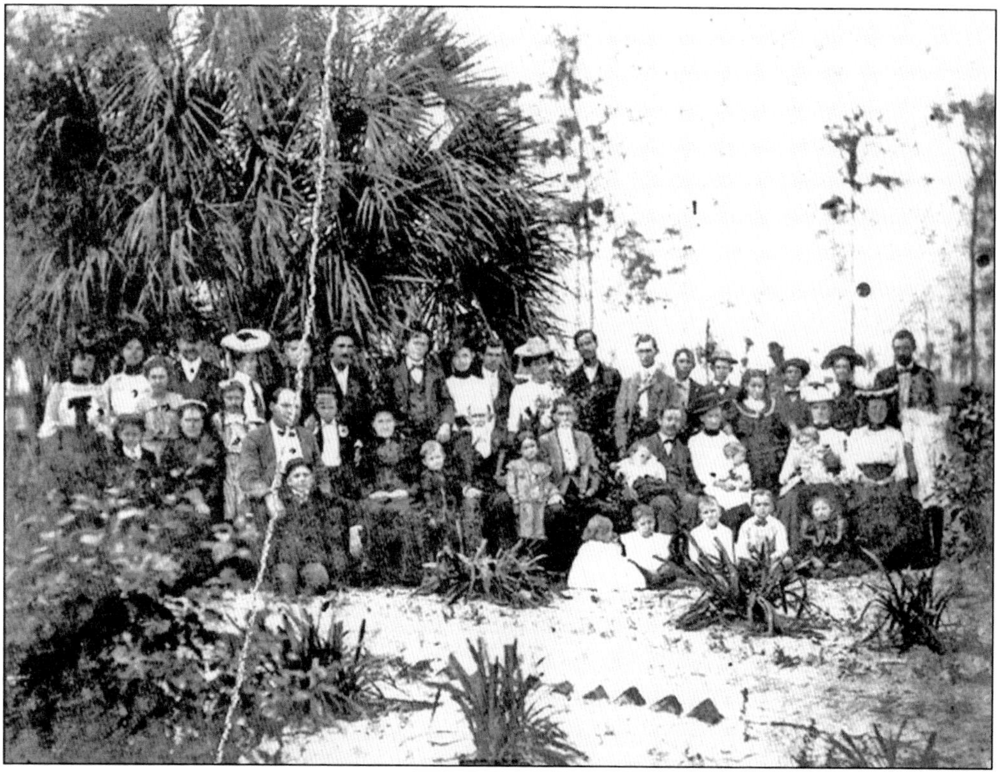

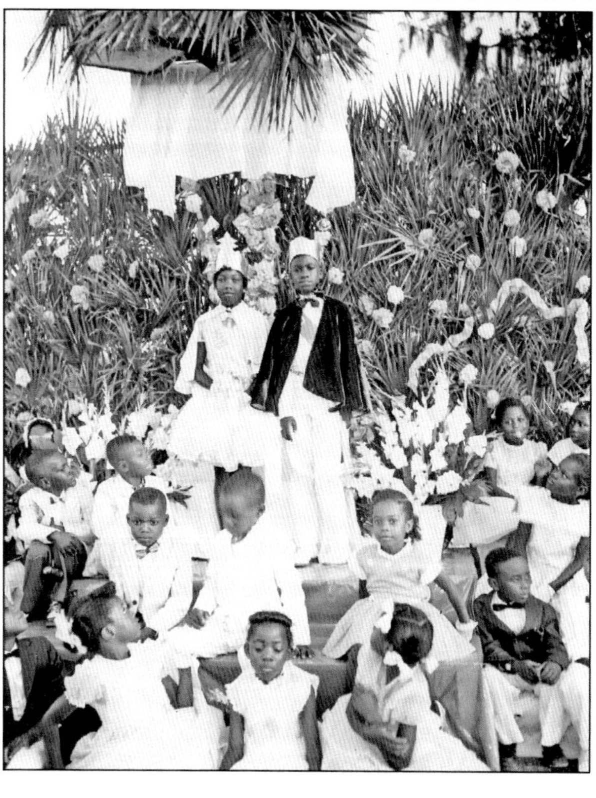

This photograph shows the Pipkin family reunion in 1902 at the home of Levi Nathaniel and Florence Beulah Proctor Pipkin. Levi was born August 18, 1866, to Nathan and Margaret Pipkin in Florala, Alabama. His family, influential pioneers, arrived by covered wagon to the area in 1883. Levi opened a general store in 1894 and organized Mulberry's first bank, the Bank of Mulberry, in 1907. (SLAF.)

On the first day of May for many years, the African American school community of Mulberry celebrated May Day. The biggest events of the day were the plaiting with colorful ribbons of the maypole and the naming of the king and queen. This 1957 photograph shows queen Sharon Anita Helper and king Robert Lewis Stevenson. (Essie N. Helper Morgan.)

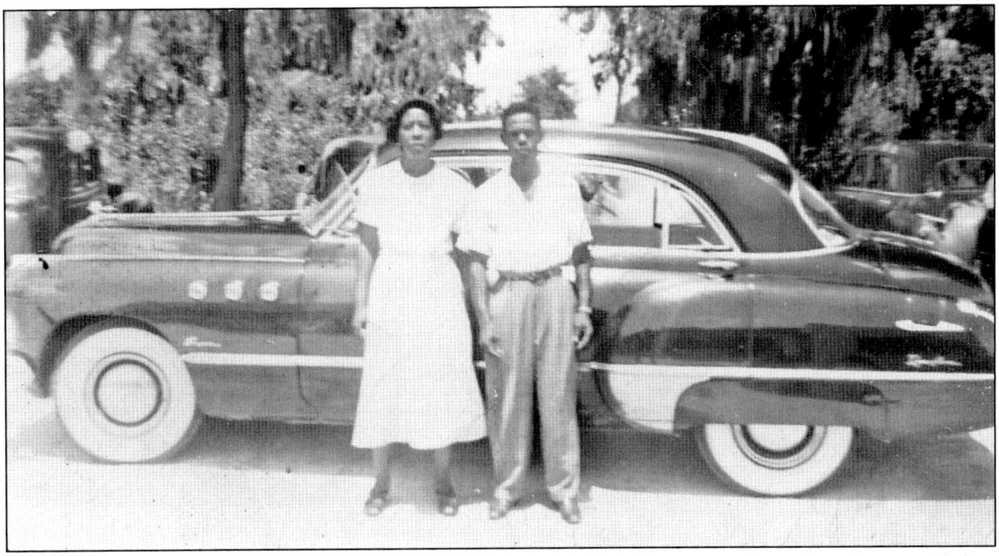

Standing in front of this 1950 Chevy are Nila B. Brown and Roosevelt Baker. The story is told that Roosevelt purchased a broken-down 1930 Chevy from Mr. Okane in the late 1940s and worked on it for two and a half years before it would operate properly, proud as he could be when he drove it around town. In 1950, he bought this brand-new 1949 Buick and put away his tools.

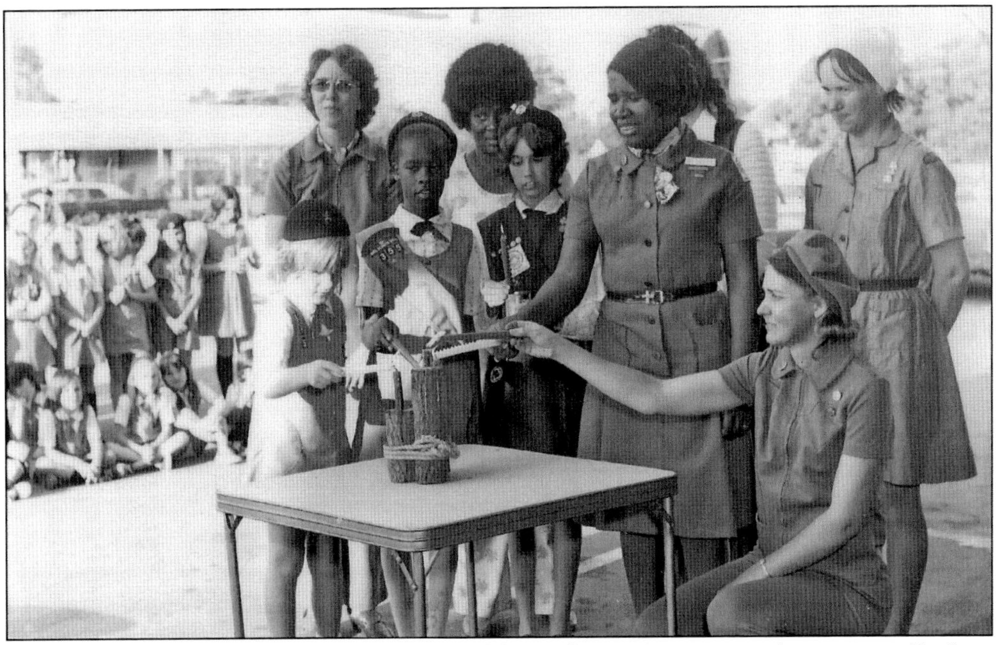

The girls scout troops of Mulberry gather to celebrate the year's activities, the earning of badges, and to renew their commitment to their communities. Pictured on stage in the first row are, from left to right, unidentified, Tangiela Lavon, unidentified, troop leader Daisy Lavan, unidentified. The only identified troop leader in the second row is Mary Smith, second from the left.

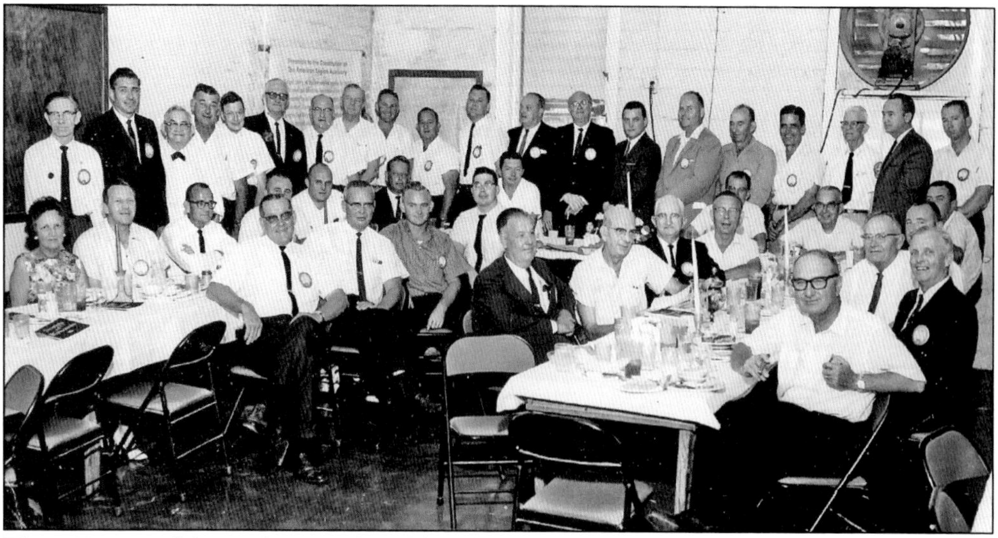

These Kiwanis club members are, listed from left to right, going around the room, (center rows, seated) Carter Kilpatrick, Teddy Aggelis, Virgil Davis, Dr. Allen Cole, B. B. Mullis, Hurton Hewett, R. N. Bryan, and unidentified; (outer rows, seated) Evelyn Badcock, John Layton, Otto Siver, unidentified, Bill Seigler, unidentified, Cecil Strange, ? Grant, E. E. Melton, unidentified, unidentified, F. R. Bergquist, W. H. Purcell, and W. S. Badcock Sr; (third row, standing) two unidentified men, E. E. Estridge, Meryl Johns, Bun Pipkin, Lawton Richardson, Dr. Gordon Taylor, Roy Gladney, Fred Marsh, unidentified, Amie Seigler, W. S. Badcock Jr., unidentified, C. Hughes, Al Caldwell, Herb Quina, Andy Bogan, Johnnie Mitchell, Gene Doss, and Robert Sweat. (The *Mulberry Press*.)

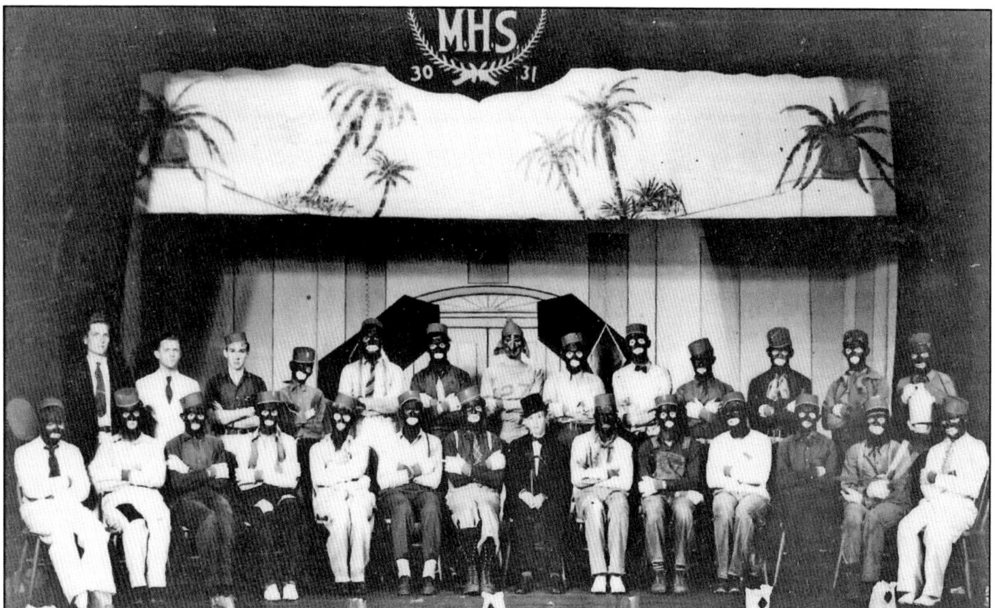

The Mulberry Kiwanis Club, a nonprofit organization, was chartered in 1935. The club supports many programs and provides meaningful services to the community of Mulberry. One of their main fund-raisers in 1940s was the minstrel variety show. The cast is unidentified. As of 2007, Michael Broders was serving as president of the club. (Henrie H. Sparkman/MBS.)

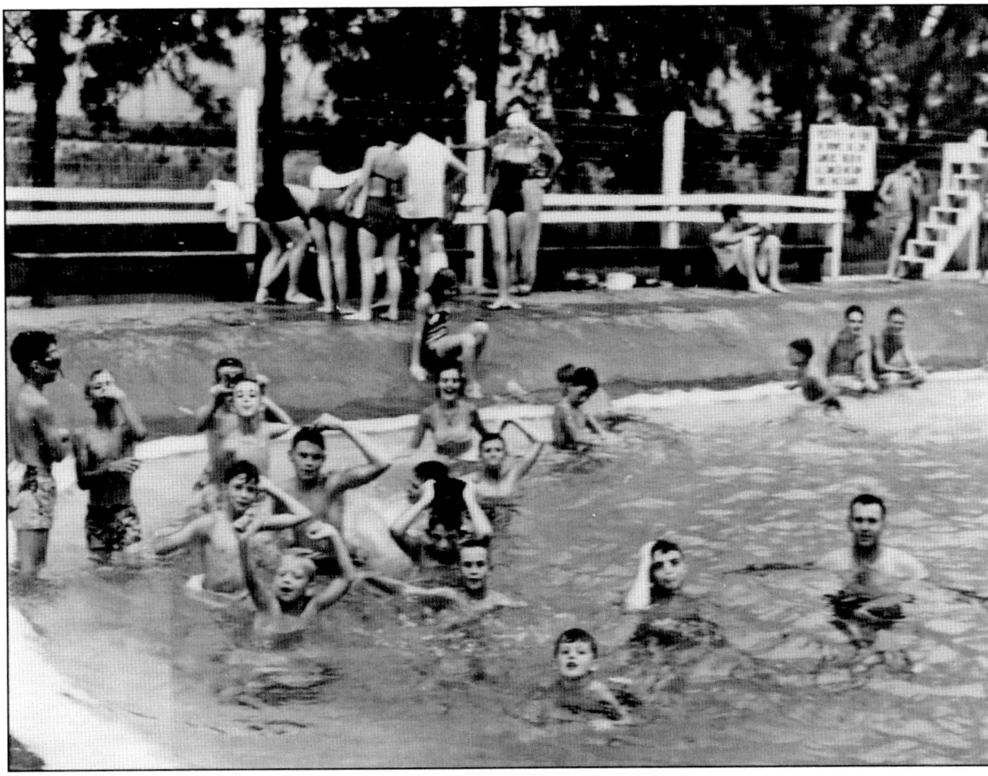

In 1937, the flow of water from a drilled well 600 feet deep was utilized to provide a swimming pool for International Minerals and Chemical Corporation employees. This water was formerly used in mining operations, according the history published in the 1950 phosphate fair program book. (Howard Wiggs/MBS.)

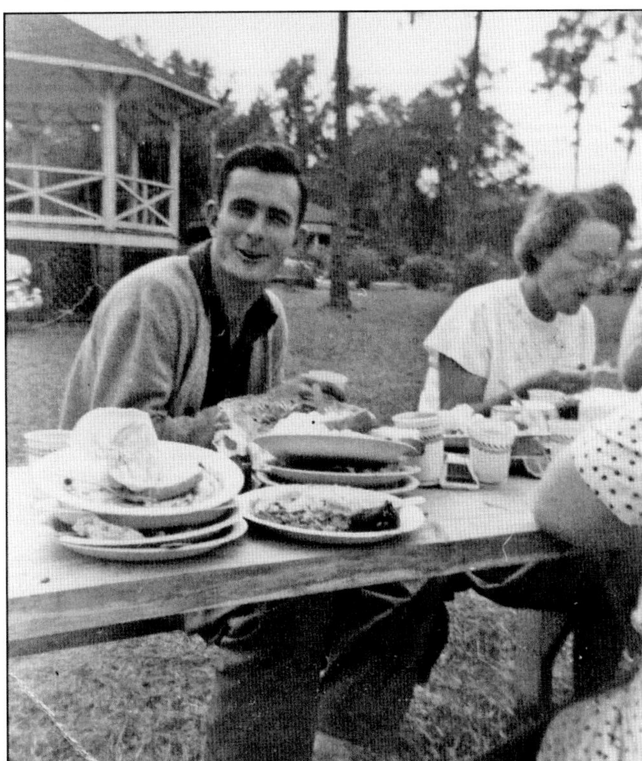

In addition to providing a swimming pool for its employees, International Minerals and Chemical Corporation's park offered a bandstand, tables and benches, and a large barbecue hut. These facilities were enjoyed by all in the community. This photograph of unidentified picnickers was taken around 1947. (Ronald Thomas.)

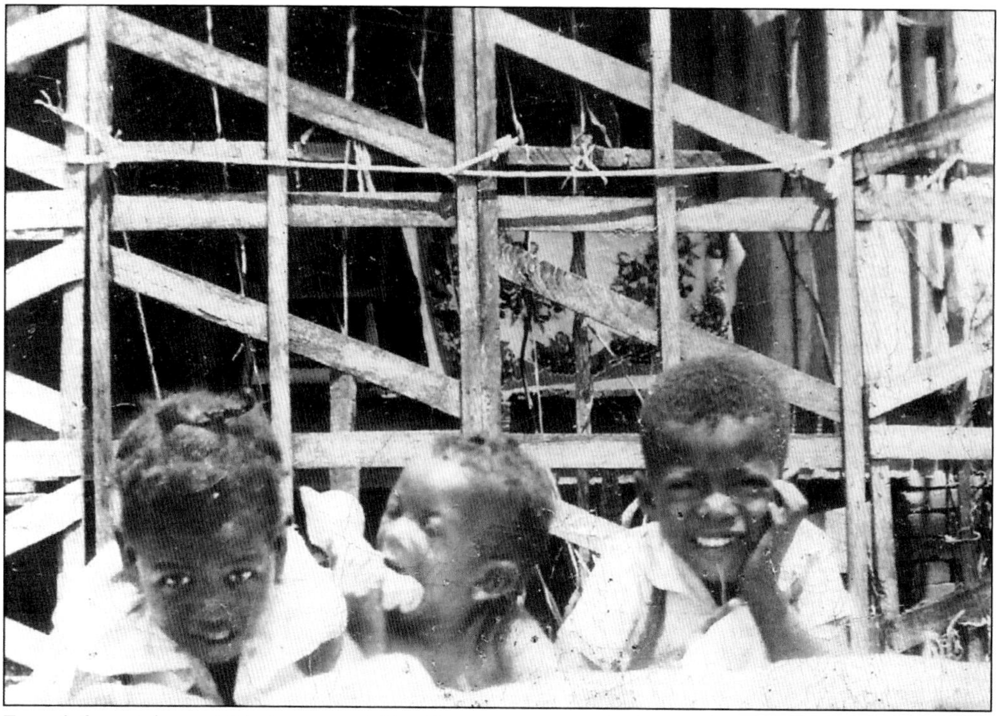

From left to right are Nila, Isom, and David, enjoying everyday living by spending time outside on the grass in about 1948, when children didn't have the luxury of television and other in-the-house entertainment. Notice the lattice work behind the kids, which the family used for plants with growing vines and vegetables. This family enjoyed the pleasure of their own garden-fresh vegetables. (Essie N. Helper Morgan.)

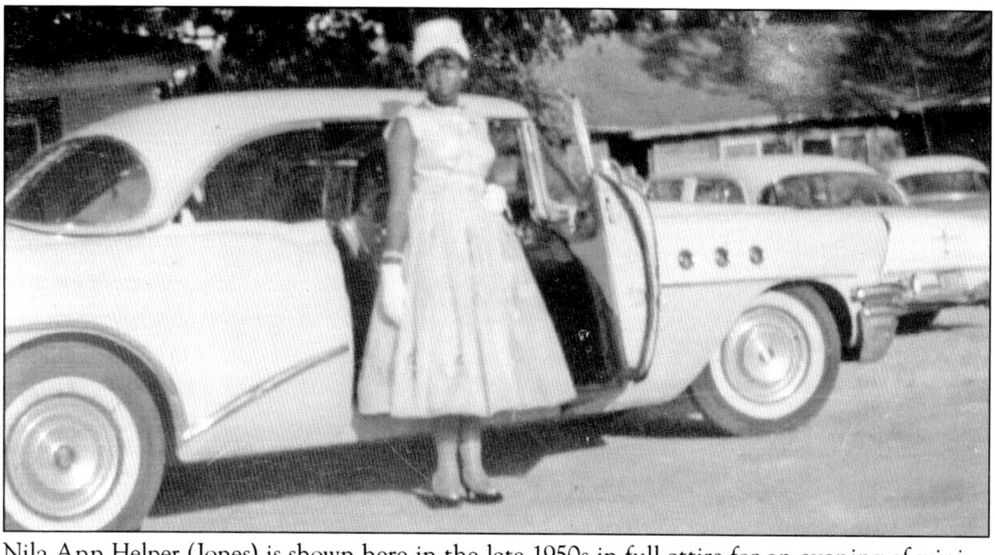

Nila Ann Helper (Jones) is shown here in the late 1950s in full attire for an evening of wining and dining. Nila was known for being dressed from head to toe—and check out those gloves! Her brother James made this dress, and the fabric cost $5.00 per yard. The car, owned by her cousin Raymond Smith, matches her style. Notice the whitewalls and the single doors on each side that open to feature a nice, comfortable back seat in the rear. (Nila Helper Jones.)

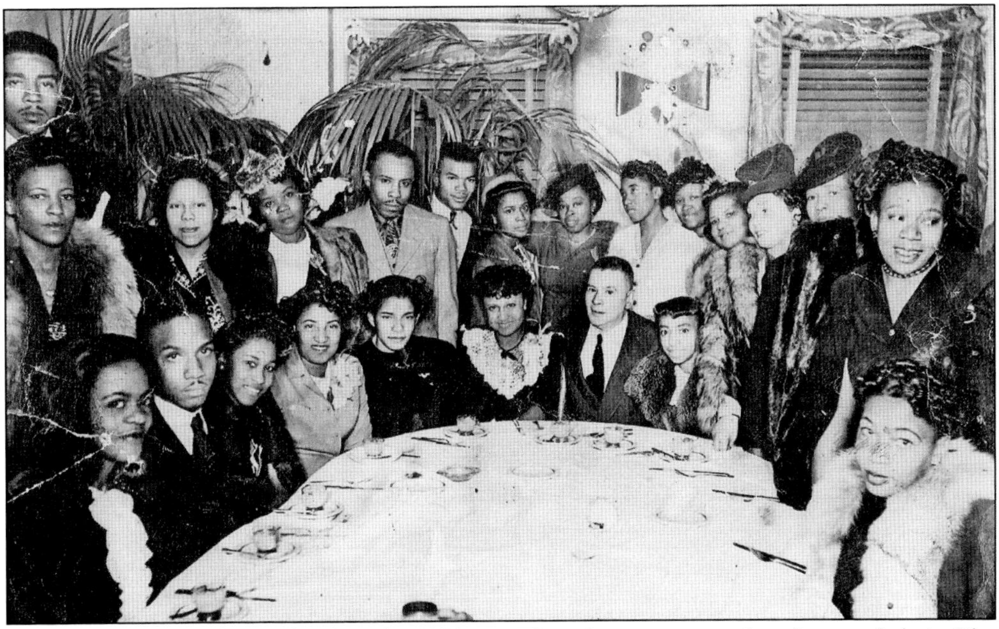

Attending beauty culture school in the 1950s was about learning more than how to do hair. The students also had to display etiquette skills by properly setting a table using fine cloth linen, fine china, crystal glassware, high-grade polished silverware. They were schooled in the proper dress attire for each time of day and occasion. The final examination activities required women to wear mink coats. Celestine Brewton Jackson is seated in the first row, third from the left; her brothers purchased her coat as her graduation gift. (Jackson family.)

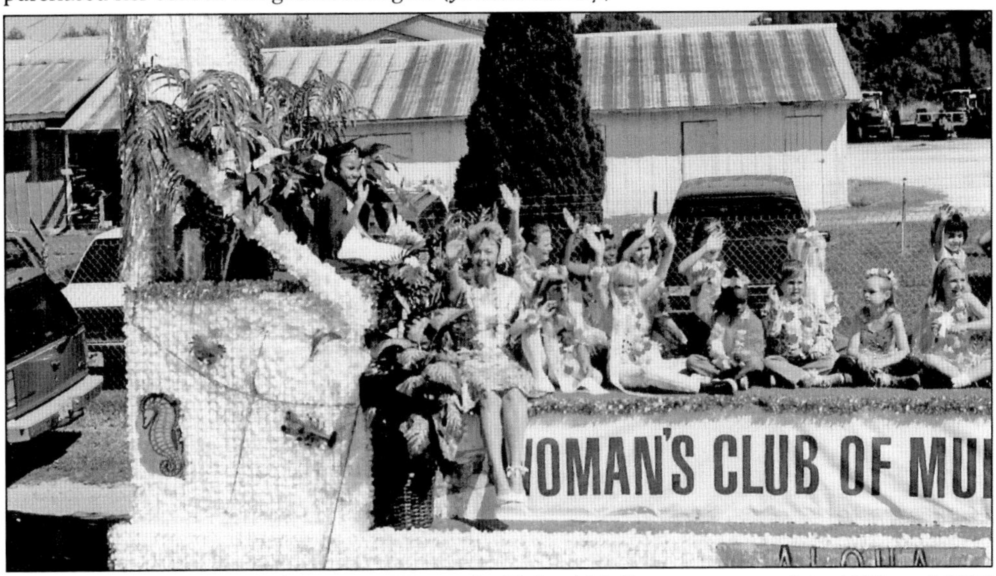

The Women's Club and the Junior Women's Club of Mulberry organized in 1899 and 1920 respectively. One of their major programs is the presentation of young ladies to society by hosting the Little Miss and Miss Mulberry pageants. Some of the young ladies formerly honored as Little Miss Mulberry are Sandra Motsinger, Sue Stewart, Sharon Grimes, Diane Alderman, and Sherry Davis. Some previous Miss Mulberry queens are Nonie Gladney, Evelyn Walker, Lynn Morris, and Beth Hattaway. (The *Mulberry Press.*)

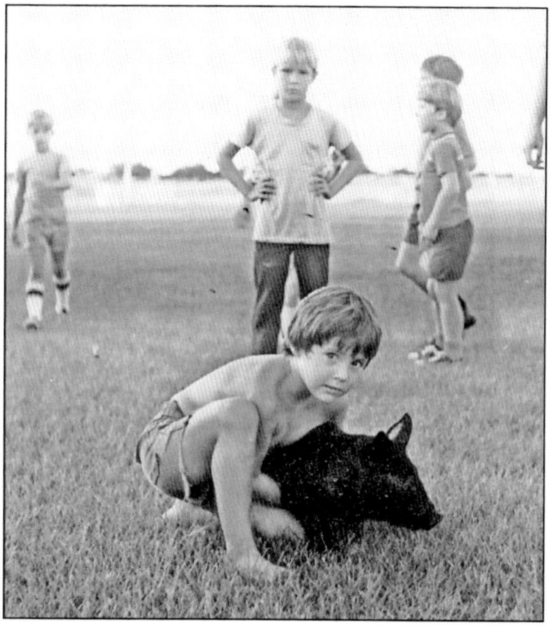

The unidentified boys shown here are participating in the greased pig contest held during Mulberry's bicentennial celebration. This event, organized by John L. Moore, took place on Monday July 5, 1976. Other events included the dedication of the mini-park, open house to view arts, crafts, and collectibles, a medicine show, a circus, a barbeque, and a birthday party. (MBS.)

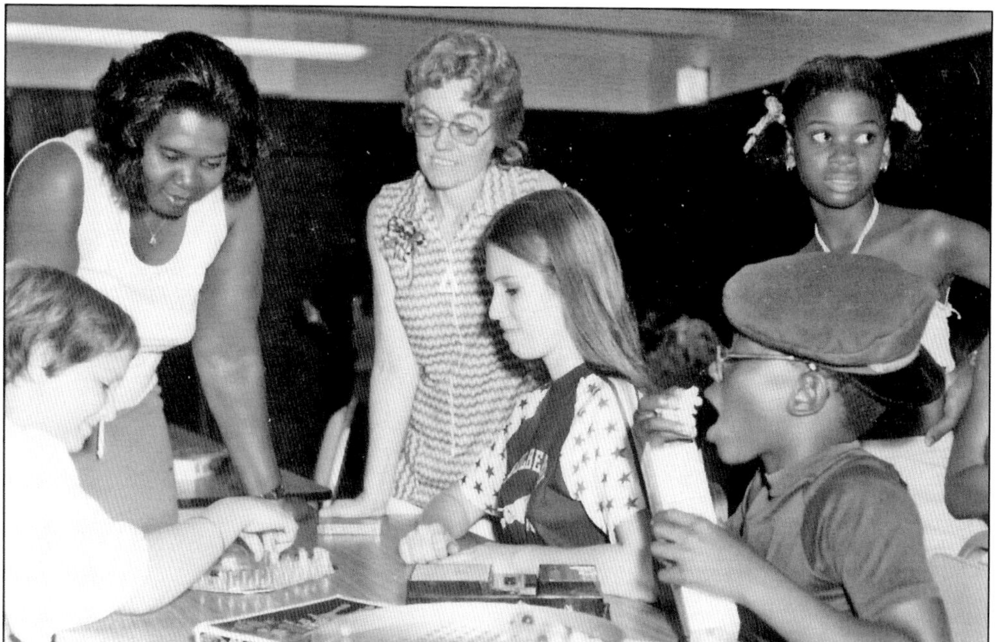

These citizens are enjoying the 75th anniversary celebration. Listed from left to right are the following: (seated) unidentified, Susan Jenkins, and unidentified; (standing) Vera Mae Hardee, unidentified, and Sonya Helper Stancil. Hardee is an inspiration; she worked two jobs—as a school bus driver and substitute teacher—to help support her family while earning an associate's degree from Polk Community College. Hardee received her bachelor's degree from Florida Agriculture and Mechanical University (FAMU) the same weekend in 1976 that her son Abraham "Billy" Hardee Jr., a professional football player, received his bachelor's degree from Virginia Tech. In 1978, she earned a master's degree from FAMU. She worked for the Polk County School Board until her retirement in 1999. Her other sons are Ronald, Raymond, and Curtis.

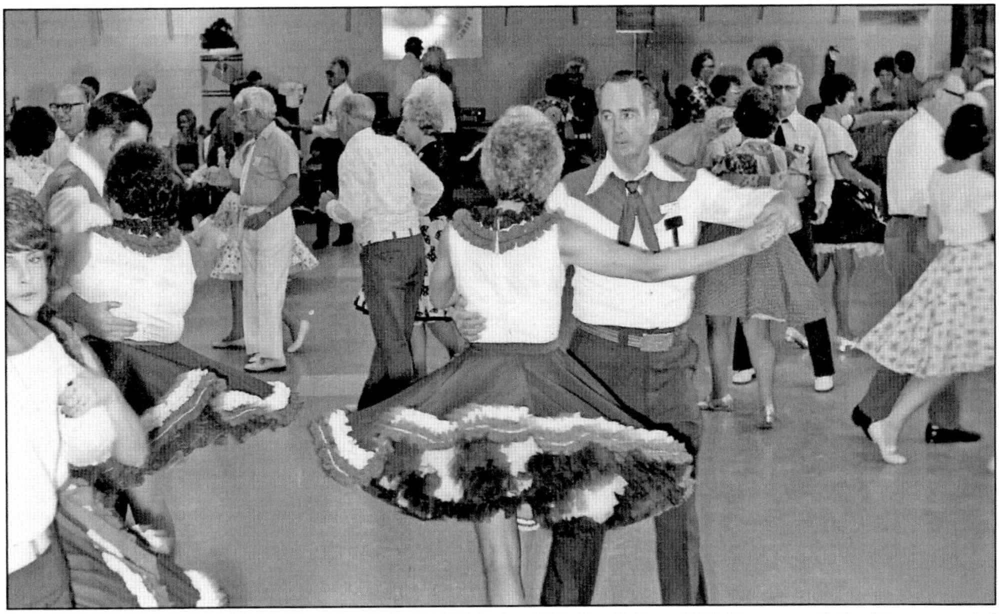

Square dancing was held on Monday July 5, 1976, the 75th birthday of Mulberry and the bicentennial celebration of our nation. The caller of the square dances was Roger Chapman. The art of square dancing continues to be promoted today and is demonstrated on a special float in each Mulberry parade. (MBS.)

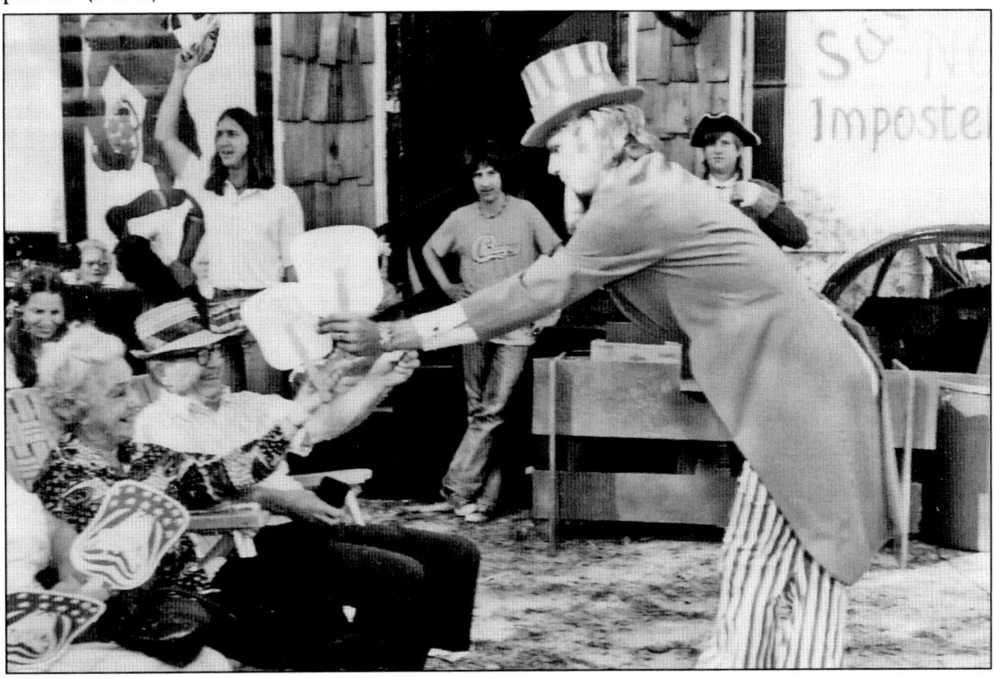

Citizens of Mulberry enjoyed the Polk County bicentennial touring medicine show with "Dr. Paten O. Pearl" on February 12, 1976. The performance is a recreation of the old-time medicine show with bluegrass and folk music. Harry Leith is shown here as Dr. Patent O. Pearl. The touring company provided two performances for the community in front of the Mulberry Civic Center. (MBS.)

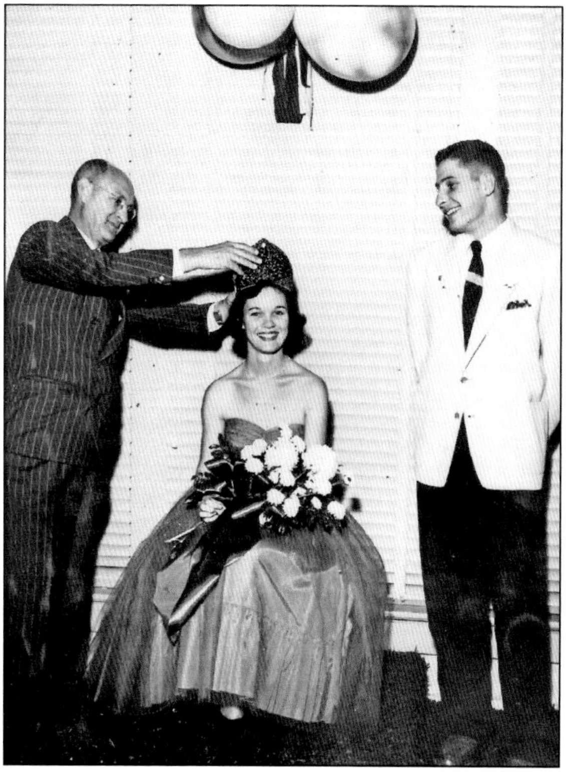

Pictured here is the 1953 Mulberry High School homecoming queen, Charlotte Burdette, flanked by principal A. E. Choate on the left and escort Dickie Harte on the right. Other contests included queens for the Phosphate Fair, Little Miss Mulberry, and Miss Mulberry. A complete list of the names of each contest queen was published in the *Mulberry Press* on February 5 and 12, 1976. (Ruby Sprott Moses/MBS.)

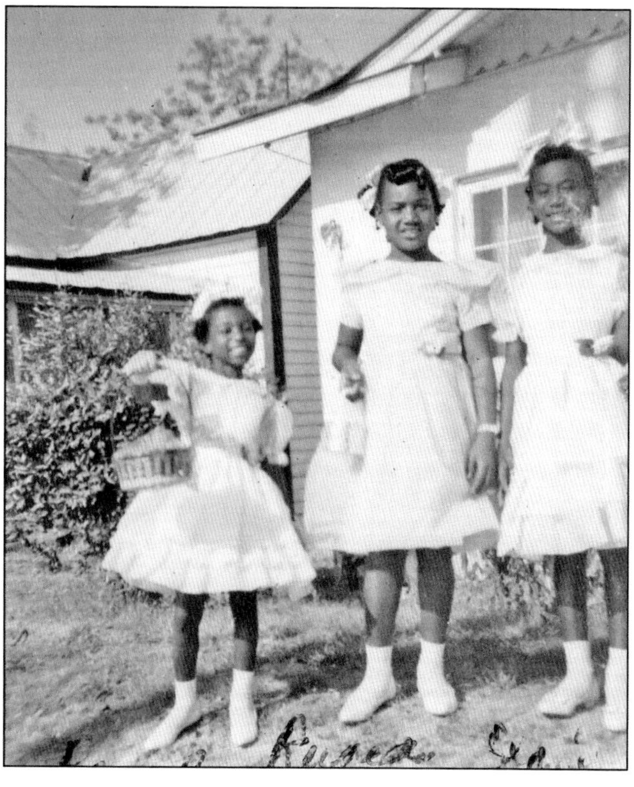

Celebrating Easter in royal style are Fifth Avenue Northwest residents, graduates of Mulberry High School (MHS) and Florida Agriculture and Mechanical University. Named from left to right are the following: Pamela Niece Morgan, who graduated MHS in 1974 and was the first recipient of the Leon Veteran Art Scholarship award; Ruenea Boyd Bigham, a 1972 MHS graduate who serves as a social worker and community activist; Jeannie Niece Satchel, who graduated MHS in 1972 after being named homecoming queen. The (1972) crowning of Jeannie and Debra Jackson (1973) as queens sparked racial tension that resulted in no homecoming queen being named at Mulberry High School for the next 10 years. (Essie N. Helper Morgan.)

This crinoline-slip Easter dress has Lauren Helper appearing a bit unhappy. Lauren graduated from Mulberry High School, earned her bachelor's degree at the University of Florida, received her master's degree from Nova Southeastern University. In 1982 she was voted Polk County's Exceptional Education Teacher of the Year. Lauren is currently employed as a staffing specialist for Miami-Dade County. She is the mother of one son, Quintin, and is recently divorced. (Essie N. Helper Morgan.)

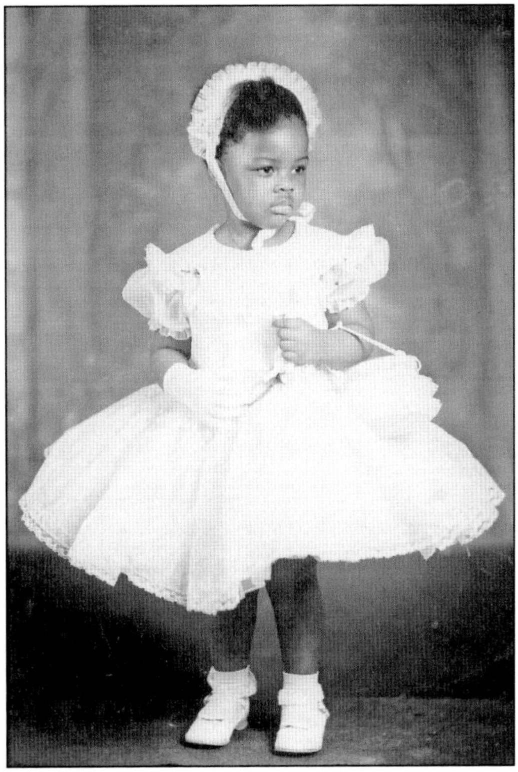

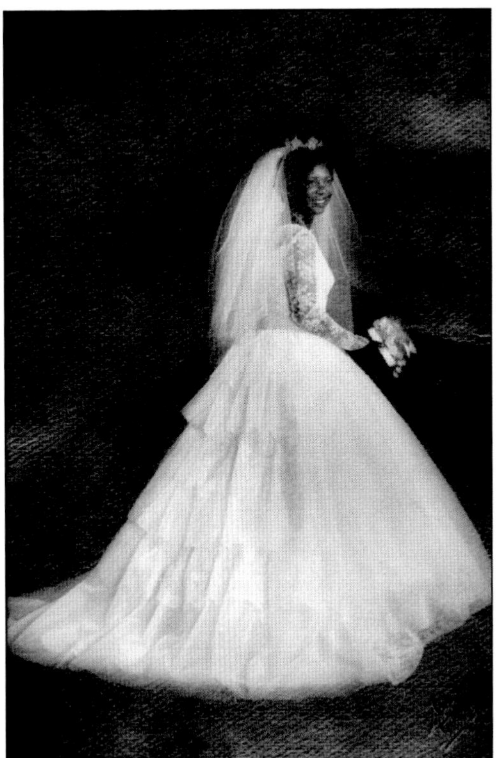

Every girl dreams of her wedding day to her Prince Charming. Every mother waits for the day her wedding dress is worn by her daughter. The blushing bride pictured here in the 1960s is Curnita Johnson, preparing for groom, Doc Clark. Curnita is the daughter of Leroy Johnson and the stepdaughter and daughter of Frank McGill and Essie M. Johnson McGill. Her siblings are Mack McGill, Aaron Johnson, Pearlie McGill Dasher, Lula McGill Scott, and Vera McGill Vandiver. (Ruenea Boyd Bigham.)

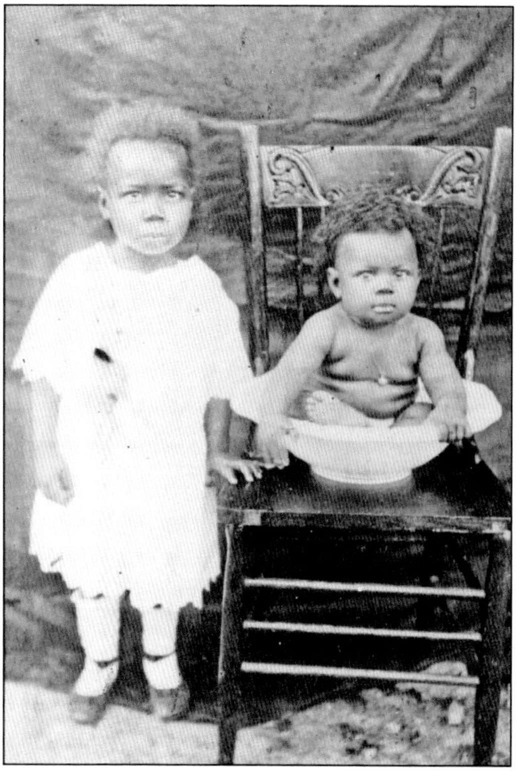

This is a late 1920s picture of Nila and Benny Green. The pitcher and bowl were used for sponge baths and for shaving. There were no bathrooms in the houses. The water was carried from the pump outside to the bowl on the dresser. (Ruenea Boyd Bigham.)

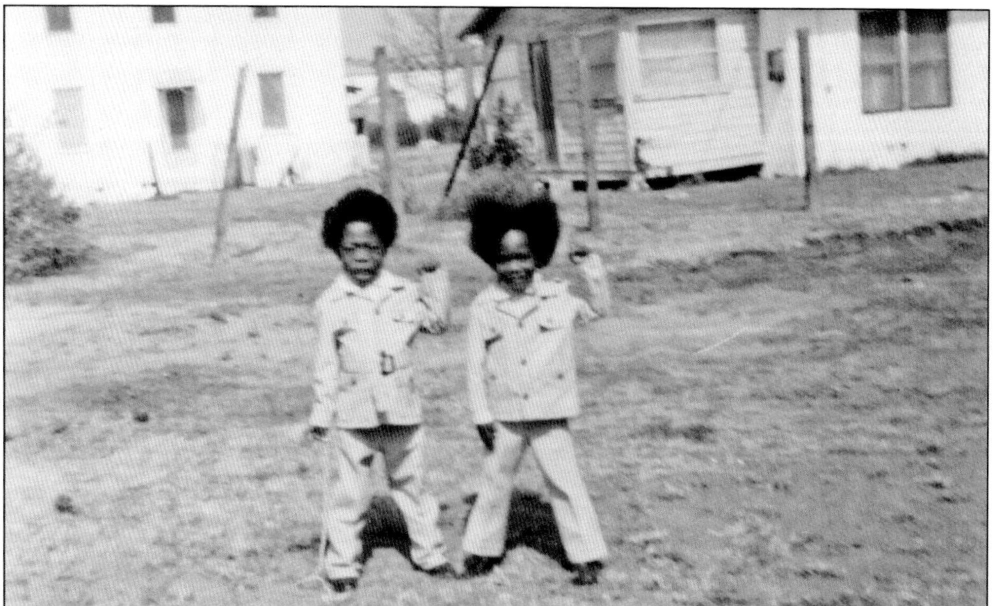

Pictured are Eugene Carson (left) and Christopher Carson in the late 1960s. The two-story building was the residence of Daisy Plummer and was the only two-story building in the African American community. Plummer rented out rooms to single working men, some of whom traveled back home on the weekends. The house to the right is a combination of wooden frame house with a brick addition. (Nila Helper Jones.)

Ten

Artifacts and Collectibles

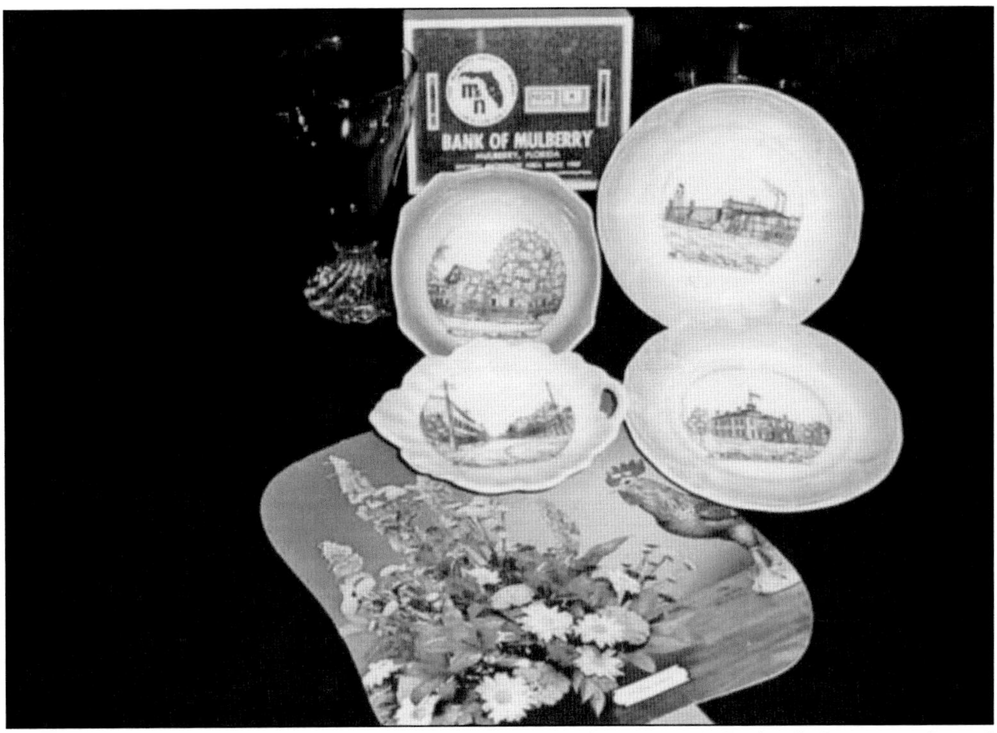

Many of the businesses in Mulberry produced promotional items. W. S. Badcock Company showed their appreciation by giving such items as glassware, matches, and fans to the community. The stemware was a gas station promotional item. The set of dishes displays scenes around Mulberry; they were the play set for the younger Theola Turner. Fans were printed with the names of businesses and were distributed to local churches, which were not air-conditioned during that time period. (Stephanie L. Dukes.)

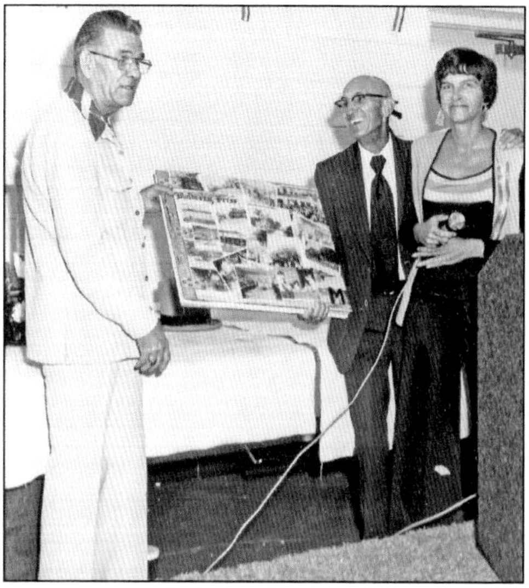

Mayor Carl "Kid" Ellis (left) receives the bicentennial scrapbook from Dick Hawkins and Henrie Harned Sparkman, members of the scrapbook committee. The keepsake includes photographs donated by Mulberry citizens showing life, buildings, and people in the town from the late 1800s up to 1976. The scrapbook is on display at the Mulberry Phosphate Museum. (MBS.)

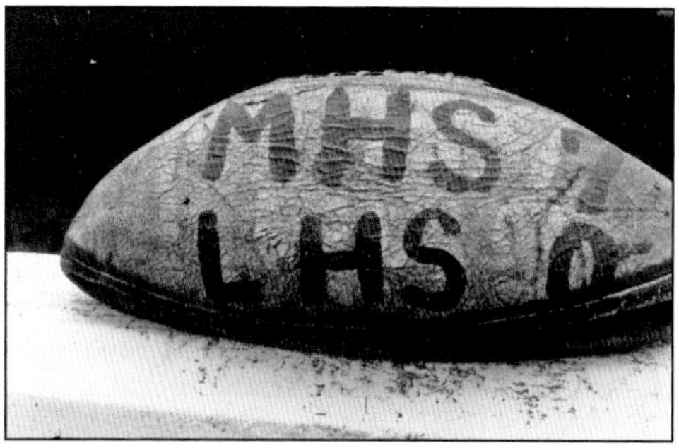

Since 1924, when a football program was established at Mulberry High School, many teams have won the district conference title and made it all the way to semifinals. This football represents the 1932 rivals of Mulberry High School and Lakeland High School. Later the biggest competitors were Bartow High School and Fort Meade High School; Union Academy's rivals were Plant City High School and Fort Meade High School. (Raymond L. Driver.)

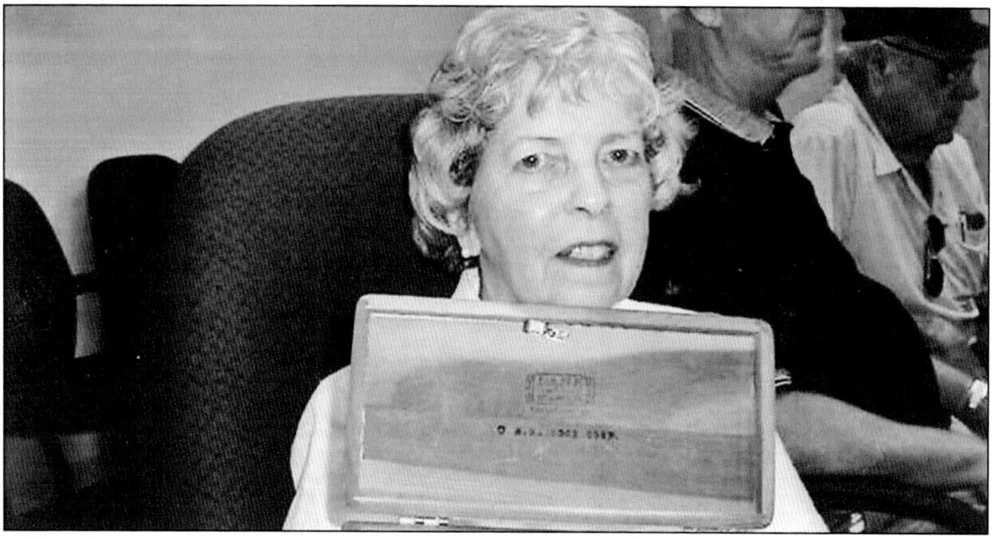

Belle Roberts shows her 1949 graduation gift, a cedar chest, from W. S. Badcock Corporation. It was a tradition for community businesses to present a gift to the graduating class. The gifts sometimes were from individual businesses and sometimes from the businesses as a group. This box has imprinted inside of the lid, "Lane Cedar Chests AltaVista, Va. Presented by W. S. Badcock Corp." (Belle Roberts and Stephanie L. Dukes.)

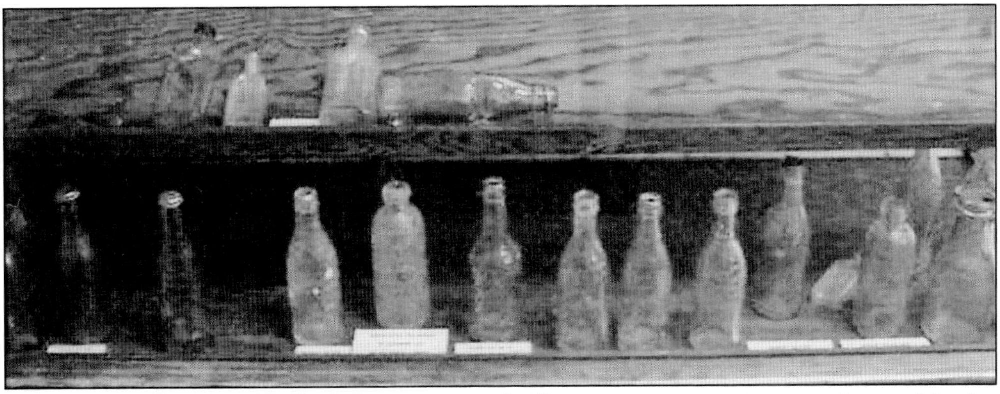

The bottle collection of Belle Roberts, a retired office services supervisor, was featured in the "Dragline," the International Mineral and Chemical Company monthly newsletter, in the March 1981 issue. For more than 12 years, Roberts collected bottles ranging from 1700s to late 1960s; she had so many that she gave them their own room! Stamped on the bottom of each bottle is the city and state in which it was manufactured. Some of the bottles were manufactured in Mulberry by the Smith Cola Bottle Company. (Stephanie L. Dukes.)

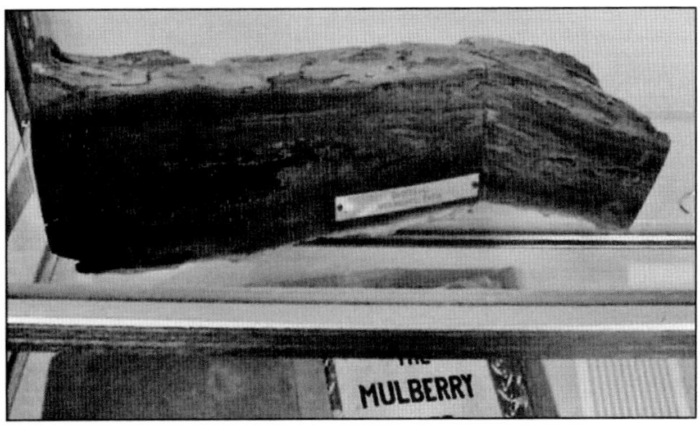

This is a part of the original mulberry tree on display at the Mulberry Phosphate Museum. Specialists attempted to save the original tree to no avail. Johnny Mitchell donated a seedling from his personal collection that now stands in the place of the old mulberry tree. The booklet on the bottom shelf is a copy of the 1934 high school annual, *the Mulberry Tree.* (Stephanie L. Dukes.)

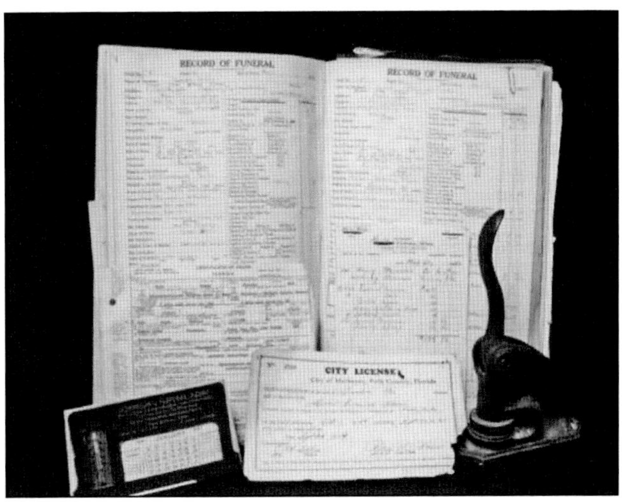

Shown here is the book of records for the funeral home owned by Isom and Essie N. Helper. The funeral home was first Johnson Funeral Home then became Lewis Funeral Home. Other items shown, from left to right, are a a death certificate, a bill of sale, the Order of Knights of Pythias organizational seal, a city business license, and a calendar with a thermometer. (Stephanie L. Dukes.)

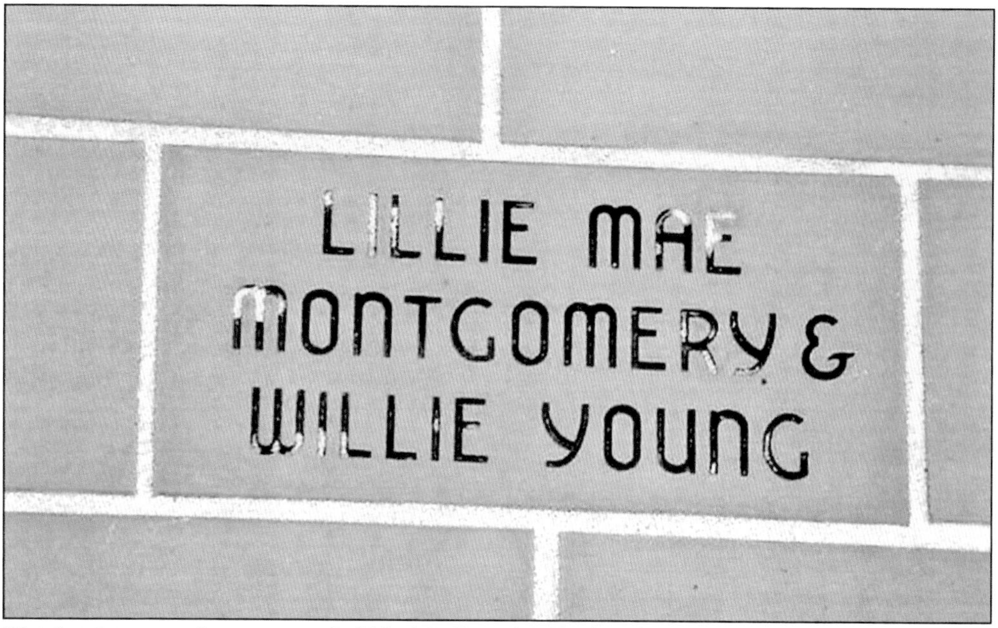

This brick is part of a campaign held by Mt. Zion AME Church. It is part of a large and beautiful red brick walkway between the church and activity center. The walkway has names of the living as well as memorial bricks. Some of the others displayed are "Robert and Nada Harrison 2003" and "In memory of Woodrow and Ruby Johnson." (Stephanie L. Dukes.)

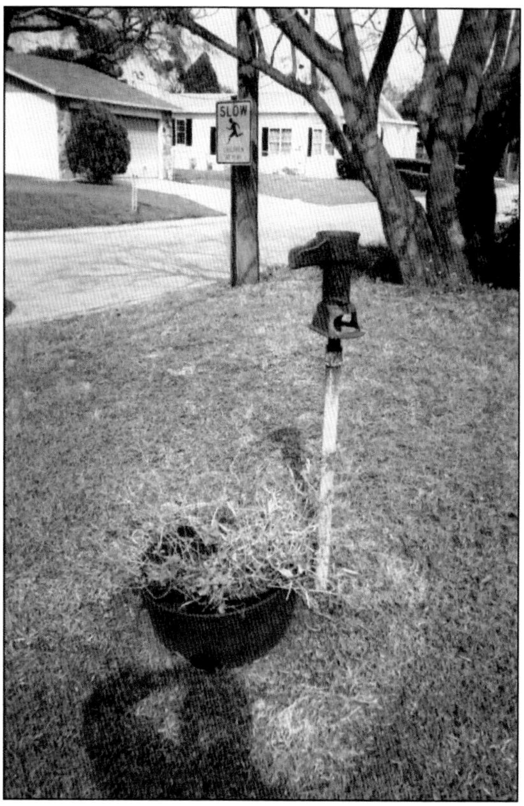

The water pump pictured here was attached to a line and brought water to the surface when the handle was pumped up and down. The boiling pot was used primarily to wash clothes. Clothes were washed using pot ash and boiling water. The clothes would come out sparkling white. (Stephanie L. Dukes.)

The quilt top shown here was made by Essie N. Helper Morgan for her granddaughter Tanya. Morgan has passed this skill on to others through the Mama Essie's Quilting Bees group. One of the members, Evelyn Durden, has quilted more than 20 full-size quilts and numerous smaller items. One of her quilts can be seen as a piece of art in the home of her daughter and son-in-law, Misha and Chris Carson. The quilting pattern shown here is the money wrench. (Tanya L. Dukes.)

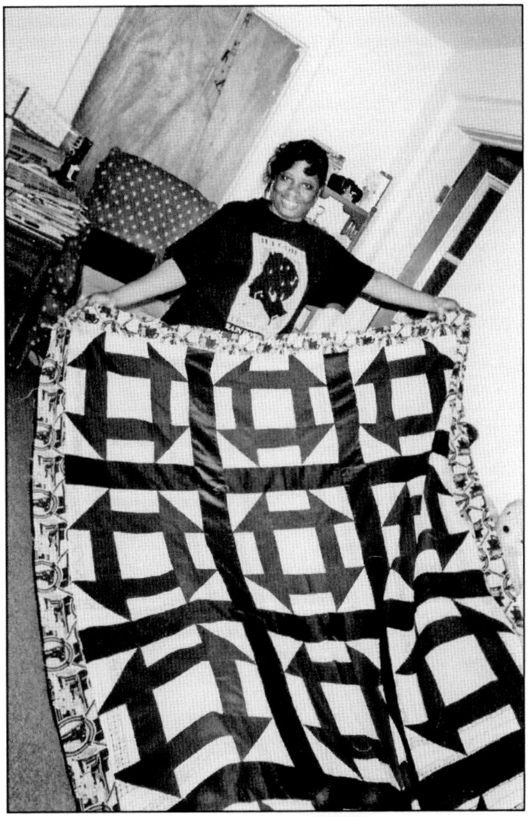

The items shown here were placed on display in the historical exhibit featured during the celebration of Mulberry's 75th birthday on February 12, 1976, at the Mulberry Civic Center. This display offered visitors a glimpse of the quality and creativity of the past. (MBS.)

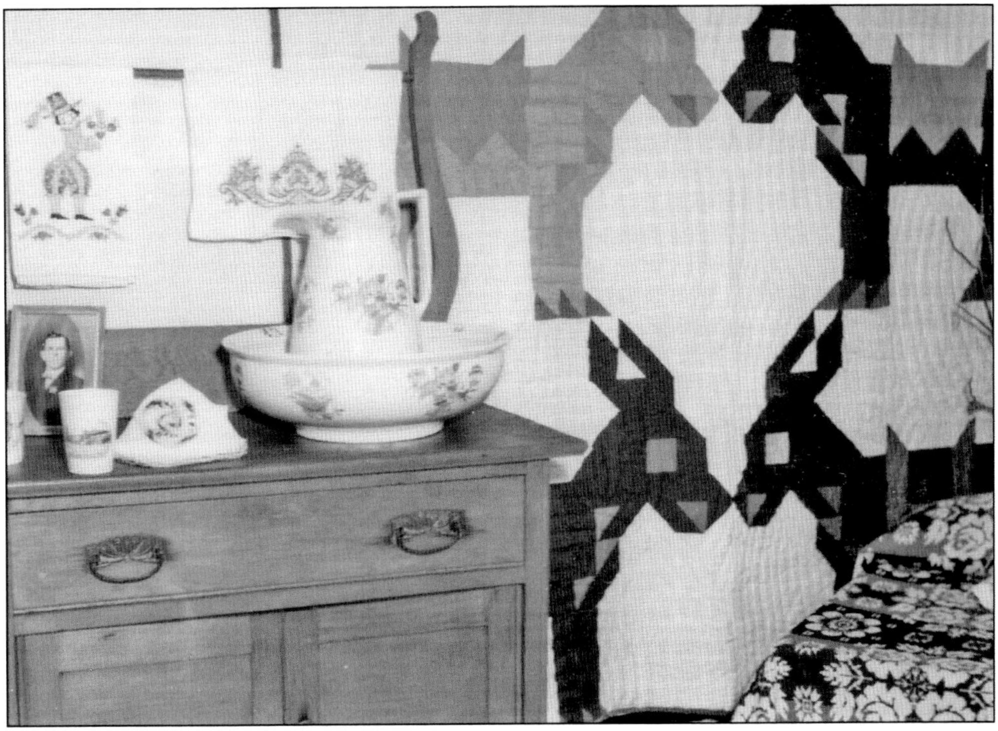

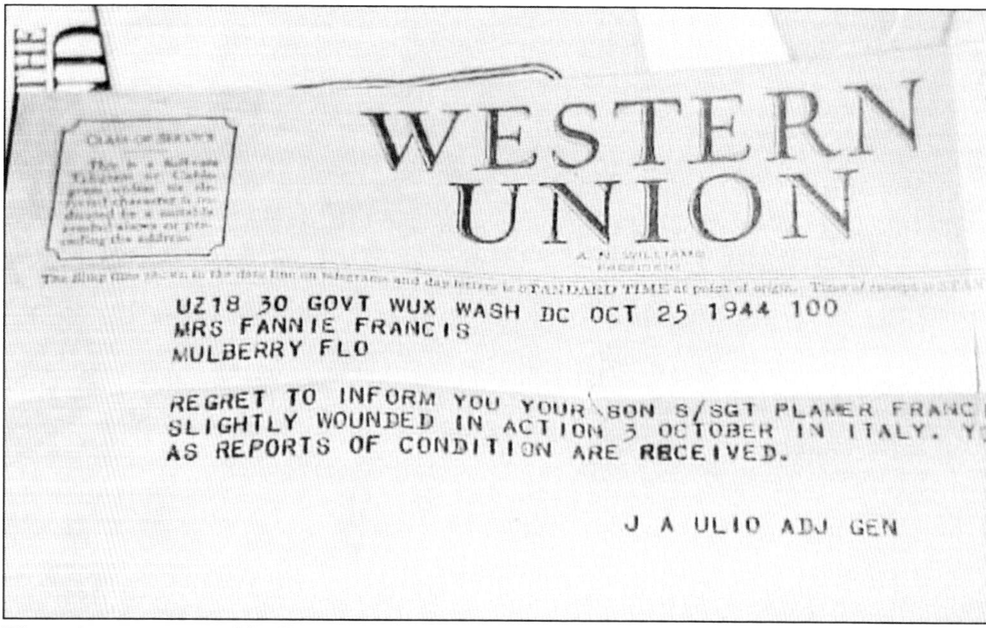

WESTERN UNION

UZ18 30 GOVT WUX WASH DC OCT 25 1944 100
MRS FANNIE FRANCIS
MULBERRY FLO

REGRET TO INFORM YOU YOUR SON S/SGT PLAMER FRANCI
SLIGHTLY WOUNDED IN ACTION 3 OCTOBER IN ITALY. YO
AS REPORTS OF CONDITION ARE RECEIVED.

J A ULIO ADJ GEN

This telegram received by Fannie Francis references her son Palmer Francis Jr. being wounded in action. To this day, Palmer has pieces of shrapnel in his body for which he earned the Purple Heart, among eight other distinguished medals. (Palmer Francis Jr.)

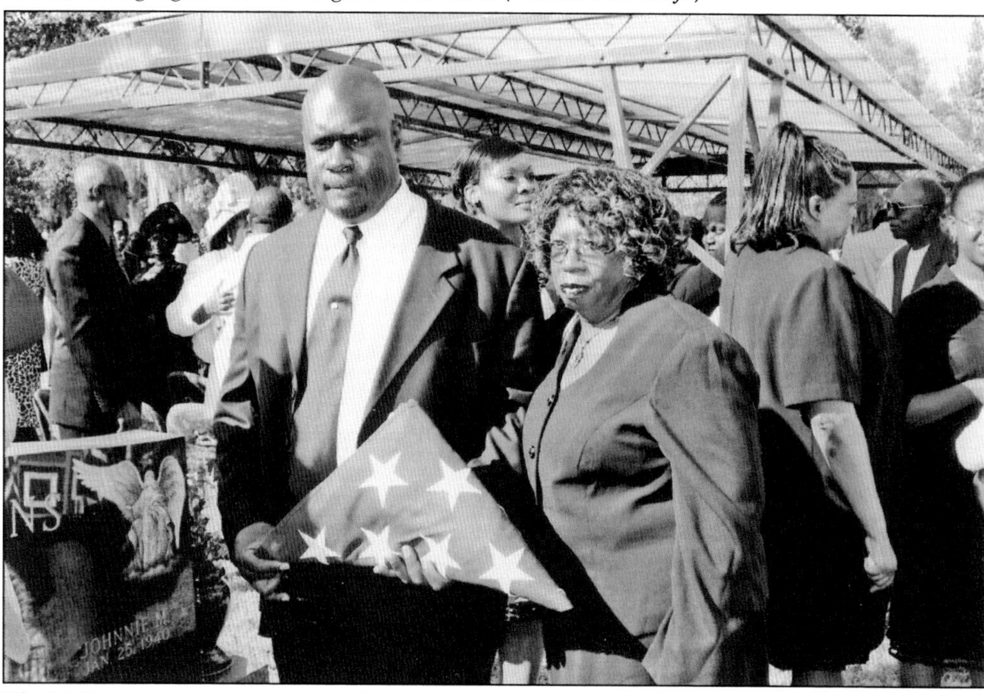

The U.S. government recognizes the contributions of every military person who either died in action or was honorably discharged by presenting the surviving family members an American flag at the burial site. Joseph "Cedric" Jones Jr. is pictured here holding the flag presented in honor of his father, Joseph L. Jones Sr. With him is Cedric's mother, Nila Helper Jones. Behind Cedric is his wife, Karen Bentley Jones. (Stephanie L. Dukes.)

The Helper family is pictured here enjoying Central Park in New York during the early 1970s. From left to right are Carla, David Jr., Emma, Daphne, Courtney, David Sr., Rawni, and Emma's sister Pamela Neloms. Not pictured is Rashid. (Emma Neloms Helper.)

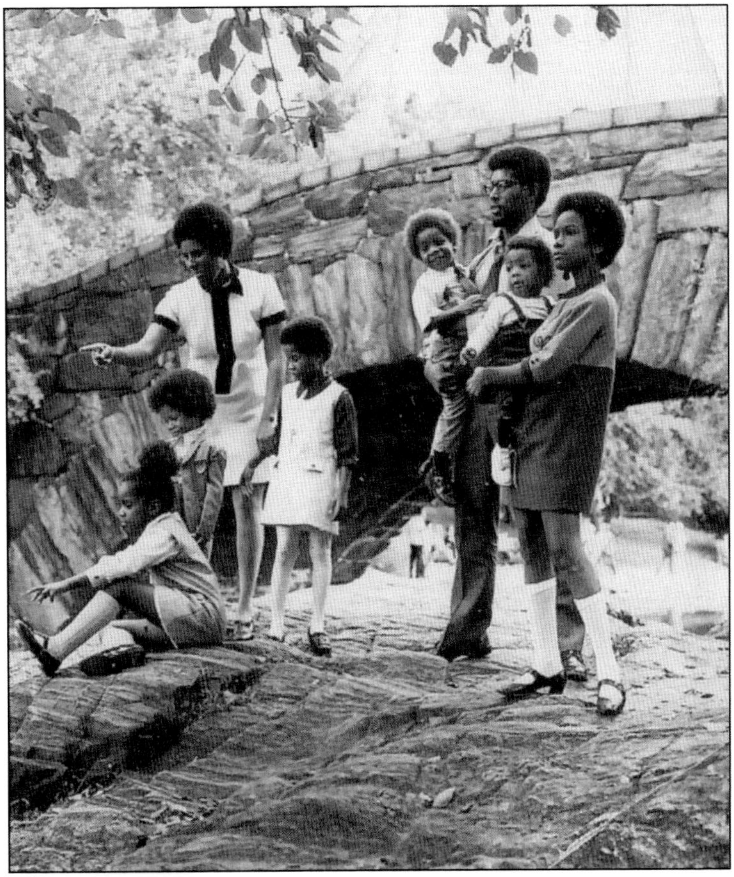

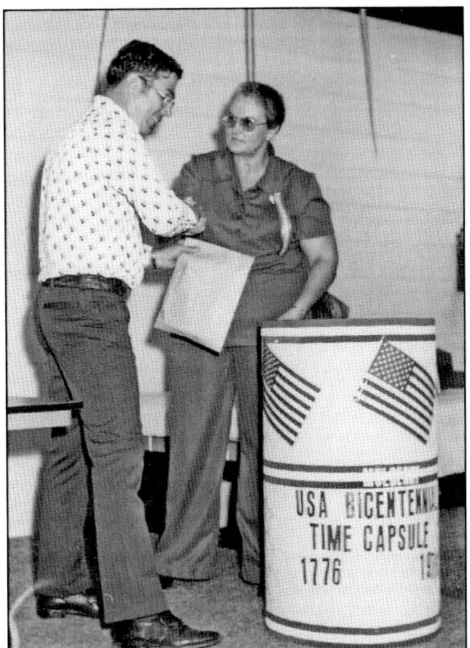

Citizens of Mulberry were encouraged to bring mementos for the bicentennial time capsule. The capsule was buried on June 12, 1977, by the Mulberry Chamber of Commerce. Items in the capsule will be revealed in 2076. (MBS.)

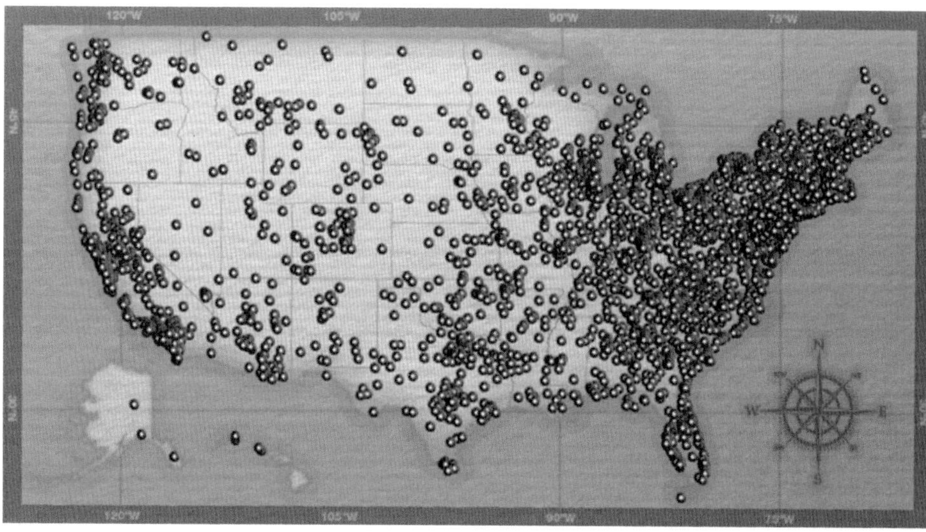